Replacement Manual

This updated and revised Reference Book and Field Guide replaces the original one issued with your ticket.

If you have lost your original ticket, this is a facsimile of the one acquired when you signed on to this Planet Earth Educational Expedition.

SPECIAL! 21st Century Planet Earth Edition

Accelerating Soul Evolution
Personal and Planetary

Ralph Genter

Pleiadian Connection©

Copyrighted at Common Law by Ralph Genter 2003

All rights reserved. Please do not reproduce any part of this book in any form without written permission from the Publisher. Brief passages may be quoted by a reviewer.

Accelerating Soul Evolution – Personal and Planetary
ISBN 0-9640829-1-8

Published by
Pleiadian Connection©
P.O. Box 51808
Albuquerque, New Mexico 87181-1808
United States of America

Web site: http://www.pleiadianconnection.org

Printed in America

First Edition

Cover photo of "Blue Marble" courtesy of NASA
Photo of Ralph Genter © Kim Jew Photography

Disclaimers: This book is intended for the learning and growth of the reader. Since each man or woman chooses how and what they make of their life within their own soul's life plan, there are no guarantees that the reader's consciousness will change and evolve.

The information in this book is not intended to diagnose, treat, cure, or prevent any disease.

TABLE OF CONTENTS

TABLE OF ILLUSTRATIONS	g
1 – INTRODUCING THE 21st CENTURY EDITION	1
Field Guide Highlights	*3*
Important Notices	*5*
Clarification of the Terms and Conditions	*8*
Important Information	*9*
To Those Expedition Participants Experiencing Their First Few Lifetimes On Planet Earth	*11*
An Open Letter To All Participants	*12*
2 – A FRESH PERSPECTIVE	14
3 – A VISIT TO THE TRAVEL AGENT	16
The Twelve Basic Principles of Creation	*17*
The Mind Over Matter	*27*
An Overview of Hermetics	*33*
4 – RETURNING TO UNITY, ONENESS, AND WHOLENESS	35
5 – COSMIC GEOGRAPHY: WHERE ARE YOU?	44
A Clearer View of Infinity	*44*
Wisdom Garnered from the Physicists	*48*
Creating Within Infinity	*51*
The Nature of Our Universe System	*52*

6 – COSMIC ANATOMY: WHO ARE YOU? 57

Trickle-down Creation — *57*
The Conscious Universe — *63*
Dimcons (Dimensions of Consciousness) — *65*
Consciousness on Earth and in the Solar System — *75*
You Are a Complex, Many-Splendored Being — *78*
The Structure of Your Individualized Nature — *79*
The Nature of Your Soul — *82*
Your Many Interdimensional Bodies — *86*
Your Auspicious Astral Body — *90*
The Seven Astral Energy Centers, or Chakras — *93*
Your Cosmic Connection — *98*
Identity Crisis: You, The Creator? — *100*
Summing Up the Cosmic Secret — *102*
Analogies — *103*
Final Summation — *104*

7 – COSMIC PURPOSE: WHAT'S THE PLAN? 106

Truth, Reality, and Illusion — *109*
Bumps on the Path of Soul Evolution — *111*
Wrestling Yourself Free of Duality — *113*
The Three Searches – Seek and You Shall Find! — *115*
Soul Groups — *115*
Guidelines for Progressing Your Soul Evolution — *116*
Everyone Enjoys a Challenge — *118*

8 – NOW, WHY DID YOU REALLY COME TO THIS PLANET? 120

Planet Earth As a Cosmic Schoolroom — *124*
You Came to Transmute Your Addictions — *125*
Your Adversary Is Your Teacher — *126*
Love Is a Many-faceted Thing — *131*

9 – CRASH! WHERE TO BUY NO-FAULT-OF-MINE INSURANCE — 133
Accidents: It Was All Their Fault — *133*
It Was Really My Parents' Fault — *135*
What Is Your Responsibility? — *137*
Hazard Insurance Is Available — *139*
Your Own Personal Security System — *142*

10 – UPGRADING YOUR SOUL DATA — 145
Self-Improvement: The Road To Transformation — *146*
Identifying Areas Requiring Transformation — *147*
Awareness – Look Sharp! Feel Sharp! Be Sharp! — *150*
On Stage and In the Audience — *152*
Action vs. Reaction — *154*
Monitoring Your Reactions — *157*
The Reaction of Anger — *159*
Ending Reaction by Transmuting Disharmonious Soul Programming — *163*
Praying for One Another — *171*
I Vow That ... Oops! — *172*
Regular Service Requirements — *173*
Your Toolbox is Full of Techniques — *174*
Receiving Guidance Through "Channeling" — *184*
Interpreting and Trusting Your Guidance — *186*

11 – SETTING A COURSE TOWARD YOUR DESTINATION — 188
Curriculum: What Courses Did You Sign Up For? — *189*
Developing an Objective Outlook — *190*
Championing the Road of Soul Evolution — *191*
Freedom of Choice — *193*

Table of Contents

12 – GAINING THE MOST FROM YOUR ADVENTURE   195

Moving Through Your Lessons More Quickly   195
Recognizing Your Personal Guidance   196
Living in "The Now"   197
Making Correct Decisions   200
Take Charge!   202
Rise Above It!   203
Humor – Umm, Umm Good!   204
Communication   205
Honoring Your Body and Your Experiences   207
On the Road to Limitless Total Love   208
Optimizing Your Experiences   210

13 – CALL 911! ILLNESS, DISEASE, AND ACCIDENTS   211

The Benefits Gained from Illness and Disease   212
Cancer   215
AIDS   217
Accidents: Your Wake-up Call   218

14 – ALTERNATIVE ROUTES AROUND THE STORMS, WASHOUTS, AND ROADBLOCKS   220

Fear: The Barrier to Love   220
Untie Your Knots   222
Judgment   223
The Astral Plane – A Barrier to Progress   225
Controlling Others   227
Excessive Ego   228
Willfulness   229
Energy Blocks   231
The Power of Thought-forms   232
Inertia   233

15 – TAPPING THE POWER OF GENDER 235
The Lessons of Romantic Love *240*
The Role of Sex in the Human Drama *241*
The Phenomena of Energy Exchange *245*
Honoring Your Chosen Sexuality *245*
Expressing Your Sexuality Responsibly *246*

16 – YOUR RELATIONSHIP TO THE OTHER KINGDOMS ON PLANET EARTH 248
The Mineral Kingdom of Mother Earth *249*
The Vegetable Kingdom *250*
The Animal Kingdom *251*
Your Responsibility to Planet Earth *253*

17 – ADDING THE MISSING INGREDIENT 255
The Role of Love in Your Soul Evolution *257*

18 – TRANSFORMATION 260
Your Relationship to Government *266*
The Magical Qualities of Total Love *266*
Establishing the Golden Age Upon the Earth *268*

Appendix: THE LAWS OF SPIRITUAL ENLIGHTENMENT AND SOUL EVOLUTION 272

DEFINITIONS 281

RECOMMENDED READING 286

NOTES ON THE CONSCIOUSNESS-RAISING MEDITATIONS 288

BOOK AND MEDITATION CD ORDERING INFORMATION 291

TABLE OF ILLUSTRATIONS

Triangle of Mind, Will, and Feeling	19
Diagram A: The Frequency Vibrational Spectrum	45
Diagram B: View of the Universe from a Perspective of Duality	47
Diagram C: Our Universe System	55
Diagram D: Realms and Dimcons	59
Diagram E: Soul Evolution and the Thirteen Dimcons	67
Diagram F: Population Distribution Relative to Levels of Consciousness within the Third Dimcon	69
Diagram G: Your Interdimensional Bodies and Union with the Godhead	87
Diagram H: The Seven Major Chakras	95
Diagram J: Current Population Distribution Relative to Number of Lifetimes on Planet Earth	277

Acknowledgments

I would like to thank every person, living or deceased, and every spiritual guide and teacher, who has contributed to the production of this field guide. Particular acknowledgements are awarded to Saint Michael the Archangel, Saint Germain, and Serapis Bey of the Hierarchal Board for their instruction and personal guidance that contributed to the concepts and subject matter contained in this book.

Special thanks and appreciation go to the following who have contributed their talents and skills in the editing of this work.

Michele Liberman
Halima Murdoc-Cristy
Bill Swearingen

Art Usher provided creative direction and produced the artwork in Diagrams H and J.

Ralph Genter

- 1 -

INTRODUCING THE 21st CENTURY EDITION

Congratulations! In the distant past, you had either been awarded or had chosen to acquire a valuable cruise ticket entitling you to participate in the Planet Earth Educational Expedition. This comprehensive excursion to the Universe's most productive educational planetary environment is the most exciting, challenging, and rewarding soul adventure in the Universe!

Earth is known throughout the Universe as "The Jewel of the Cosmos" for its unique geophysical environment and the vast variety of minerals, flora, and fauna it supports. Its atmosphere is rich in both oxygen and carbon dioxide providing sustenance for vegetable, animal, and human life forms. A phenomenal array of spectacular marine, animal, reptile, bird, and insect life forms constantly captivate the attention of Expedition Participants (human beings in this case, but the term also applies to all beings throughout the universe endowed with freedom of choice).

Unique unto itself, Earth is known as a pristine planet. Its primary attractions feature clear, turquoise oceans, spacious skies, vast grassy plains, and rivers flowing through enchanting canyons. Majestic purple mountain ranges blanketed with stately forests, ranging from sea to shining sea. For millennia, spirit intelligences have diligently labored to create these natural wonders, justly earning enthusiastic and resounding kudos from Expedition Participants for their brilliant performances. Their efforts have been a major contribution toward establishing Earth's reputation as the sparkling gem of the Galaxy.

The Earth Embodiment Physical Cruise Vehicle (the human body) is another marvel of creative bio-nuclear engineering. Many prior models were developed but subsequently discarded, having failed centuries of meticulous stress, function, and performance tests. This latest standard model off the production line is the sleekest, most aerodynamic, structurally sound, problem-free edition ever produced. Design ingenuity permits Participants to execute all basic physical, feeling, and mental functions with unparalleled dexterity, in view of Earth's unusually dense atomic environment. It is available in five stunning basic colors—red, white, brown, yellow, and black. A limitless assortment of intermediate hues is available at no additional charge.

A wide selection of body styles is offered to provide Expedition Participants with endless opportunities for truly phenomenal experiences. These styles include family, sport, utility, and cargo models. Almost any custom modification can be accommodated. Most models have low frequency-of-repair records. Many technologically progressive service and repair stations (clinics and hospitals) have been franchised in numerous areas of the globe.

Of particular interest on this magnificent planet are the unique reproductive procedures practiced by its vegetable, animal, and human kingdoms. This has been a never-ending source of fascination to Expedition Participants, who have developed and perform a variety of rites, customs, ceremonies, and obsessions around these practices.

Around 300,000 years ago, the pride of Planet Earth was the renowned Garden of Eden. However, the conditions prevalent in this legendary Garden no longer exist. The primary purpose of this field guide is to suggest how Planet Earth may again be transformed to emulate the original, higher dimensional state of the magnificent Garden of Eden.

Field Guide Highlights

The production of this revised reference book and field guide is sponsored by the spiritual Hierarchical Board of this galaxy, which has a local area branch office in The Pleiades Star Cluster. The branch office of this area, which includes Planet Earth, is currently presided over by the exalted being now known as Saint Germain (perhaps more familiarly recognized from previous incarnations as Samuel the Prophet, Saint Joseph, Merlin, Saint Alban, and others). In addition, Saint Germain and Mother Mary presently occupy the esteemed positions of Patriarch and Matriarch of Planet Earth.

This field guide has been extensively revised, updated, and expanded from the previous edition published just after the Great Flood. We are responding to millions of questions and complaints received from Expedition Participants concerning ambiguities in previous field guides issued thousands of years ago.

Many early ticket holders have expressed a desire to progress beyond fear-based, third-dimensional teachings and dogmas, by replacing them with more accurate, spiritually oriented truths. This new edition, therefore, clarifies the original purpose and objectives of this educational expedition and offers Participants a fresh perspective as to how they fit into the scheme of things. We hope this will clear up the confusion, prejudice, and judgmental attitudes which have developed from seemingly conflicting belief systems postulated on this planet.

After much research, we have discovered the most productive approach to encourage Participants to make constructive behavioral modifications within themselves. This entails laying a strong foundation by examining and understanding the broad cosmic picture, then analyzing the unique challenges confronting each Participant on this adventure. We include an analysis of the universal environment (the macrocosm), an overview of your personal anatomy (the microcosm), the reasons you chose to participate in this Expedition, and the rewards for having completed your objective. Also, this updated field guide conveys the reasons underlying our support of your use of suggested proper modes of behavior.

Since many Participants have gotten lost in the maze of fascinating distractions on this cruise, we discuss changes in itinerary and offer suggestions for getting back on a straight course. This will aid Participants to graduate to a more expansive experience on a higher vibrational frequency.

With a view toward accomplishing these objectives, this new edition reveals to ticket holders some facts that were previously considered classified information. Up until the 20th century AD, these more accurate, higher truths had been divulged only to dedicated students in the peaceful atmosphere of secluded temples, monasteries, and ashrams. The populace was fed a primitive, unsophisticated, and watered-down version of Truth in the form of myths, parables, and metaphors.

Ages ago, misuses of the power inherent in higher Truths necessitated these Truths being withdrawn from general circulation. This eventually resulted in a depletion of spiritual knowledge and wisdom, and an increase in the overall level of ignorance. Subsequently, it was relatively easy for humanity to be manipulated and dominated by a small minority of clever, entrepreneurial Participants. In their quest for material wealth, pleasures, and power, this forceful, elitist group has been extremely successful in controlling the general populace for their personal benefit.

The vast majority of Participants do not have an inkling they are functioning at a level of consciousness and self-expression far below their intended physical, feeling, mental, and spiritual potentials. Fortunately, many Participants are beginning to wake up, having become frustrated with this situation, and are pleading for progress and constructive change.

Frankly, this updated edition is in response to countless requests we have received lately from Participants who have found themselves flunking courses by making mistakes they did not even realize were mistakes. To advance their graduation date, they are clamoring for a better curriculum in this learning adventure. Many already have submitted applications for an adventure cruise on a higher, spiritual vibration.

Important Notices

In the past, field guides let you believe that you are "down here" and "God," who created all of this stuff, is somewhere "up there in heaven." We do not apologize for this gross inaccuracy because it boils down to what a Participant is capable of understanding and willing to accept.

Participants will best comprehend the perceptions presented in this updated field guide by processing them through their *intuitive* minds. The intellectual mind, in which the third-dimensional consciousness places so much importance, is virtually useless when it comes to comprehending abstract, intangible concepts of a fourth-dimensional or higher nature.

Therefore, if certain ideas and perceptions presented in this field guide seem foreign to you upon first reading, we suggest you do this:

1. Stop right there.
2. Relax, close your eyes, and take a few deep breaths.
3. Repeat to yourself the words of the concept in question.
4. Ask for clarification. Say to God, your guides, whomever, "I want to understand this concept. Please help me."
5. Wait patiently—a few seconds or minutes; it may be a few hours, even days—well, weeks, or months, depending.
6. Be aware of all coincidences in your life. Know that you will receive your answers when you are ready to understand them.

We recommend that you store unfamiliar concepts on a storage shelf in your mental closet, notebook, or daily journal to be readily available for the day, year, or lifetime when the necessary comprehensive tools and perceptive abilities become available. It is wise not to discard them outright.

Keep in mind that the words used in this field guide are just that—only *words*, only *symbols* and *guides*. Words are, however, necessary tools for Participants to physically communicate with one another through the dense medium of air molecules encountered on Planet Earth. Words are great for describing things of a tangible, concrete, literal nature, but when attempting to convey and comprehend intangible manifestations (like consciousness, spirit, and soul) and abstract ideas and concepts (like spiritual evolution), words fall very short of providing a suitable thought picture.

Human beings depend upon mutual agreements about the meanings of certain verbal sounds, which are designated as words. As these definitions of a word in a particular language are learned from many sources throughout one's life, various people can give a word different meanings. Also, the concepts, feelings, and ideas inherent in certain words may not be clearly and definitively translatable from one language to another. This is because a word in one language may not trigger the intended mental, feeling, and psychological responses in the available words of another language.

For instance, it is generally accepted that Jesus of Nazareth spoke Aramaic, the common language of that time. However, certain Aramaic words are not directly translatable into English, Latin, or Greek and, therefore, when translated, do not retain the full implications of their meanings. For example, the words *sin* and *evil*, used in the English language, are derived from Aramaic archery terms. *Khata*, representing "missing the target," was translated as *sin*, and *bisha*, meaning "off target," where the arrow went when it missed, is translated as *evil*. These Aramaic words imply the meaning "not on the mark," contrary to Latin, Greek, and English interpretations implying immorality and wickedness.

Since they are only symbols, words describing abstract and intangible ideas and concepts can only point the speaker or listener in a certain general direction. It then is up to the reader/listener to go inside and use their intuitive mind to translate these words into clear ideas and concepts. The intuitive mind is then able to communicate an understandable translation of the idea to the Participant's intellectual mind.

The challenge in communicating fourth-dimensional ideas and concepts through the use of third-dimensional words is immense. Therefore, either new, specific meanings need to be given to existing words, or new words need to be created. For clearer communication, it is necessary to narrow down the definitions of certain words.

In the third-dimensional English language, many words do not make a clear distinction between what is harmonious and disharmonious or constructive and destructive. As an example, dictionaries currently state that the words *feelings* and *emotions* may be used interchangeably, with emotions connoting more vigorous and forceful feelings. In fourth-dimensional language, we prefer to make a clearer distinction between these two words: *feelings* being harmonious and constructive; *emotions* being disharmonious and destructive.

feelings – harmonious psychological sensations of Love, Gratitude, Compassion, Enthusiasm, and Joy experienced as a constant state or mode of being.

emotions – feelings that have been distorted by the illusions presented to one's consciousness through the disharmonious programming inherent in duality. This condition is prevalent on fear-based planets.

Another word is "love." In English this word has so many different meanings that descriptive adjectives must be used to clearly communicate the intended type of love. Other languages, like Greek, have separate words that describe the various aspects of love.

To clearly delineate words describing spiritual qualities as opposed to third-dimensional qualities, we begin them with upper case letters, like Love, Trust, Power, Knowing, as well as using descriptive adjectives when appropriate.

In effect, what you are creating is similar to a gigantic picture puzzle in which many or most of the pieces are laying about without any apparent place to fit. Eventually, however, with diligence, these pieces will interlock to afford you a beautiful, seamless mosaic of spiritual understanding. In other words, with patience and perseverance, you will eventually "get the picture."

Clarification of the Terms and Conditions

As the various discourses progress, we shall introduce or redefine certain terms or words, so the concepts to which they relate may more clearly pertain to the spiritual context of this field guide. This provides Participants with a more realistic perspective of spiritual realities, in particular who and where they are, and how to optimize this Planet Earth educational experience. Now, some definitions.

evolution – the process of continuous change, development, or growth from a lower, simpler condition to a higher, more complex condition or state of existence.

consciousness – the quality or state of being aware and cognizant of one's external environment and of one's internal thought, volition, and feeling processes.

The inherent characteristic of awareness that gives life forms the capacity to think, learn, grow, and expand in instinct, intelligence, knowledge, intuition, and wisdom.

dimension – the degree or measurable range over which something extends. A realm of existence or level of consciousness.

dimensions of consciousness (dimcons) – are analogous to different levels or degrees of awareness, learning experience, understanding, and wisdom, similar to graded school systems. There are thirteen dimcons in this Universe system. Each higher dimcon allows its inhabitants a broader perspective and comprehension of Love, Truth, and Wisdom. Dimcons are not related to dimensions of place, time, and space. Each dimcon is divided into seven major levels or progressive steps.

Until now, the majority of Earth-based teachings have emphasized progress only as it applies to Participants' immediate Earthly experiences, particularly personality traits and flaws. Where this field guide differs significantly from previous editions is that the emphasis is on *personal soul evolution*.

There are two fundamental aspects of the evolutionary process: outer evolution and inner evolution. Outer evolution is concerned with the physical transmutation of mineral, plant, animal, and human organisms and body types and forms. Inner evolution is concerned with one's soul and spiritual progress and development. The true purpose for which you signed onto this Earth Educational Expedition was to progress your soul's spiritual evolution.

Due to ignorance on the subject of soul evolution, many arbitrary rules of conduct postulated by various religious and governmental institutions have significantly limited the scope of Participants' experiences. It is not only preferable, but actually necessary, that Participants have more freedom of movement and self-expression to fulfill their self-chosen life and soul objectives.

It is, therefore, strongly recommended that ticket holders carefully review the "Important Information" section (the fine print) which follows. Seasoned Expedition Participants who have lost their original ticket stub and field guide will appreciate a review of these *terms and conditions* accepted upon issuance of their cruise tickets.

Important Information

1. This cruise ticket entitles the purchaser, hereafter referred to as "Participant," to one exciting cruise of Planet Earth for as many lessons and bodily lifetimes as are necessary to acquire a spiritual consciousness. Graduation from Planet Earth is bestowed upon this event, whereupon a return trip is a choice rather than a requirement.
2. This cruise ticket is non-refundable. Once Participants begin this cruise, it is their responsibility to complete it. There are no dropouts.
3. It is understood by all parties concerned that trips to Planet Earth entail an extreme loss of consciousness due to the limited confines and atomic density of the earthly physical body and brain. Participants are issued an intellectual mind that will enable them to cope with the condition of duality and mundane, earthly affairs. A major goal of this expedition is for Participants to recognize, develop, and use their intuitive minds, thereby advancing their soul evolution.
4. To make this adventure an exciting and thrilling challenge, the designers of this cruise require that Participants begin each new bodily

experience on Planet Earth with partial amnesia. Most Participants will not know who they are, why they came to this planet, anything regarding past lifetimes or the purpose of that particular trip. As Participants mature, they must learn to rely on data received from their personal soul programming as well as information received through the assistance of other responsible Participants. Participants assume total responsibility for their acceptance of any misinformation or distortions of cosmic truths.

5. Participants will each be assigned a minimum of four astral and/or spiritual guides (guardian angels) upon the beginning of each earthly bodily experience. As the Participant evolves, the nature, characteristics, and number of guides may fluctuate to satisfy current requirements. How effectively one utilizes the services of their guides depends upon the degree to which each Participant develops their intuitive mind and spiritual awareness.

6. There is no guarantee that this educational cruise will progress as smoothly or as quickly as anticipated without interruptions, accidents, or errors. Participants must accept total responsibility for any unforeseen circumstances, as they may have attracted these situations or experiences to themselves because of their own erroneous soul programming, thoughts, and/or actions.

7. Planning and coordinating any one lifetime are the sole responsibilities of the Participant. We strongly advise you to give due and serious consideration to prompt implementation of life plans suggested by the Board of Karma. It is acceptable to have no life plan.

8. Periodic tests and quick-quizzes will be given frequently during the cruise to assess Participant's accumulated soul knowledge and wisdom. If a lesson does not receive a passing grade, it will be repeated until one is attained. Do-overs are provided to Participants at no additional charge.

9. Spirit will not interfere with Participants' individual experience. Guidance, advice, counseling, and protection are provided upon a Participant's request via the Higher Dimension Hotline.

10. Many erroneous or half-erroneous teachings are postulated on Planet Earth. If a Participant believes them, they serve a purpose and, eventually, these will test the degree of discernment and wisdom attained.

11. Spirit will not provide bail for serious offenses for which Participant is incarcerated on either Planet Earth or the Astral Plane. Participant is responsible for any karmic lessons or debts incurred. These are understood to be beneficial learning experiences and are an integral part of this adventure.
12. When an Expedition Participant completes all prerequisite and optional curriculum requirements with passing grades and, thereby, attains a spiritual fourth-dimensional consciousness, upon Participant's return to spirit's side, Participant will be greeted with a huge celebration to include a seven-layer triple-chocolate spiritual dream-come-true and a discount voucher for the next cruise on a higher dimcon.

To Those Expedition Participants Experiencing Their First Few Lifetimes On Planet Earth

We give you this one basic fact to remember:
You are an evolving soul.

Understanding this basic concept is important to you. If you are not able to comprehend or relate to any other idea or concept in this field guide, be at ease. Know that with perseverance, and at the appropriate time, you will.

Considering your current physical, feeling, mental, and spiritual state or condition, what matters is that you do your best to evolve. To make each moment in your life a step toward a fourth-dimensional spiritual consciousness, we suggest you say each day:

"My soul evolution is *now* progressing successfully."

1 - INTRODUCTION TO THE 20TH CENTURY EDITION

An Open Letter To All Participants

Dear Expedition Participants,

In all the billions of years that educational adventure expeditions have been conducted throughout the galaxies of this Universe, those to Planet Earth have proven to be the most challenging. Viewed from our perspective, an educational trip to Planet Earth appears to be relatively easy to conclude. We now realize that, due to the multitude of distractions, most Participants have found this Planet Earth Educational Expedition to be quite difficult and time consuming. Only a relatively small percentage of Participants have remembered the true purpose of the cruise and graduated to a spiritual, fourth-dimensional consciousness.

Therefore, we have developed some special educational resources to facilitate your progress. This revised *Expedition Field Guide and Reference Book* will give you an advantage in successfully completing your Earth experience by revealing *where* you are, *who* you are, *why* you chose to take this cruise, and *how* to follow a direct course toward achieving your spiritual goals.

There are four major lessons which, as a group, Participants are having difficulty mastering:

1. Self-discipline

2. Honesty and integrity

3. Responsibility

4. Harmlessness

Resistance on the part of many Participants to integrate these principles in their lives has all but halted humankind's spiritual soul evolution.

Your Earth Expedition was intended to be a happy, cheerful, exciting, enthusiastic, motivated, and loving experience; not the miserable, wretched, depressing, tormented catastrophe some Participants are creating for themselves. Their learning experiences are much more traumatic than is necessary because they are unaware of the basic principles governing harmonious behavior.

The information in this updated field guide is intended to help you clearly recognize and identify your soul blueprint, or plan, for this lifetime. By so doing, you will proceed more smoothly and harmoniously through your life experiences, and avoid many obstacles with which you have been colliding.

We anticipate there will be a steady upsurge in worldwide mass consciousness as an increasing number of Participants choose to learn how to live in harmony with the Universal Laws and the true nature of their being.

Respectfully Yours in Light and Love,

The Hierarchal Board of the Milky Way Galaxy

- 2 -

A FRESH PERSPECTIVE

The Kingdom of God cannot be observed, for it is within you.

As humanity progresses into the twenty-first century, we have entered the space age. However, we must not only explore outer space, but the realms of *inner* space as well. The vibrations interpenetrating Planet Earth are now rising higher than they have been for thousands of years. This is an exhilarating time for those inhabitants who possess the awareness, ingenuity, insight, and visionary foresight to ride the waves of spiritual as well as material progress.

A rare opportunity therefore exists for the citizens of Planet Earth to make a giant leap in evolution—not only in their physical, outer evolution, but also in their inner, spiritual, soul evolution. What this requires is a transformation in the level and degree of humanity's conscious awareness of spiritual ideals and concepts.

What is the Kingdom of God? A state of *consciousness*. Consciousness – an abstract, intangible concept that is everywhere, in everything, yet is so little understood. Consciousness – the quality of mind through which one perceives and evaluates their basic nature, their environment, their life, and their destiny.

This field guide is about consciousness and the journey of the human soul striving to achieve ever higher levels of awareness and understanding. This journey cannot be explained, only experienced, for each soul's path is unique unto itself. Only general guidelines, with a few pertinent examples, can be suggested. It is through personal experience that a suitable orientation is obtained to enable you to fly free of Earth confines.

Spiritual progress requires an inquisitive mind and a bountiful heart. A mind that desires to expand and understand the wheres, whys, and hows of human existence. A heart that yearns to develop its *feeling* nature. A heart that realizes that Love is the ingredient that literally makes the worlds go around. The mind and heart that yearn to evolve into higher, vaster realms of awareness and experience.

The information, knowledge, and wisdom contained in this volume have been affirmed through the personal experiences of the scribe who, with much spiritual guidance, persisted and pursued the path from a material to a spiritual consciousness within this lifetime. Personal experience was gained by bouncing off the restrictive walls of the physical adventure to seek that narrow, fine thread of higher truths that lurk behind and within Earth's everyday life events.

What is Truth? Pure, spiritual Truths are non-linear, abstract, intangible concepts and ideas that cannot be adequately expressed in words. Therefore, to the physical Earth brain-mind we can only talk around Truths in linear terms, very different from the infinite nature of cosmic realities.

Just as there are many facets to a cut precious stone, and many windows through which to view the interior of a mansion, there are various perspectives from which to view spiritual Truths. Truth, as viewed from the Earthly level, is like a pie divided into twelve pieces— twelve viewpoints to help one approach a philosophy of life. This field guide presents one piece, one-twelfth of the pie. This piece presents a unique approach to the understanding of our spiritual natures and destinies. For broadness of perspective, familiarity with more than one of these paths is helpful, but it is preferable that a man or woman chooses one path as their primary direction.

- 3 -

A VISIT TO THE TRAVEL AGENT

When planning a journey, it is usually advantageous to have some general ideas regarding the destination(s) you wish to reach and the best routes for getting there. For those of you desiring to arrive at a fourth-dimensional consciousness, know that reliable travel guides have been assigned to assist you.

We will begin by presenting some important ideas and concepts to familiarize you with the route and nature of your destination. You will find the understanding of these concepts very helpful to your comprehension of the subject matter presented herein, and the direction in which you are traveling. These include—

1. The Twelve Basic Principles of Creation.
2. The various categories of mind.
3. The basic precepts of Hermetics.
4. A comprehension of infinity.
5. Realms of existence.
6. Dimensions of consciousness.
7. The nature of soul.

These, and other concepts included in this field guide, are intended to broaden your understanding of the true nature of this adventure.

The Twelve Basic Principles of Creation

Within the range of infinite possibilities, there are countless designs by which a universe could be created and then function. There are twelve Basic Principles or Powers of Creation involved in the fabrication of the Universe we are now experiencing. These twelve Principles relate to, and are inherent in all life and everything created.

Within everything, visible or invisible, there exists Three Primary Principles, or Infinite Qualities, of God The Absolute: 1) Mind, 2) Will, and 3) Feeling. These are the basic energies by which the creation process was initiated to produce this Universe system and everything in it.

Infinite Being also formulated Four Elemental Principles that are at the basis of our Universe's structural characteristics.

Then, there are Five Personal Principles that are necessary for Participants to develop as personal attributes, in order to evolve and co-create in harmony with the highest principles of The Godhead.

At times, you may feel captive to outer circumstances. It is your destiny, however, to learn, develop, and use these twelve creative principles to enhance your life and the lives of others on this planet and beyond. Through first becoming the Master of yourself, you may then learn to become the Master of your life and, thereby, in control of your destiny.

Following is a list of the twelve Basic Principles, including a brief analysis of each, and some practical applications. For some, we will refer to their polarity, which we define as:

> **polarity** – The condition whereby two principles complement or are diametrically opposed to each other. Qualities or conditions having contrasting properties or opposite extremes. Regarding electricity, the relative condition of opposite charges having two poles, referred to as positive and negative.

The Three Primary Principles of God The Absolute

1. Mind – the Principle of <u>Life</u>

 Highest Attribute: Omniscience – All Knowing.
     Sense: Consciousness, awareness, communication, speech, hearing.
   Energy Form: Mind and Kinetic Power (kinetic: energy relating to animated, active, lively movement).
     Function: Thought, observation, communication. The designer. To formulate ideas, plan, and design the Universe.
     Polarity: Neutral (both electric and magnetic).
     Gender: Androgynous
 Associated Color: Emerald Green

2. Will – the Principle of <u>Light</u>

 Highest Attribute: Omnipotence – All Powerful
     Sense: Vision.
   Energy Form: Willpower.
     Function: Authority. The decision-maker. To direct the Universe.
     Polarity: Electric / Dynamic.
     Gender: Masculine – The Father Principle
 Associated Color: Blue-violet

3. Feeling – the Principle of <u>Love</u>

 Highest Attribute: Omnisentience – All Feeling.
     Sense: Feeling (Enthusiasm, Compassion, Joy).
   Energy Form: Productive Power.
     Function: Manifestation. The producer. To produce the Universe.
     Polarity: Magnetic / Receptive.
     Gender: Feminine – The Mother Principle.
 Associated Color: Rose-pink

The Twelve Basic Principles of Creation

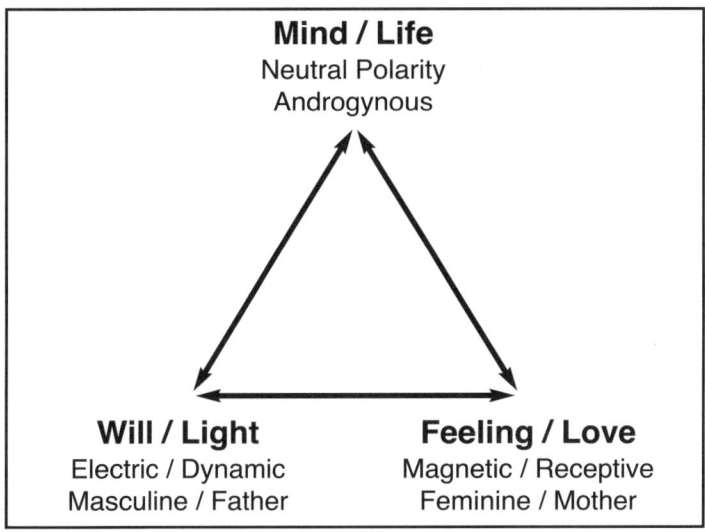

Within God The Absolute, these Three Primary Principles of Mind, Will, and Feeling are always in perfect balance and harmony, and equally interact with each other. Will/Light balances Feeling/Love; Mind/Life, being neutral in polarity, is common to both Will/Light and Feeling/Love. The Absolute is a Father-Mother God, for it is balanced in both polarity and gender. These Primary Principles are the basis of and permeate all of creation, for creation could not take place without them. They comprise what you are striving to balance and harmonize in your thoughts, words, feelings, and actions that you may attain a spiritual consciousness.

The Principle of Mind is given special emphasis throughout this field guide, as Mind is the master key to actuating and maintaining the balance of all Three Primary Principles. Why? Because the correctness and the accuracy of your thought processes are at the core of how you feel about every facet of your life experiences, and, thereby, how you respond through the direction of your willpower. Mind, Will, and Feeling form the key triangle wherein the Three Primary Principles work together in harmony as one. This principle is fundamental to all existence.

Note the colors associated with these Three Infinite Primary Principles: emerald green, blue-violet, and rose-pink. What happens when you combine these three in equal proportions? The result is the color golden-white. Golden-white is the color of balance and harmony. It is the color that permeates the spiritual and higher dimensions of consciousness. This is the color that you are striving to emulate and radiate in your bodily auras. You can practice visualizing this color and use it to protect yourself or communicate your desires and decrees to the Universe.

There are no mathematical equations or scientific theories for Mind, Will, and Feeling. Why? Because these are abstract, intangible, directly unobservable attributes, whereas physical science and the "scientific method" relate primarily to observable, material, concrete, tangible reality.

Each of these Primary Principles, or Qualities, however, is *energy* and *power*! These three qualities of Mind/Life, Will/Light, and Feeling/Love are the basic energies that actuated the creation of the Universe and everything in it! Also, everything created, whether animate or seemingly inanimate, incorporates all Three Primary Principles.

Where a deficiency of one or more of these Primary Principles exists within a Participant, this indicates the area(s) in which they need to work to eventually bring all three qualities into balance within themselves. This is an ongoing task throughout the advancement of one's soul evolution.

When these three Primary Principles are underdeveloped and out of balance with one another, ones thoughts, words, and actions tend to be disharmonious. For instance, Participants with sufficiently developed intellectual minds and willpower, but possessing undeveloped Feeling / Love / Heart natures, have been guilty of performing the most despicable brutality and crimes against their family members, neighbors, strangers, and people of different religious, ethnic, or political groups. An extreme example of this is the Holocaust of World War II in Europe and Asia.

An imbalance in these Three Primary Principles inhibits one's achievement capabilities. Participants may have a strong mind/feeling nature but lack the willpower to achieve constructive action in their lives. This is evident in Participants who have good, creative ideas and are passionate in their beliefs, but do not have the energy, determination, and drive to manifest their concepts into physical reality.

The Three Primary Principles function in varying degrees within yourself, in your environment and throughout the cosmos on every level and dimension. They are used daily by Participants to accomplish all their tasks, simple or complex. They are required to accomplish and create anything. Consider this simple process at work when you wake up in the morning.

First, there is **a mental recognition** that the wake-up alarm is sounding.

Second, there must be **a decision** as to what to do: turn off the alarm and go back to sleep; push the "snooze" button and get up later; or get up now. The decision is, "I **will** do … (*choice*)!"

The **third** step, in order to produce the willed effect, is to *feel* the desired effect **and do it!** That is, to either turn off the alarm, push snooze, or get up. This step is known in your slang lingo as "putting your money where your mouth is!"

This tri-fold process applies to the invention, management, and production of anything—the steam engine, automobile, airplane, washing machine, the harvesting, processing, and packing of fruits and vegetables—virtually every product you eat, use, feel, watch, or listen to.

Here are some other examples as to how these Three Primary Principles function throughout your everyday experiences. We will match the appropriate experience category to each applicable major Primary Principle and its corresponding polarity: Mind – Neutral; Will – Dynamic; Feeling – Magnetic.

1. a. Planning a dog house   Mind / Neutral
   b. Deciding to produce it   Will / Dynamic
   c. Constructing the dog-house   Feeling / Magnetic

2. a. Inventors / Designers   Mind / Neutral
   b. Management   Will / Dynamic
   c. Labor   Feeling / Magnetic.

3. a. Composer   Mind / Neutral
   b. Conductor / Director   Will / Dynamic
   c. Orchestral players   Feeling / Magnetic

4. a. Lesson Plans and Texts   Mind / Neutral
   b. Teachers   Will / Dynamic
   c. Students   Feeling / Magnetic

In some situations, one Participant can perform all three functions themselves. In other instances, more Participants are required. As you can observe, all three factors are required to effectively complete a productive creative process.

The Four Elemental Principles were purposely formulated and created by The Absolute out of Its infinite nature, to endow our Universe with certain unique characteristics. Who is to say that these are the only possible factors? They are, however, the only ones with which we are familiar.

The Four Elemental Principles of Creation

4. Air

Elemental quality: Light and wispy. Weightless.
Principle: Movement, intelligence.
Function: Projects the pattern, plan, design, and mold into the "space" required for the new creation.
Polarity: Positive.
Nuclear derivative: Electromagnetism.
Associated Color: Yellow

5. Fire

Elemental quality: Fiery-hot and dry.
Principle: Expansion.
Function: Projects the raw materials, etheric, subatomic, and atomic particles, into the newly created space.
Polarity: Positive.
Nuclear derivative: The strong force.
Associated Color: Orange

6. Water

Elemental quality: Icy-cold and wet.
Principle: Contraction.
Function: Controls the rates of expansion, cools the raw materials and conforms them to the pattern and mold of the plan.
Polarity: Negative.
Nuclear derivative: The weak force.
Associated Color: Light Turquoise-blue

7. Earth

Elemental quality: Heavy and dense.
Principle: Stability, materialization, completion.
Function: Condenses the raw materials into various forms of etheric and material matter and substance.
Polarity: Negative.
Nuclear derivative: Gravity.
Associated Color: Indigo Blue

These Four Elemental Principles originate in and emanate from the Three Primary Principles. The Three Primary Principles are always in existence within and supporting the Four Elemental Principles, which cannot exist by themselves. Mind, Will, and Feeling must constantly interact with each Elemental Principle to further the creative processes.

Note that these four Elemental Principles **are always in perfect balance,** that is, their total combined energies always equal **zero**. Air balances Earth; Fire balances Water—neutralizing or canceling one another if united.

Consider a simple example illustrating the operation of the Primary Principles and the Elemental Principles. A sculptor wishes to cast a statue in bronze. Here is the basic process.

1. **Mind**   The sculptor has an idea to create a bronze statue from a stone statue they have already produced.
2. **Will**   The sculptor decides to do it.
3. **Feeling**   The sculptor assembles the necessary materials and proceeds with the production process.
4. **Air**   The sculptor casts a suitable hollow mold from the stone statue.
5. **Fire**   The sculptor then pours red-hot, molten bronze into the mold.
6. **Water**   The molten bronze fills up and conforms to the shape of the mold, then slowly cools down to room temperature.
7. **Earth**   The mold is removed, some finishing work is performed, and the bronze copy of the original statue is completed for public exhibition. The bronze statue is a physical reality.

As you may wonder how these seven Principles of Creation were applied in the creation of this Universe, let us examine the processes involved in this feat.

1. **Mind**   Infinite Mind thinks up the basic idea to create a unique universe system out of Itself, formulates the design and computes the technical details.

2. Will   When all the major principles and details are formulated, Infinite Will makes the final decision and initiates the *electric/dynamic* energies required to proceed.

3. Feeling   Through the projection of Infinite Love, The Absolute initiates the *magnetic/receptive* energies to produce the universe through the projection of the Four Elemental Principles. Humanity refers to this event as "The Big Bang!"

Intelligent extensions of The Absolute—individualized beings with varying levels of consciousness—are also created to function throughout the various realms to implement and enhance the original design. Everything is alive and has a creative job to do.

4. Air   Movement projects the pattern and mold of the design into a newly created "space."

5. Fire   The very hot raw materials, electrically charged particles and waves, and subatomic and atomic particles, are projected into the space created by the air principle.

6. Water   The cooling principle of water reduces and controls the intense heat of the initial explosion. The atomic raw materials are eventually contracted into various groups and forms.

7. Earth   Through gravity, the raw materials condense into etheric and material matter according to the designs and patterns projected by the Principle of Air.

As the creative process continues, heavier and denser combinations of atomic particles develop, and galaxies, stars, and planets eventually take form.

Always keep in mind that these seven Principles have been in operation since the Big Bang, being continually operative not only throughout the entire Universe, but also throughout your daily life.

As every created thing vibrates, and order permeates the Universe, the following table illustrates how the rhythms of color and tone apply to the first seven Principles of Creation.

	Love / Feeling	Fire	Air	Life / Mind	Water	Earth	Light / Will
Color	Rose-pink	Orange	Yellow	Green	Turquoise	Indigo-blue	Blue-violet
Tone	C do	D re	E mi	F fa	G sol	A la	B ti

Next, we shall examine the nature of **The Five Personal Principles** with a short statement as to their applications. These are basic evolutionary tools essential to an Earth Participant's spiritual progress, and are an integral requirement to manifest one's needs. They are presented in the form of affirmations, that must be stated with *feeling;* the power of which is explained in a later section.

The Five Personal Principles of Creation

8. Trust
- I Trust my unity with everything!
- I Trust I am safe, secure, and protected!
- I Trust all my needs are supplied!

9. Confidence
- I have Confidence in myself!
- I have Confidence my requests are granted!

10. Knowing
- I Know that I Know!
- I Know that All Is Well!

11. Courage
- I have Courage to live my personal truth!

12. Fortitude
- I have Fortitude to persevere and advance my soul evolution!

The colors associated with these Personal Principles are pastel, spiritual colors that cannot be easily described by human languages. To associate the color of golden-white with each of them is the best suggestion we can offer.

The Mind Over Matter

At this point it is important to analyze and understand the various facets of Mind, so that Participants seeking spiritual progress may more readily establish the most direct route to their destination with the least stress and discomfort. You obviously possess a Mind, or you would not be reading this text, much less comprehending it.

The Principle of Mind states that The All consists of one, infinite consciousness, and this mind exists in everything.

Can you think of anything that has ever been conceived, assembled, manufactured, or created on this planet without thought, ideas, and inspiration? Being one of the abstract and intangible three Primary Qualities of The Absolute, the Principle of Mind has been misunderstood as it pertains to the esoteric side of life in general, and personal soul evolution in particular.

Each Earth Participant's Mind possesses four basic aspects: the unconscious mind (automatic life processes), the subconscious mind (recorded soul data), the conscious mind (everyday awareness), and the superconscious mind (spiritual attunement).

Mind is at the basis of all life and consciousness. Mind enables a being to relate to its environment through thought. Mind potentially possesses the attributes of awareness, observation, evaluation, induction, deduction, logic, conclusion, decision-making, intuition, and Knowing.

The spiritually appropriate use and direction of your conscious mind is the primary means by which you will reach your spiritual goal on Planet Earth. Proper *Thought* determines, influences, and directs the most appropriate use of *Willpower* and *Feelings*.

The conscious mind has three facets as experienced by human beings on Planet Earth. You have heard that animals, and in certain ways humans, function through **instinct:** the *instinctual mind*. You are familiar with the **intellect:** the *intellectual mind,* which is in constant use during your daily, wakened hours. Then, there is **intuition:** the *intuitive mind*. What is the purpose of each and how do they relate to your experiences? Note in this discussion that the three types of conscious mind each have a different *polarity,* a principle that applies to anything and everything existing in the Universe.

The Instinctual Mind

The Instinctual Mind serves the animal kingdom to perform the basic necessities of life existence, namely the quest for food and rest, social behaviors, reproductive activities, and survival. A group instinctual mind and group soul guides each animal species giving it unique, basic characteristics. The instinctual mind is *neutral* in polarity.

The Intellectual Mind

The Intellectual Mind is developed by human beings and assists them to analyze, organize, and relate to objects, events and circumstances in the outer, tangible, material world. The intellectual mind can learn to calculate mathematical data; it relates, thinks, and communicates in terms of words and language.

Cosmically speaking, the rational, human intellectual mind, although more evolved than the instinctual mind used by the animal kingdom, is very limited. A major part of the human experience involves learning to develop and use the intellectual mind. Thereby, a Participant evolves from simply running on "auto-pilot" (instinct), to being able to make cognizant choices through thinking before acting.

The intellect learns to make choices through outer physical experience. The intellectual mind is *dynamic* and serves Participants by *doing things* throughout the mundane affairs of daily life such as thinking, calculating mathematical problems, memorizing data, using logical reasoning, and executing technical sequences. In the area of religion for example, the intellectual mind is only capable of understanding concrete dogma which relate to physical conditions that can be described in *words,* like "burning in the fires of hell" or "entering the pearly gates of heaven." The intellectual mind was designed to comprehend only what it assumes to perceive through the physical senses. It is not a spiritual mind.

The Intuitive Mind

The Intuitive Mind is developed by human beings and enables a Participant to relate to and comprehend abstract, intangible ideas and concepts. The intuitive mind is initially developed through participation in the many forms of art, painting, sculpture, music, dance, literature, poetry, and the like. It is further developed through studies of a variety of abstract metaphysical and spiritual subjects. The intuitive mind is fully operative in life forms functioning on the spiritual realms.

The intuitive mind is greatly broadened and expanded through the practice of meditation. The intuitive mind can relate to and communicate with the unconscious, subconscious, and superconscious minds. Regarding abstract, intangible topics, one's intuitions are verified through their feeling nature. They *feel* right. Intuitive ideas and concepts relating to tangible, material reality may be verified by the intellectual mind through observations, such as the unfolding of future events and scientific research and discovery.

The intuitive mind is not limited by time and space and opens one's consciousness to comprehend the secrets of the Universe. Since the intuitive mind's polarity is *magnetic,* it is *receptive;* it *receives* information. It is able to send and receive mental communications to and from anywhere in the Universe, through thought-pictures. **A thought-picture** is a mind-to-mind transmission whereby a complex idea and concept is sent, received and comprehended in an instant. A thought-picture cannot be accurately translated into words.

Thought-pictures communicate ideas in a manner far beyond the limited scope of words. Thought-pictures are utilized by spiritual beings to communicate with one another through inner space and the vacuum of outer space. The intuitive mind has two basic functions—

1. To receive data transmissions in the form of dreams, visions, ideas, inspirations and word-pictures from inner, non-physical, etheric sources, such as one's soul consciousness, the universal mind, and astral or spiritual guides and teachers.
2. To assimilate, process, and understand abstract, intangible, non-material ideas, concepts, perceptions, and realizations. These latter may be of an esoteric, metaphysical nature such as dream symbols, the concepts of spirit and soul, the principles of cause and effect (karma) and reincarnation.

In response to direct questions, the intuitive mind can receive answers through a process that is beyond the scope of the intellectual mind to comprehend. The answer may reside in the Participant's physical brain memory, their soul memory bank, or be received from astral or higher, spiritual intelligences. Some Participants have the ability to receive *directly* from the data bank of the Universal Mind out in the ethers, which contains this Universe's accumulated knowledge and wisdom. The intuitive, creative mind functions primarily through the *right* hemisphere of the human brain, whereas the intellectual, analytical, thinking mind operates primarily through the *left* hemisphere.

Since the intellectual mind plays an important role in the development of a Participant's spiritual consciousness (the pieces have to fit together), it needs assistance in relating to abstract, intangible concepts. This is where intuition comes into play. The intuitive mind is the greater mind that wants to grow, expand, and reach out into vaster spiritual concepts and realities. It connects into the universal consciousness, the source of all knowledge and wisdom. To eventually achieve a fourth-dimensional consciousness, it is necessary for *all* Participants to develop their Intuitive Minds.

The level of spiritual consciousness a Participant has achieved does not necessarily correlate with the measure of their intelligence quotient (IQ). An intellectually *brilliant* Participant may have a totally undeveloped intuitive mind. The renowned physicist Albert Einstein possessed and demonstrated a brilliant intellectual mind and a well developed intuitive mind. By observing physical phenomena, he was able to comprehend their intangible, non-physical basis.

He is an example of a balanced, scientific mentality, both left brain and right brain. Most of his scientific associates, however, miss this point and choose to remain rigidly confined to their dazzling, but limited, intellects. To quote one of Einstein's observations on his intellectual/intuitive thought processes—

> "All great achievements of science start from intuitive knowledge, namely, in axioms, from which deductions are then made. ... Intuition is the necessary condition for the discovery of such axioms."

As Participants progress in their soul evolution, certain aspects of their instinctual drives are first brought under the control of their intellectual mind, and then their intuitive mind.

An example of this is the requirement for food and nourishment. Rather than indiscriminately eat any food or drink available or desired, you may ask, "Is this food nutritious for me? Am I eating too much or too little? Am I eating a nutritious, balanced diet? Does it contain the full extent of vitamins, minerals, and other nutrients my body requires? Do I need food supplements and if so, what dosage? What does my intuition tell me is ideal for my body's health?"

To summarize the three types of Conscious Mind:

The Instinctual Mind
- Serves the Animal Kingdom.
- Fulfills the basic necessities of life existence.
- Neutral in polarity.

The Intellectual Mind
- Is developed by human beings.
- Assists Participants to reason, analyze, organize, plan, and act.
- Relates to objective, tangible, material reality.

- Can calculate mathematical data and use logic.
- Uses words in the form of language to think and communicate.
- Polarity is dynamic (active, electric).

The Intuitive Mind
- Is to be developed by human beings.
- Relates to and comprehends abstract, intangible ideas and concepts.
- Fosters imagination, inspiration, and ideals.
- Verified by one's feeling nature.
- Not limited by time and space.
- Able to comprehend universal, infinite concepts.
- Can communicate in thought-pictures.
- Polarity is magnetic (receptive).

As a Participant's soul evolves, the more they look towards a higher purpose in their lives, and toward what the most harmonious, constructive, loving course of action may be for themselves, their immediate family, their friends and neighbors, their community, and the world. It is only through the integration of one's intuitive and intellectual minds that one can receive and comprehend the knowledge and wisdom required to clearly answer the questions that arise.

An Overview of Hermetics

Hermetics – The study of spiritual science and technology. Hermetic Principles explain the basic conditions, structures, and premises behind the creation and continuing existence of our Universe and everything in it.

The Hermetic Principles explain, from a unique perspective, the manner in which the Twelve Basic Principles function throughout the universe and in your daily lives. The student of metaphysics who is aware of these principles will find their application useful.

A serious study of Hermetics is invaluable for those who desire a better understanding of the nature and workings of "God," and, thereby, the mechanics of how everything was and is created. It can assist Participants to develop and use their inherent creative nature on a practical, everyday basis utilizing higher, spiritual principles. For instance, in accord with your soul development, you can learn and implement various creative tools that enable you to purify your food, protect your person and property, and attract your needs.

Since the term "The All" is used in the following statements which elucidate the Seven Basic Hermetic Principles, we begin with its definition.

The All – The whole of everything that exists. The consciousness and energies of God The Absolute which extend throughout all creation.

"While all is in THE ALL, it is equally true that THE ALL is in all. To him who truly understands this truth hath come great knowledge."

The Kybalion – Hermetic Philosophy, Yoga Publication Society

The Seven Basic Hermetic Principles (from *The Kybalion*)

1. The Principle of Mentalism
The All is Mind. The Universe is Mental.

2. The Principle of Correspondence
As above, so below. As below, so above.

3. The Principle of Vibration
Nothing rests. Everything moves. Everything vibrates.

4. The Principle of Polarity
Everything is Dual. Everything has poles. Everything has its pair of opposites. Like and unlike are the same. Opposites are identical in nature, but different in degree. Extremes meet. All truths are but half-truths. All paradoxes may be reconciled. [Paradoxes are opposing truths, having opposite polarities.]

5. The Principle of Rhythm
Everything flows, out and in. Everything has its tides. All things rise and fall. The pendulum-swing manifests in everything. The measure of the swing to the right is the measure of the swing to the left. Rhythm compensates.

6. The Principle of Cause and Effect
Every Cause has its Effect. Every Effect has its Cause. Everything happens according to Law. Chance is but a name for Law not recognized. There are many planes of causation, but nothing escapes the Law.

7. The Principle of Gender
Gender is in everything. Everything has both its Masculine and Feminine Principles. Gender manifests on all planes [realms].

Special Note: For clarification as to the specific meaning of the word "spiritual" as used in this guidebook, we present the definition, although we have not yet defined some of the words contained therein:

spiritual – That which relates to the fourth or higher dimensions of consciousness, or to the fourth or higher realms.

– 4 –

RETURNING TO UNITY, ONENESS, AND WHOLENESS

    The original intent was for the Planet Earth experience to take place in an atmosphere of Limitless Total Love. Since the majority of Participants choose to accept the current general conditions on this planet as their only available choice, we will offer an alternative perception.

    Throughout this vast Universe, as physical planets were created, all Participants were endowed with the awareness of their **unity** and **oneness** with God The Absolute, the Infinite Source of everything. These Participants functioned through spiritual, astral, or physical-etheric bodies, and knew and expressed only Limitless Total Love. Thus, the planets they inhabited were *Love-based*.

- **Love-based planet** – The planet in any solar system whose inhabitants choose to live in and express only Limitless Total Love.
- **fear** – An error condition in one's consciousness based upon a lack of Trust, manifesting as a disharmonious, self-defeating emotional reaction to a situation wherein one anticipates great physical, emotional, or mental harm to themselves or to others.
- **fear-based planet** – The planet in any solar system wherein the vibrational frequencies have degraded to the point wherein its third dimcon inhabitants experience aspects of fear.

duality – 1. The most extreme aspect of polarity that exists on fear-based planets wherein Participants experience both harmony and disharmony relative to Natural Law. Duality is experienced as the opposing forces of good and evil; Trust and fear; Love and fear; Love and hate.

2. The perception in one's consciousness of separation, division, and isolation from their Divine Source, their intrinsic spiritual nature, and everything that exists.

evil (see **fraud** also) – 1. Power used as force directed toward interfering with another person's freedom of choice (free will).

2. Intentionally harming another's body or possessions.

3. The use of undue negative influence on a man or woman through the indoctrination of false truths.

4. The negative energy resulting from erroneous soul programming whereby a man or woman has denied their inherent goodness (Godness).

5. The use of mental, emotional, or physical fear tactics to direct another's focus toward disharmony and doubt, whereby they can be controlled.

fraud – An intentional perversion or concealment of truth to induce another to part with a valuable possession or to surrender a legal right. A false representation or concealment of a fact which should have been disclosed, with the intention to deceive another so that he shall act upon it to his legal, financial, or bodily injury. Deceit or trickery used to gain an unfair advantage over another.

Planet Earth was originally a *Love-based* planet wherein the Participants functioned in harmony through a spiritual state of consciousness in full realization of their unity with everything. "Evil," or separateness from the will of The Creator, was not a condition they experienced, for they lived in a state of Limitless Total Love, which transcends the duality of conditional and unconditional love.

Participants in some civilizations, however, desired to experience *both* Good and Evil, or *duality*. Therefore, not only were their levels of conscious awareness and overall intelligence greatly reduced, but the frequency vibration of their bodies and of the entire planet was also lowered. Subsequently, these Participants were required to function in dense, lethargic, physical-material bodies, which were subject to different natural laws, including aging and death. They previously had functioned through bodies of a higher vibrational frequency, which were extremely intelligent, lighter, and did not experience death as humans do.

By choosing to embrace error and conflict—out of harmony with the intrinsic nature of their being—humanity's ancestors thereby created the state of **duality, division, separateness** and, therefore, **judgment.** Spiritual truths, including their inherent unity and oneness with the whole of creation, became foreign concepts to these Participants. They developed ego-oriented and self-centered perspectives, viewing themselves as separate, in opposition to, and in conflict with the greater good of the whole. Being aware of only separateness and division, they fell into judgment and anger, bickering and fighting over their seeming differences.

Under the influence of duality, all of the various facets of Earthly living have been reduced to two fundamental components: **Love and fear.** For countless centuries, these two opposites have been the basic learning tools and guidelines for Participants of this educational adventure. All decisions made by the majority of Participants have had aspects of these two choices—Love and fear—at their foundation.

As long as the majority of Participants with a third-dimensional consciousness desire to experience both the harmonious and the disharmonious aspects of duality, they will continue to run up against the challenges encountered in choosing between good and evil, peace and violence, happiness and sadness, wealth and poverty, pleasure and suffering, power and weakness, victory and defeat. Like mountains and valleys, wave crests and troughs, these extreme opposites have created the seesaw of life in the third dimcon.

As most Participants are currently constrained in the perception of duality, the majority of the major institutions on this planet—such as government, religion, education, information, entertainment, business, and industry—are rooted in fear and are used by their administrators to enhance their own personal agendas, rather than being dedicated to serving the best interests of humanity as a whole. For Earth to be a Love-based planet, all institutions that do not project , promote, and support the principle of Limitless Total Love need to be transformed.

Over the past thousands of years, there have been many attempts by spiritually oriented Participants to raise Mother Earth out of the denseness of these lower frequency vibrations, and back to her original condition as a spiritual, Love-based planet. Why have these efforts been unsuccessful?

The downfall of humankind has been that most people have failed to live and act in the highest principles that they know.

Observing the Universe as a whole, the condition of duality is the exception, not the rule. To encounter and participate in evil is not a prerequisite to the experience of a third-dimensional consciousness. The vast majority of planets in other solar systems wherein Participants experience the third dimcon have remained Love-based. Participants on Love-based planets are aware of the principles of unity, oneness, and wholeness. Love-based planets function at a much higher vibratory rate than is now encountered on Earth.

Since it does not exist, the perception of separateness and isolation from anyone or anything in the universe is an aberration. The state of duality has been a trap for humanity on Planet Earth from which relatively few have escaped. The challenge for Participants has been to evolve out of the quagmire and tangle of seemingly conflicting rules, opinions, and belief systems. The more you comprehend and merge your identity with the oneness and wholeness of everything in the universe, the more surely you progress toward acquiring a fourth-dimensional consciousness. This is the major step in progressing along your spiritual path toward Enlightenment, Truth, and Wisdom.

Since all Participants on this Earth Expedition are endowed with the attribute of free will, each man and woman always has the option of choosing between Oneness and Duality. Each Participant needs to be aware of the current situation and informed of the means to transcend it. According to myth and tradition, in order for a Participant to achieve or return to a fourth-dimensional, spiritual consciousness, there are five tests or initiations to be mastered. They are the tests of—

1. **air** – the purification of one's mental processes, by releasing all disharmonious, self-defeating thoughts and ideas;
2. **fire** – the purification of one's will, by releasing one's small, ego will to the greater, Higher Will;
3. **water** – the purification of one's feeling nature, by dissolving disharmonious emotions;
4. **earth** – the purification of one's sensual desire nature, through the lack of attachment to mental, emotional, and physical addictions, habits, and attractions;
5. **ether** – the purification of one's soul.

On Planet Earth, the souls of the vast majority of human Participants originated here—this is their first planetary experience. These souls' mission is to bridge the span extending from the animal consciousness to the attainment of a spiritual consciousness. When viewing the spectrum of Participants' consciousness on Earth today, a large number of humanity is comprised of new or young souls with little or no experience in confronting the disharmonious wiles of the world. These "youngster" souls' programming is inadequate to assist them in delineating the differences between constructive and destructive behaviors. As their souls have never experienced harmonious, Love-based planets, these native Earth souls have no frame of reference to distinguish the disharmonious state of duality from the ideal state of Unity and Oneness. At the other end of the spectrum, some Participants have experienced over two hundred or more bodily incarnations on Earth, and have yet to graduate to the fourth dimcon.

The fascinating lure of Earth attractions and adventures is very great. From birth, Participants on this Planet Earth Expedition have been programmed by virtually every institution on the planet to believe that duality and material conditions are the only realities. The result has been that Participants are constantly conditioned to live in doubt, distrust, and fear. A Participant remains functioning in the third dimcon until these disharmonious, self-defeating qualities are transmuted into a higher vibrational awareness of constructive, spiritual attributes.

Due to the low vibrational level of awareness Participants experience on Earth, many unscrupulous Participants, both young and old souls, ignorant of the severe karmic consequences of their actions, have found it relatively easy to mislead, manipulate, and control their fellow Participants. They have done this through dictatorial rules, governmental laws with hidden agendas, fraudulent tactics, deceptive sales practices, and mind control techniques, to name a few.

For instance, based on an agenda of increasing viewership and revenues, the news and entertainment media constantly broadcast productions depicting crime, unethical behavior and practices, and sensual emotional gratification. The effect of this brainwashing is to desensitize Participants into accepting disharmonious activities as a normal, fundamental component of the Earth experience. Amoral behavior is increasingly being viewed, and accepted, as standard and routine. As disharmony perpetuates fear, and Participants can be controlled through fear, this is an unsatisfactory situation at best.

As a result, most Participants are unaware of constructive, spiritual alternatives to materialism and fear. Few people are aware that participating, even indirectly, in the duality of both good and evil is not in harmony with a spiritual consciousness. The majority feels resigned to accept life on Earth as it is presented and as it appears to the relative reality of their physical senses. Separateness, division, and judgment have been considered normal, to the point where they are taken for granted. Constructive options based on spiritual truth and wisdom rarely are seriously offered or considered.

Many Participants are taught and believe that when they complete one bodily experience, they have reached the end of the road; the decisive moment has arrived wherein one's eternal destiny is determined.

This is a fear-based concept, designed to control Participants through threats and coercion. Perhaps the outer intent has been for people to concentrate on doing their best with this lifetime, but has fear resolved the problems inherent in the extreme polarization of good and evil?

The soul requires many physical incarnations and countless higher vibrational experiences along its path of evolution. Actually, graduating from a third-dimensional consciousness on Planet Earth is equivalent to having completing kindergarten (the sand box experience) and the first grade in your elementary schools. There is a long way to go; more expeditions to experience on many realms, and there are more dimeons through which to evolve. There is much soul growth to be achieved in cosmic experience, knowledge, and wisdom than can be acquired in only one lifetime on Planet Earth.

Historically, there are three misdirections of energy that resulted in humanity's many falls from Grace. These still typify the present condition on Planet Earth. They are—

1. the misuse of **Power;**
2. the misuse of **Money and Wealth;**
3. the misuse of **Sex.**

Due to its prevalence, a fourth, more contemporary error has befallen the world:

4. the misuse of **Drugs.**

The misuse of these four spiritual responsibilities, rewards, and gifts has produced the greatest barriers to the advancement of the soul evolution of both individual Participants, and all Participants as a group. The majority of karmic lessons and imbalances reside within these four misuses. They are where humanity needs to come into harmony before it can move forward into enlightenment.

The karmic lessons resulting from the **misuse of power** have their greatest impact on Participants in government, financial, business, and educational institutions, and upon the wealthy class of people. Positions of power over other Participants are only temporary roles one plays, and they bestow great responsibilities on humanity's leaders to place public and planetary interests over their own personal self-interests. The world's greatest leaders recognized that they were the servants of all the people. They were most sensitive to the populace and strove to provide them with their real needs. The misuse of power for one's own material gain—at the expense of others and the planet's environment—is out of harmony with Natural Law, as everything is God, and everyone is equal.

Currently, the false god of Planet Earth is **money.** This situation demands transformation. The attitude that the rules for the acquisition of money and wealth supersede moral spiritual principles is a gross error. Money needs to be honored only as a medium of exchange. It represents the value of energy expended for services rendered. Money was intended to be the servant, not the master. Perspectives regarding money and its role in one's life requires change. Money needs to be viewed in a more realistic manner.

Many of those who are overly concerned with the accumulation of money believe that the amassing of material wealth is a confirmation of their self-value. Participants who handle money appropriately by allowing it to flow back and forth with ease, have no problem with self-worth. Ask yourself whether in your thoughts you place too much value on money, or if in your actions you misuse money. When you know your own true self-worth and self-value, abundance comes not only in the form of money, but in friends, gifts, help, and support.

Participants need to be humble when honored with success, abundance, and monetary wealth brought about through their talents, ingenuity, intelligence, hard work, and good karma. Giving back a portion of one's income is being grateful to the Participants, the Planet, and the unseen innerplane intelligences that assisted them to acquire their material abundance. Money is a form of power. To use one's wealth to exercise control over other Participants—to force them into submission and treat them as slaves—is out of harmony with everyone's nature as The Absolute.

The **misuse of sex** is a major pitfall that is little recognized. From a spiritual perspective, there is much misunderstanding surrounding one's sexuality. Sex is a sacred gift bestowed upon humanity to be honored, respected, and used discreetly—with wisdom. The misuse of sex has been a major factor in the deceleration of soul evolution on this planet. Human sexuality is completely out of balance. It needs to be brought back into harmony before humanity can evolve to a higher level of consciousness.

For a soul to evolve through constructive action when embodied in human form, the body needs all the awareness, willpower, and functionality of which it is capable. The **misuse of recreational and pharmaceutical drugs** greatly inhibits these abilities and eventually deteriorates one's mind, feeling nature, and physical body. Participants come to Planet Earth to progress their soul evolution and this purpose is thwarted by the addiction to any substance or obsessive action.

We have been pointing out the major pitfalls and traps that have been stagnating soul evolution on Planet Earth. The good news is that **this present extreme condition of duality can be reversed and the planet returned to a harmonious, spiritual frequency vibration and condition.** Duality does not have to exist on Planet Earth. If a sufficient number of Participants desire to live in a pleasant, harmonious environment, the present condition can be transformed into an atmosphere of LimitlessTotal Love.

When more people pray for the transformation of Planet Earth, and a sufficient number of Participants acquire a fourth-dimensional, spiritual consciousness, the scales will then tip to raise Earth's vibration to the status of a Love-based planet. Disharmony will cease to exist.

Considering the present size of the population on Earth, a minimum number of two million Participants with a spiritual consciousness is required to accomplish this feat. Greater efforts are needed to propel Earth vibrations over the top!

Please understand the importance of your participation in this Expedition. For a Participant to have experienced and then graduated from the realm of duality, to Unity and Oneness, they indeed have acquired a potent knowledge, wisdom, and a strength that will fortify and empower them throughout their climb up the ladder of soul evolution.

- 5 -

COSMIC GEOGRAPHY: WHERE ARE YOU?

It is apparent that the vast majority of Participants on Planet Earth have a lack of comprehension as to *where they really are* in relationship to the whole scheme of things—the physical world, and whatever else is *out* there, or perhaps more importantly, *in* there.

A Clearer View of Infinity

> *If the doors of perception were cleansed, everything would appear to man as it is—infinite.*
> William Blake

By obtaining a clearer concept of infinity, the dark glass through which Participants on this Earth adventure have been looking can easily become transparent. Let us begin by examining some definitions of the words *infinite* and *infinity*.

infinite – Being limitless and without boundaries. Endless and inexhaustible with no beginning or end. All encompassing beyond measure or comprehension.

infinity – Limitless space, distance, time, quantity, or number.

After examining these definitions, we may state certain conclusions concerning the nature of infinity and its properties.

Diagram A: The Vibrational Frequency Spectrum

Frequency – in cycles per second		Wavelength – in meters (where applicable)
∞		
	Cosmic Rays	10^{-20}
10^{25}		
	Gamma Rays	10^{-15}
10^{20}		
	X-Rays	10^{-10}
10^{15}	Ultraviolet Light	
	VISIBLE LIGHT	
	Infrared Light	10^{-5}
10^{10}	Microwaves	
	Radar Waves	
	Television Waves	
	FM Radio Waves	1 meter
10^{5}	Shortwave Radio Waves	
	AM Radio Waves	
10^{2}	**HUMAN HEARING**	10^{-5}
10	Ten Seconds of Time	
1	One Second of Time	
10^{-5}	One Day on Planet Earth	
	One Orbit of Planet Pluto	
	One Rotation of a Galaxy	
∞		

Conclusions regarding the Properties of Infinity

1. That which is infinite cannot be made larger or added to.
2. That which is infinite cannot be made smaller or subtracted from.
3. Nothing can be separated from that which is infinite.
4. Nothing can exist outside of that which is infinite, which having no limits, is everywhere and includes everything.
5. Infinity is equal everywhere. Nowhere can there be more or less.

As the Hermetic Principle of Vibration states, everything in the Universe, on all planes of existence, is vibrating or cycling at a specific rate, or within a particular frequency range. For instance, a tuning fork tuned to the note "G" vibrates at a fixed frequency, whereas the sun emits a very broad frequency spectrum covering a multitude of octaves. Taking all creation into consideration, whether it is an atom, sun, planet, galaxy, or realm, the vibrational frequency range is *infinite*.

vibrational spectrum – A progressive scale of measure of infinite range that depicts the specific or average rate of rhythm, vibration, or cycle pertaining to anything in the Universe.

When considering the notion of infinity, Participants generally think of infinity as being outside of their experience of time/space, which appears to be limited. However, if one con-siders that the vibrational spectrum is infinite, and that nothing can exist outside of infinity, the vibrational spectrum Participants are experiencing as time/space must exist somewhere *within* the limitless range of infinity. (see Diagram A)

In other words, the physical planetary experience to which Participants are now relating is connected to everything in the infiniteness of creation. A problem may arise because the infinite nature of Participant's Earthly experience is not readily apparent to the intellectual mind's analysis of data perceived through the five physical senses. The solution for Participants is to develop an ultra-sensory nature—one that perceives from a state of Spiritual Unity rather than from separation.

The illusions created by the condition of duality and division have produced the misconception that this Universe and the life forms

Diagram B:
View of the Universe from a Perspective of Duality

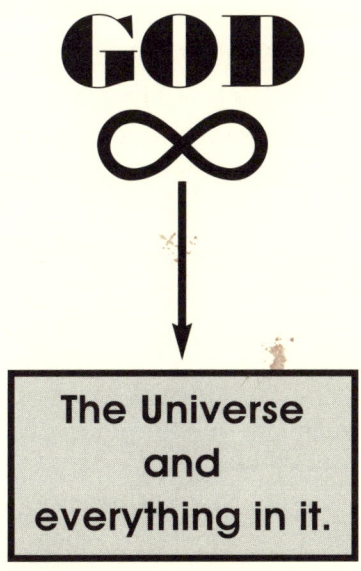

experiencing it are outside of and separate from The Infinite Intelligence that created them. (see Diagram B) As you may now realize, this is impossible. There can be no inside or outside of infinity, for by definition, *all* facets of infinity are infinite.

The concept of infinity becomes clearer once a Participant has achieved a spiritual, fourth-dimensional consciousness, wherein one is more cognizant of the principles of unity, oneness, and wholeness. Participants with a third-dimensional consciousness usually experience great difficulty when relating to the limitless nature of infinity, as their perspective is filtered through the dark glass of duality, division, and separateness and is, therefore, severely distorted and inaccurate.

Our purpose in providing a clearer comprehension of where you are is to assist Participants in acquiring an understanding of the relationship between themselves as unique individuals, the physical environment of the planet they are inhabiting, the cosmos "out there," and all of creation in general.

Wisdom Garnered from the Physicists

Science without religion is lame, religion without science is blind.
Albert Einstein

You may wish to read the book *God and the Astronomers,* by Robert Jastrow, an eminent astrophysicist and author of many scientific books. In *God and the Astronomers,* Robert Jastrow guides the reader through the discoveries, theories, and thought processes of the astro- and nuclear-physicists from around the beginning of the Twentieth Century to the present. This very informative little book is laced with an underlying humor that uncovers the point at which science and spirituality find a common meeting ground, bridging the gap that had separated them for many centuries.

Simply stated, the big-bang theory of the creation of the Universe, which contemporary scientific evidence supports, contends that at the beginning instant, everything in the Universe originated from a tiny, infinite point in which all matter was compacted under staggering pressures, and heat and cold. When the rapidly expanding Universe was one second old, the temperature had decreased by one billion degrees. It took a million years in Earth terms for the expanding fireball to cool down enough to begin forming atomic particles and the simple building blocks of matter.

The highly respected physicist, Stephen Hawking, made the following statements concerning calculations in relation to the creation and nature of the Universe, particularly pertaining to infinity:

> All of the Friedmann [a Russian physicist and mathematician] solutions have the feature that at some time in the past (between ten and twenty thousand million years ago) the distance between neighboring galaxies must have been zero. At that time, which we call the big bang, the density of the universe and the curvature of space-time would have been infinite. Because mathematics cannot really handle infinite numbers, this means that the general theory of relativity (on which Friedmann's solutions are based) predicts that there is a

point in the universe where the theory itself breaks down. Such a point is an example of what mathematicians call a singularity. In fact, all our theories of science are formulated on the assumption that space-time is smooth and nearly flat, so they break down at the big bang singularity, where the curvature of space-time is infinite.[1]

At the big bang itself, the universe is thought to have had zero size, and so to have been infinitely hot.[2]

In order to predict how the universe should have started off, one needs laws that hold at the beginning of time. If the classical theory of general relativity was correct, the singularity theorems that Roger Penrose and I proved show that the beginning of time would have been a point of infinite density and infinite curvature of space-time. All the known laws of science would break down at such a point.[3]

The obvious question with which the physicists were confronted was, "If the Universe had a beginning, what started it?" For many scientific reasons, the only logical answer points to *an infinitely powerful intelligence*. Scientific theories, calculations, and discoveries have supported this answer. Here are a few examples of physicists' questions and observations:

> Why did the universe start out with so nearly the critical rate of expansion that separates models that recollapse from those that go on expanding forever, that even now, ten thousand million years later, it is still expanding at nearly the critical rate? If the rate of expansion one second after the big bang had been smaller by even one part in a hundred thousand million million, the universe would have recollapsed before it ever reached its present size.[4]

---

1 *The Illustrated Brief History of Time,* p. 61, by Stephen Hawking
2 Ibid, p. 147
3 Ibid. p. 171
4 Ibid. p. 156

The initial rate of expansion also would have had to be chosen very precisely for the rate of expansion still to be so close to the critical rate needed to avoid recollapse. This means that the initial state of the universe must have been very carefully chosen indeed if the hot big bang model was correct right back to the beginning of time. It would be very difficult to explain why the universe should have begun in just this way, except as the act of a God who intended to create beings like us.[5]

A human being is a part of the whole called by us the Universe, a part limited in time and space. He experiences himself, his thoughts and feelings as something separated from the rest—a kind of optical delusion of his consciousness. This delusion is a kind of prison for us, restricting us to our personal desires and to affection for a few persons nearest to us. Our task must be to free ourselves from this prison by widening our circle of compassion to embrace all living creatures and the whole nature in it's beauty.
Albert Einstein as quoted in *Self-Realization Magazine, Summer, 1979*

(In the following quote by Einstein, it would perhaps have been more accurate to state that "nearly everyone" or "many" who are seriously involved in the pursuit of science ...)

Everyone who is seriously involved in the pursuit of science becomes convinced that a spirit is manifest in the laws of the Universe—a spirit vastly superior to that of man, and one in the face of which we with our modest powers must feel humble. In this way, the pursuit of science leads to a religious feeling of a special sort, which is indeed quite different from the religiosity of someone more naive.

Albert Einstein.

---

5 Ibid. p. 163

Creating Within Infinity

If infinity cannot be made larger, smaller, or separated, and nothing can exist outside of it, just how was the Universe and everything in it created? The answer lies in an understanding of The Seven Basic Hermetic Principles, particularly The Principles of Correspondence, Polarity and Gender. Physicists have discovered some other interesting particulars in this regard.

We now know that every particle has an antiparticle, with which it can annihilate. There could be whole antiworlds and antipeople made out of antiparticles.[6] [RG: also antiuniverses]

Where did they (atomic particles) all come from? The answer is that, in quantum theory, particles can be created out of energy in the form of particle/antiparticle pairs. But that just raises the question of where the energy came from. The answer is that the total energy of the universe is exactly zero. ... In the case of a universe that is approximately uniform in space, one can show that this negative gravitational energy exactly cancels the positive energy represented by the matter. So the total energy of the universe is zero.[7]

The positive atomic charges in the Universe, like protons, pions, and certain kaons, exactly balance out the negative charges, like electrons and taus, with some particles being neutral, like neutrons, photons and neutrinos. In addition, nuclear physicists can observe in the laboratory that matter and antimatter exist in equal proportions. However, this exact balance is not found in our universe through observation by the astrophysicists. Some antimatter is observable streaming from black holes, which are also singularities. However, if matter and antimatter existed in equal proportions, our Universe would most likely annihilate itself. This is why there exists an antiuniverse, an opposite to ours, in which, to its Participants, our Universe appears to be the antiuniverse.

---

6 Ibid., p. 89
7 Ibid., p. 166

So now, you may comprehend how everything, and everyone, was created out of infinity without changing the basic Laws inherent in infinity. The basic ingredients of matter and consciousness in everything created are in perfect balance. Everything was given polarity—equal but opposite energy "charges."

In all of creation matter equals antimatter; positive polarity equals negative polarity; male equals female; neutral polarity being balanced within itself. Throughout this process, infinity was not made larger or smaller or separated from itself, and nothing exists outside of infinity. The origin and composition of everything and everyone is infinite!

The Nature of Our Universe System

> *There are more things in heaven and earth, Horatio,
> than are dreamt of in your philosophy.*
>
> Hamlet, Act 1, Scene 5, by William Shakespeare

Have you on occasion stopped to search the nighttime sky and ponder the possible implications of what you observe—the Moon, the planets, the wavy sea of billions of stars, some near and bright, others dissolved in misty star-clouds? One might ask, "If there is other life out there, why doesn't it talk to me? Why is it hiding? Why do I feel so isolated in this vast Universe?"

Did you ever stop to think, though, that perhaps the Universe was actually teeming with life, with angelic and other forms of intelligence unseen to human eyes, inaudible to human ears, untouchable to human hands? Have you recognized that the earth-body experience to which your physical senses are attuned is akin to a radio tuned to a station transmitting a narrow band of electromagnetic energy? That the rest of the infinite spectrum is unobservable directly to your human senses?

"In my Father's house, there are many rooms."

This quote is very familiar to many Earth cruise Participants with a Western religious orientation. However, few understand the true implications of the statement. Perhaps it would be more accurate to state,

In my Father's house, there are many floors, or levels.

... or, even more accurately,

In my Father's Universe, there are many realms and dimensions of consciousness.

realm – A dimension of place or existence within a universe system, occupying a specific, distinct range of vibrational frequencies. There are numerous octaves of energy frequencies within a realm. (For instance, human beings' hearing is within a range of vibrational octaves; their vision is within a higher vibrational octave.) A realm offers a place of existence for the experiences of beings functioning through various dimcons.

universe system – An organized network of many realms. All realms are connected sequentially. The vibrational range of each realm is separated from the next by "transformers" of both power and vibrational frequency. Each realm has its own unique energy spectrum, and each realm is connected to and based upon another, like the links of a chain.

By now, many of you Expedition Participants know that Earth is a medium-size planet in a solar system containing nine planets, an asteroid belt, and many comets, all orbiting around a relatively small-size sun. This solar system is in an outlying arm of a "spiral" galaxy containing billions of stars. The "Milky Way Galaxy," as the locals call it, is just one of hundreds of billions of galaxies in this Universe.

From the spiritual realms, we are able to perceive a much broader range of frequency vibrations than is possible from an Earth perspective. Therefore, we wish to take this opportunity to share our viewpoint as to the composition of this Universe. You are actually experiencing **a universe system of twelve realms**—three physical, six spiritual, and three transcendent. This means that the material realm you observe and to which you relate has an underlying, interior foundation of eleven other realms, each pulsating at proportionally higher vibrational frequencies. All twelve realms exist within the same area of "space," in much the same manner that many sound, radio, TV, radar, and other frequencies can all exist within a given sector of atmosphere on Earth. (see Diagram C)

As human beings function in material bodies, most Participants living on Planet Earth are conscious of functioning in only one of these realms—the first, the heaviest and most dense of all. Participants have at times referred to this first realm as "the third dimension" based on the geometry of its linear extensions. This phrase, however, is not useful when examining the whole system of realms. The second to the twelfth realms offer experience to Participants functioning at progressively higher levels of awareness through body forms and densities which harmonically correspond to that particular realm. As these other realms exist beyond Earth concepts of time, space, and matter, they definitely come under the heading of abstract, intangible concepts.

The concepts behind the existence of many realms and dimcons within the nature of God are very sophisticated. An in-depth understanding of them requires that Participants be ready, willing, and able to set aside their intellectual minds in order to pursue greater comprehension through their receptive, intuitive minds. Until now, few have desired to do this, for to examine the principles behind the existence of twelve realms and dimensions of consciousness requires an ability to understand and relate to abstract, intangible concepts. This process is beyond the limited realities that the human intellectual mind can perceive through the five physical senses.

The nature, intricacies, and workings of this Universe system that you are experiencing, although based on simple basic principles, are too complex for the average intellectual mind to grasp by itself. This is why it had been much easier in previous centuries for some sectors to teach Earth Expedition Participants, "You are here; God is there, or everywhere; and that's that!"

Concerning this Universe system, the three lowest vibrational realms of this Universe system, the first to the third, are the Physical Realms. They give Participants the very familiar "hands-on" planetary experiences, "down there" in the under-worlds, with their various aspects of physical reality.

Diagram C: Our Universe System

Symbolic Frequency and Power		Realms	∞	
10^{∞}	**The Godhead**		God The Absolute	
$10^{10,000}$			God The Creator	
$10^{1,000}$			God The Manifest	
10^{12}	**Transcendent Realms**	12th		
10^{11}		11th		
10^{10}		10th		
10^{9}	**Spiritual Realms** (no space or time)	9th		
10^{8}		8th		
10^{7}		7th		
10^{6}		6th		
10^{5}		5th		
10^{4}	"The Kingdom of God"	4th		
10^{3}	**Physical Realms**	3rd	**Astral Realm** (Space; no time)	
10^{2}		2nd	**Physical-etheric Realm** (Space and time)	
10		1st	**Material Realm** (Space and time)	

The next six realms, the fourth to the ninth, are the Spiritual Realms. These give Participants a "wings-on" experience of creation relative to planets, solar systems, and galaxies.

The Transcendent Realms, the tenth to the twelfth, are the three highest vibrationally speaking. These realms blaze at incredibly high frequency vibrations, and are not so much a "place" of existence as a state or condition of pure consciousness. They give Participants the experience of a galactic and universal consciousness, and an intimate awareness of the functioning of the Twelve Basic Principles throughout this Universe system.

For more scientifically oriented Expedition Participants, we offer some ideas from a different perspective for you to consider. You are aware that *atomic particles,* tiny solar systems of electrical charges, are the basis of matter in this first, material realm. Consider that *subatomic particles* are the basis of matter of the second realm, and *light particles,* similar to photons, the matter of the third realm. This is an interesting situation, for time and space exist in the first and second realms, but only space, not time, exists in the third realm.

The Spiritual Realms, the fourth to the ninth, are made up of etheric light particles of proportionately higher frequency vibrations. There is no space or time in these realms, for the speed of etheric light particles is instantaneous.

There is a barrier separating the three lower, physical realms, which contain space, from the next six higher spiritual realms. Earth Participants will require a higher-dimensional spiritual consciousness and an ethereal body to penetrate the mysteries of these finer realms.

Infinity did not end at the Big Bang just because space/time, which appears to be finite, began then. Our Universe system of twelve realms is only one part of the infinite "spectrum" of infinity. Confusion has arisen around this point since most Participants on Earth are conscious of experiencing only one small segment of infinity—the lowest frequency, densest, and most restrictive realm created to date.

- 6 -

COSMIC ANATOMY: WHO ARE YOU?

"You are Gods!"
(but you wonder how this can be true.)

"Who am I, really?" Have you ever asked yourself this question? Have you received a definitive answer that really rang true for you? With a clearer understanding of both *where* you are, and *who* you are, the fog of isolation begins lifting to reveal your true purpose and objectives in "signing up" for this Planet Earth Educational Expedition.

Trickle-down Creation

The All – The whole of everything that exists. The consciousness and energies of God The Absolute which extend throughout all creation.

God The Absolute – The highest aspect of The All which is the Limitless Prime Source and Master Mind behind all creation. Infinite unmanifested potential. Primordial consciousness, will, feeling, energy, and creative power.

God The Creator – The infinite point constituting the Twelve Basic Principles, or Energies, inherent in the creation, formation, and structure of everything in our Universe system.

God The Manifest – The point of consciousness in which the Twelve Basic Energies of God The Creator are combined and blended, then radiate out to create, maintain, and transform all the realms and dimcons of our Universe system.

This is the **Unity Point** of manifestation. It may be thought of as **the thirteenth dimcon,** as all individualized life and all forms of environmental substance have their origin, are unified in, and radiate throughout the Universe from this infinite point.

For you to truly understand *who you are,* we must begin before the creation of this Universe. In actuality the *real you* is a very complex organism, or more correctly, a series of organisms. There is much more to John and Mary than appears on the surface.

To begin, let us presume that our Universe system, comprised of The Godhead and twelve realms, was all created in one singularity, or "big bang" event. Let us also observe that the each of the twelve realms chronologically correspond to the twelve dimcons. The matter of the first realm (the slowest in frequency oscillation) is composed of and supported by beings with a first-dimensional consciousness, the least aware dimcon, comparably for the second dimcon, and so forth up the line.

Beings can function (within limits) through bodies in realms at or lower than their corresponding dimcons, but not in realms above it. For example, a spiritual being with a fifth-dimensional consciousness may experience an incarnation on Earth, the first realm, but may not experience the sixth realm until graduation to the sixth dimcon. "Diagram D" will make this clearer.

As previously noted under the heading "The Twelve Building Blocks of This Universe," there are Three Primary Principles of Creation: Mind, Will, and Feeling. These three fundamental qualities are called "primary" because they are intrinsic to the nature of **God The Absolute,** are vital elements in the creation process, and exist in everything created.

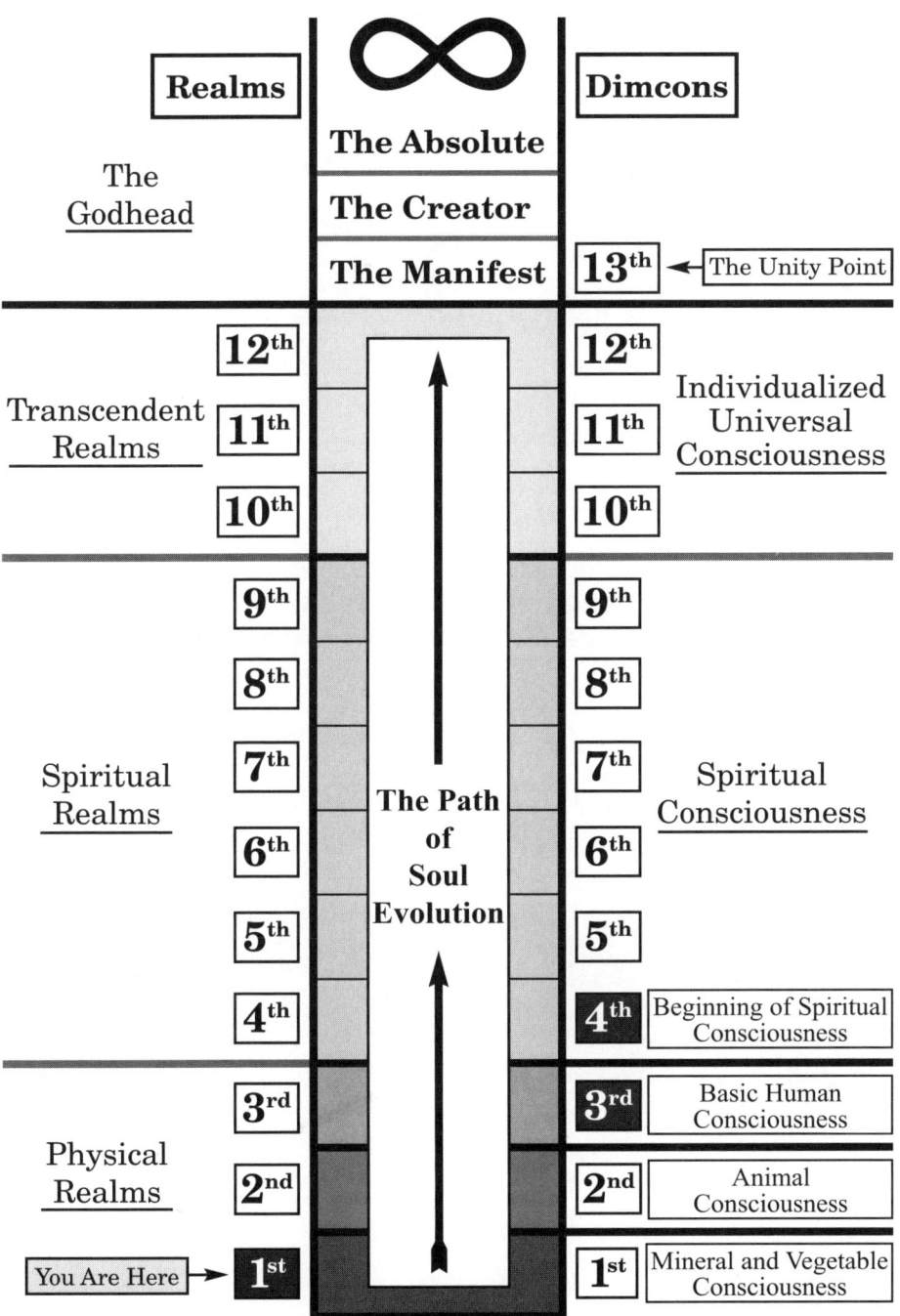

Diagram D: Realms and Dimcons

No constructive, creative action can be performed on any level or realm without their combined activity. Every being and everything in existence possesses the Three Primary Principles of Mind, Will, and Feeling.

To create matter and lower life forms out of infinity and within infinity, God The Absolute had to project Its energies to a lower level of vibrational frequency and power, always keeping these extended energies in perfect harmony, balance, and equilibrium. Since The Absolute was extending facets of Itself, and within infinity nothing can be added, subtracted, or separated, the Primary Principles It projected had to be fundamentally identical to Itself. Although these projected facets exist at lower vibrational frequencies than The Absolute, they are identical in content, but not in power (the available amount of energy) or degree of awareness or consciousness.

To better understand how everything is connected in unity and oneness, let us examine the mechanics of this creative endeavor. It is obvious that the fundamental nature of The Absolute is to be Creative. Since everything and everyone exists within the limitless expanse of infinity, everything and everyone has some active or passive role to perform in the ongoing creative process.

The hermetic Principle of Correspondence states, "As above, so below. As below, so above." Examine the nature of the Sun of your solar system and the three-fold process involved in the transformation of its energies. The Sun is basically 1) composed of a huge ball of fuel, hydrogen atoms, which, 2) being compressed under the Sun's crushing force of gravity, causes a thermonuclear fusion reaction at its very center. This process transforms the hydrogen atoms into helium atoms. This results in 3) the release of tremendous amounts of energy in the form of wave/particles which radiate in all directions. Participants on Planet Earth sense the Sun's radiation primarily as light and heat.

Now, with our greater understanding of infinity, as well as adhering to the Hermetic Principle of Correspondence, "As above, so below. As below, so above," let us observe how the process operative in the suns of the galaxies parallels the process of creating this Universe, and perceive just how it was accomplished.

Once upon a "no-time," and "no-thing" else for that matter, **God The Absolute** willed the creation of a new, grand universe system. As we established in the previous section, to create this within the laws of infinity, it is required that two universes be created simultaneously, each with energies equal to and polarities the reverse of the other—each, thereby, being an antiuniverse to the other. One way to perceive this is to observe the symbol for infinity: ∞ It has two parts (loops), that are connected, *as one.* Even God The Absolute must adhere to the laws of infinity, although It most likely views the situation as simply working within the intrinsic, infinite nature of Its Being.

As The Absolute needed to formulate this grand universe system out of Itself, Its Three Primary Principles (Mind, Will, and Feeling), had to go along for the ride. Researching Its vast storehouse of knowledge, experience, and wisdom, the Prime Source then had to "decide" what Elemental and Personal qualities, chosen out of the limitless range of infinite possibilities, would be included in this new project, thereby satisfying Its creative instincts. The final choice was the Twelve Basic Principles of this Universe system we are presently experiencing. Note that eight of them are intangible (the Primary and Personal), and four are tangible (the Elemental), as they relate to your five physical senses. (Refer to p. 17, The Twelve Basic Principles of Creation.)

As the inherent nature of God The Absolute is limitless and formless, the second creative step was to compress these Twelve Basic Principles into an *infinite point* at a power level and vibrational frequency lower than that of The Absolute Itself, The Limitless Source. We will name this power point **God The Creator.**

Being an infinite point of consciousness, God The Creator is not only the center point of this Universe system but also the center point of each thing contained within it. In other words, the infinite point of God The Creator is somewhere, anywhere, and everywhere at the same time, for it is the basis of every *thing* created. God The Creator's twelve energies are each infinite in scope, just more itemized, customized, and specific than The Absolute's broad spectrum of limitless energies and unmanifested potential.

To better comprehend God The Creator, visualize a brilliant, blazing point of blue-white light radiating an aura, a circular rainbow of twelve colors. Or, think of twelve knights sitting at a round table whose energies combine over the table's center as a brilliant point of blue-white light. These twelve principles vibrate throughout all of the realms and correspond to the twelve notes of a musical octave—on a piano, the seven white and five black keys. These twelve keys make up one musical octave. As above, so below.

The third step is the manifestation process. As in music, these Twelve Basic Principles may be endlessly combined to yield an infinite variety of manifestations. This process involves the outward radiation of these Twelve Creative Energies from the central point of God The Creator to form and eventually develop this entire Universe system and all its inhabitants. We will name the radiance of these energies, **God The Manifest.** In keeping with trickle-down creation, God The Manifest functions at a lower power level and vibrational frequency than God The Creator.

This three-step creative process resulted in the twelve realms of experience and the twelve dimensions of consciousness in our expanding Universe system. The central point from which the energies of God The Manifest radiate is also known as **The Unity Point of All Individualized Consciousness.** This Unity Point is the origin and creative source wherein all environmental and individualized forms of life are unified and connected. Therefore the saying, "All is One!" Think of and visualize each "ray" of Light radiating from God The Manifest as being a single, conscious, individualized aspect of the godhead, experiencing the various realms of the Universe.

By necessity, this presentation is a simplification of an extremely complex and convoluted procedure. However, it covers the basics and provides an Earth Participant with sufficient information regarding the creative process to comprehend and use within the scope of this field guide.

The original creation of our Universe system began in the instant we refer to as the Big-Bang Singularity. The energies comprising this singularity created what eventually has become the twelve realms, twelve dimcons, countless galaxies, solar systems, suns, planets, every grain of sand, every atom, and the various life forms and individualized beings associated with each realm.

The trinity comprised of The Absolute, The Creator, and The Manifest is **The Central Sun of the Universe.** From this primordial power base emanate all the endless details inherent in the complex nature of our Universe system.

Do you now comprehend how God The Absolute did not create everything (The All) out of nothing, but out of Itself? Everything created is but an aspect of The Absolute, transmuted to become The All by keeping each element balanced by its anti-element and polar opposite. Throughout this process, The All has never been added to, subtracted, or separated from anything, and nothing exists outside of it, for being infinite, this is impossible. From a fresh perspective, begin to contemplate these ideas surrounding creation, for it is important that you clearly understand these concepts.

The Conscious Universe

Everything created is infinite. As a part of The All, everything, including consciousness, is but an extension of God The Absolute. You are a conscious being because you are an extended aspect of The Absolute's consciousness. The Three Primary Qualities of The Absolute —Mind, Will, and Feeling—trickled down to *you*. If you look around, you can observe and feel awareness, consciousness, and intelligence everywhere.

We can project this concept of consciousness to other life forms on Planet Earth. Do you see how this principle of Eternal Life applies to the multitudes of animals, insects, plants, and other vegetation and, yes, even to the mineral kingdom? The mineral kingdom seems to be inanimate because it does not appear to grow and have legs on which to move around. There is, however, a kingdom of ethereal spirit consciousnesses *within*, supporting the atoms, molecules, the grains, chunks, and groups of minerals. These intelligences are ranked and known as the elementals, nature spirits, devas, angels, and archangels— the angelic kingdom.

While touching on this subject, let us simply state that there are two basic lifestreams of consciousness in this Universe:

1. the **dynamic lifestream,** which is electric.
2. the **angelic lifestream,** which is magnetic/receptive.

Humans are part of the dynamic/electric lifestream which relates to the Primary Principle of Will. The angelic lifestream is magnetic/receptive, relating to the Principle of Feeling. This is another example of polarity at work.

An example of how human beings use the power of this polarized combination is during *prayer!* You may ask for a particular favor from a supernatural being, like healing for either yourself or another. So far, you are using your mind and your willpower. You are broadcasting your decree like a radio or television station, sending your thought waves out into the ethers in an electric/dynamic manner.

The angelic kingdom, being magnetic/receptive, receives your message and, if the action is permissible by spiritual standards, proceeds to produce your request/decree. The more power you can put behind your request/decree by adding or increasing the vision of Light and the feeling of Love, the more power the angelic kingdom has to work with to produce the effect you desire. Like any radio or TV transmitter, the more power behind the signal, the clearer and further reaching the reception.

The more energy (vision, will, feeling, and persistence) a Participant can put behind their prayer decrees, the more likely their request will be granted.

Additionally, when two or more Participants unify their thoughts, words, willpower, and feelings through prayer, their combined power factor is greater than the actual number of people participating. The power factor is the square of those participating when both male and female individuals are present in equal numbers. Thereby, the likelihood of the desired result being attained is greatly increased.

Dimcons (Dimensions of Consciousness)

Many spectrums of consciousness flow from The Absolute in a fashion similar to the spectrums of matter. Within infinity, consciousness is projected throughout the realms of experience by the same laws that govern infinity—not added to, subtracted or separated from, or outside of it.

The thirteen dimcons correspond to different levels of awareness and learning experience, like graded school systems. Again, there are seven major levels to each dimcon. For reasons related to the nature of soul, a subject covered later in this section, some dimcons overlap, and some do not. (see Diagram E) There are many subjects to be covered and lessons to be learned at each grade level. There are certain prerequisites a soul must experience and complete within each dimcon before it may graduate to a higher dimcon. The highest dimcon through which a being or other life form can function is directly related to its degree of *soul evolution*. The determining factors include—

1. the degree to which the life-form or being accurately perceives its own nature and its relationship to other life-forms in its environment (whether tangible or intangible to that species),
2. the proficiency with which a Participant functions within the principles of The 22 Laws of Spiritual Enlightenment and Soul Evolution, and,
3. the degree to which a being identifies with and functions in spiritual union with their Divine Spirit, and thereby relates to The All and everything created.

In our Universe system of twelve realms and thirteen dimcons, **the first dimcon** encompasses the mineral and vegetable kingdoms of the first realm. This is the realm of the elementals—the sylphs of air, salamanders of fire, undines of water, and gnomes of earth, and the nature spirits—wispy, energy life forms also known as elves, fairies, sprites, leprechauns, and so forth. Think of the variety of products the mineral and vegetable kingdoms provide to support your everyday lives. Do you not admire and praise the beauty and vast abundance produced and sustained by the intelligences behind these kingdoms—the beautiful rocks, the precious metals and gemstones, the exotic trees, fruits, plants, vegetables, and flowers?

The second dimcon embraces the animal kingdom. The lower levels offer experience to the insect and more primitive animal forms. The wild animal's consciousness resides in the middle of the second dimcon. At the higher, sixth and seventh levels are the group souls of the farm and ranch mammals, the loving, domesticated pets and the more highly evolved ocean mammals. Each particular life form contributes its own unique experiences to the Creator's storehouse of wisdom and beauty.

The third dimcon offers the human kingdom its experiences through which Participants begin to develop and refine their intellectual and intuitive minds, and their volition and feeling natures. Each Participant with a third-dimensional consciousness has a soul-evolution number, from one to seven, based upon their level of soul achievement to date. (see Diagram F) This number may be determined by the corresponding symbol in their astral body, as seen over their heads.

At the lower, first and second levels are those Participants experiencing their first few lifetimes on the planet, usually leading simpler, technically uninvolved lives, close to the naturalness of the Earth. These individuals usually live in peace and harmony with natural law. In many ways, these young souls are more attuned to their spiritual natures than their seemingly more evolved fellow Expedition Participants.

When individuals of these youthful soul groups are born into more elaborate, industrialized societies, they tend to be confused by complex concepts foreign to their impressionable, inexperienced souls. In other situations, more evolved groups of Participants attempt to take advantage of their younger neighbors' simplicity and lack of modern expertise. The resulting clash of cultures occasionally erupts into feelings of hysteria and desperation, resulting in waves of crime, violence, and war.

Diagram E: Soul Evolution and the Thirteen Dimcons

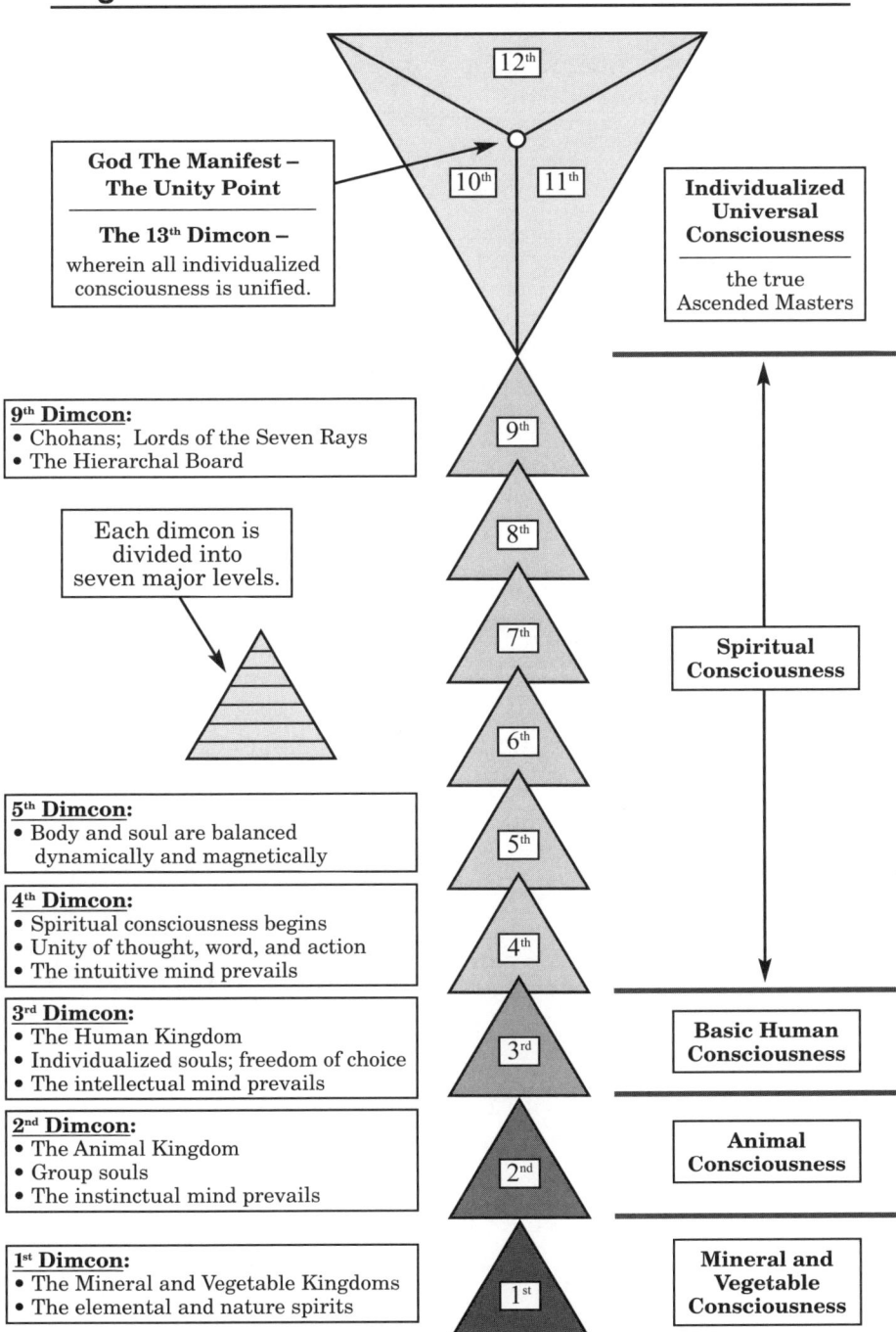

God The Manifest – The Unity Point

The 13th Dimcon – wherein all individualized consciousness is unified.

Individualized Universal Consciousness

the true Ascended Masters

9th Dimcon:
- Chohans; Lords of the Seven Rays
- The Hierarchal Board

Each dimcon is divided into seven major levels.

Spiritual Consciousness

5th Dimcon:
- Body and soul are balanced dynamically and magnetically

4th Dimcon:
- Spiritual consciousness begins
- Unity of thought, word, and action
- The intuitive mind prevails

3rd Dimcon:
- The Human Kingdom
- Individualized souls; freedom of choice
- The intellectual mind prevails

Basic Human Consciousness

2nd Dimcon:
- The Animal Kingdom
- Group souls
- The instinctual mind prevails

Animal Consciousness

1st Dimcon:
- The Mineral and Vegetable Kingdoms
- The elemental and nature spirits

Mineral and Vegetable Consciousness

As a soul evolves up through the third dimcon, it becomes more aware of the intricacies of physical life. The soul gradually experiences a greater range of human feelings and observes the interplay between one's own free will and the free will decisions and experiences of other Participants.

At the third, fourth, and fifth levels of the third dimcon, the search for a self-identity relative to the whole receives more emphasis. This large group tends to be focused on the material aspects of life and, since they are concentrating on developing their intellectual minds, can best relate to the concept of an infinite God in concrete, physical terms. These Participants tend to interpret words in literal, material terms since they are unable to conceptualize abstract, intangible ideas and concepts. Many search for their self-identity and self-worth through their possessions and their status in the community. Outer security issues are of major concern, and these Participants find themselves mentally and emotionally embroiled in a variety of everyday learning situations in the home, at work, and in the community. Whether they know it or not, they are learning millions of basic, but important, cosmic lessons.

Through these middle levels of the third dimcon, Participants are limited by their five-sensory natures. Therefore, they have no frame of reference to relate to the concept that there may be higher vibrational experiences beyond the physical. They think this planet is the full extent of creation and do not realize how low a level of consciousness they are experiencing relative to their potential. In part, this is due to the low, sluggish density of the first realm, which severely limits any Participant's brain functioning, intelligence, and awareness in general.

Most Participants in the higher echelons of government, from the President and the Executive Branch, those in Congress, and persons appointed to the Supreme Court, are functioning at the fourth level of the third dimcon. More evolved Participants usually avoid politics, choosing not to be involved with the formulation of man-made rules that exercise power and control over others, or with political and business game-playing. Also within this fourth-level group are most clerics of

Diagram F: Population Distribution Relative to Levels of Consciousness within the Third Dimcon

[Bell curve chart: Y-axis labeled "Percent of the Population"; X-axis labeled "Major Levels of Consciousness within the Third Dimcon" numbered 1 through 7. Regions labeled: "New and young souls" (levels 1-2), "The Middle Range" (levels 3-5), "Beginning comprehension of Unity and Oneness" (level 6), "Overlaps the first level of the fourth dimcon" (level 7).]

traditional religions, and business and industrial executives, all learning very important lessons in the cosmic sandbox.

Participants with more Earth experience and soul growth function through the higher sixth and seventh levels of the third dimcon, which in this cosmic schoolroom, is the equivalent of the first grade in a human school system. To enter these upper levels, a Participant must have begun to comprehend their true spiritual identity and the unity and oneness of everything. They begin to understand that God is not an external consciousness and power, but exists *within* them.

Many in these levels choose to be self-employed. Although still confronted with the intricacies of daily Earth living, they become more detached from the importance placed upon physical possessions and encumbrances.

This group of Participants are more inquisitive and philosophical, and begin to question the common values and beliefs held by the majority of the populace. They are presented with opportunities to develop and use their intuitive minds—the doorway to a spiritual consciousness. These Participants begin to delve into studies of their relationship to the intangible, abstract spheres of existence. Here,

Participants begin to look beyond the obvious and engage in the search for higher meanings and more accurate truths hidden behind their everyday Earth life experiences. They tend to lead lives enriched by their love and respect for nature, the environment, and *all* life, whatever its level of intelligence or degree of soul evolution.

Each higher dimcon allows a broader perspective and comprehension of Love, Truth, and Wisdom. In the third dimcon, humans learn valuable lessons through solving the multitude of daily challenges with which they are confronted. These manifest when Participants are confronted with others' seemingly conflicting agendas, paradigms, and paradoxes. Participants' major lessons of the third dimcon revolve around the development and use of their intellectual and intuitive minds, willpower, and feeling natures. Participants can thereby learn to reconcile their apparent differences in an atmosphere of Limitless Total Love. Oneness of thought, word, action, and purpose, is a spiritual concept. The initial comprehension of Unity, Oneness, and Wholeness begins with the sixth level of the third dimcon.

Considering the entire range of twelve dimcons in this schoolroom we call the Universe, when a Participant receives a certificate of completion from the third dimcon, they have in effect graduated to the equivalent of the second grade. As we shall see, there is still a long way to go and seemingly endless lessons are offered. There is a completion point, but it is a long, adventurous journey far beyond the constrictive environment and elementary experiences offered by Planet Earth.

There is no minimum requirement as to the number of lifetimes a soul must reincarnate on Planet Earth to experience the third dimcon. However, some Participants have experienced over 200 incarnations on this planet and have yet to graduate to the fourth dimcon. It is really each Participant's choice as to how quickly they evolve. Many Participants report they would have acquired a fourth-dimensional consciousness sooner had they been fully conscious of who and where they were, and been better informed that the purpose of life on any planet is to acquire sufficient experience, knowledge, and wisdom to evolve to a higher dimcon.

The spiritual dimcons of higher learning and evolvement begin at **the fourth dimcon** and extend **to the ninth,** each of which offer higher degrees of awareness, knowledge, and wisdom. Normally, these Participants have higher vibrational bodies capable of experiencing interplanetary, interstellar, intergalactic, and interdimensional travel. To achieve a specific objective, spiritual beings with a fourth to an eighth-dimensional *consciousness,* may choose to incarnate in a material or physical-etheric body on the first or second *realm* of a physical planet. However, they must thereby endure the limitations inherent in these lower realms. Also, the higher evolutionary status of a being with a spiritual consciousness is barely recognizable when they function on Earth through a material body, due to the very low and restrictive vibratory environment.

On the ladder of soul evolution, each higher dimcon provides Participants with much broader levels of awareness, perception, and abilities. Observe the vast difference in consciousness and freedom of movement that the animals experience relative to the minerals and plants. Then compare the much higher levels of consciousness the third-dimensional human kingdom possesses compared to the animals. In the spiritual fourth dimcon, there is a proportionate expansion of consciousness relative to the third dimcon.

The fourth dimcon is the beginning of spiritual consciousness, and is the equivalent of achieving the second grade level in this cosmic schoolroom. The fourth dimcon is not simply an extension of the third dimcon. The fourth dimcon is entirely different. One must have mastered the third dimcon before they can move on to the fourth. This is a giant step in a Participant's soul evolution. From a third dimcon perspective, a Participant cannot comprehend the nature of the fourth dimcon. Only when a Participant has achieved a fourth-dimensional consciousness can they begin to perceive and appreciate what it is all about.

Participants with a fourth-dimensional consciousness have certain minimum requirements they must fulfill before they can graduate to the fifth dimcon. One requirement is that a Participant must experience an entire lifetime with one partner in a dedicated, exclusive, heterosexual relationship. Another is that one must spend a lifetime of service to the populace. These and other requirements usually take five or six lifetimes to complete.

For the most part, the truths of the fourth dimcon are one-hundred and eighty degrees in the opposite direction from the third, particularly on a fear-based planet. For instance, the concept of *Oneness* is opposite that of *duality*; *Total Love* is opposite to *romantic love; harmony* is opposite *disharmony* and *discord*. In the third dimcon, one perceives their reality and truths from *outer*, physical, tangible phenomenon. In the fourth dimcon, one's reality and truths are based and founded upon *inner,* abstract, intangible ideas and concepts. You experience the Kingdom of God as being within, not outside of you.

Spiritual beings have a wide variety of tasks in which they may chose to participate. These may include the cleansing of contaminated air and water on a planet; the elimination of deadly fungus affecting plants; the creation of minerals, plants, and life forms on a newly formed planet. They may choose the role of guides and teachers to assist various lifeforms, such as humans, to progress their soul evolution.

Beings, like St. Germain, with a ninth-dimensional spiritual consciousness are referred to as Chohans, and oversee the evolutionary progress of their assigned portion of a galaxy. They do not incarnate on the physical realms. However, as spiritual guides and mentors, these exalted beings have the ability to create an aspect of themselves on any or all the realms from the Astral Plane on up, with each segment functioning through a consciousness relative to that realm. This enables these very advanced beings to offer lessons and teachings from the inner realms (either directly to an individual or through a channel) that relate to a student's personal understanding and level of consciousness.

The "Ascended Masters"[8] reside in and function from **the tenth to the twelfth dimcons,** which we shall refer to as the dimensions of

---

[8] In this context, the term "Ascended Masters" refers to spiritual beings who have attained a tenth-dimensional consciousness or higher, not to Earth expedition Participants with spiritual consciousnesses who may have ascended with their physical bodies upon leaving Earth or who function through a sixth to eighth-dimensional consciousness.

Individualized Universal Consciousness. (see Diagram E) At this level, these Ascended Masters apply the uniqueness of their individualized consciousnesses to the Twelve Principles of Creation supporting this Universe system. They learn to work with the Twelve Basic Principles and use these energies to enhance the evolution of the planets, stars, and galaxies—the whole universe—much as a musical composer plays with the infinite variety of tempos, rhythms, colors, and tones a philharmonic orchestra is capable of producing.

The Unity Point of God The Manifest **is the thirteenth dimcon,** from which all individualized life and all forms of environmental substance originate, are connected to, and radiate from. Upon completion of their evolutionary journey, all beings and their souls, united with their Divine Spirits, return to this infinite creative point. These illustrious beings exist in a realm beyond your ordinary concept of "place," for they exist and function in a condition as close as one can get to being unified in God-oneness, and still retain an aspect of individuality.

To clarify an issue which has been a source of confusion to most Participants, we shall illustrate the life of Jesus of Nazareth. Jesus' soul name was Sananda, which experienced many incarnations in human bodily form (Noah, Moses, Isaiah, Gautama Buddha, and Socrates are examples). Before his incarnation as Jesus, this great being had a history of leading the Beings of Light in their innerplane conflict with the Forces of Darkness. The Beings of Light have in many ways assisted their brothers and sisters on Earth to attain or regain a spiritual consciousness.

The Hebrew people were originally from a planet in the solar system of Arcturus. The primary purpose of Sananda's lifetime as Jesus was to help the Jews regain their spiritual consciousnesses through his teachings of Total Love. When the Jews rejected his teachings, he taught anyone who would listen, including the Gentiles, who were not held in very high esteem, since most of them had never experienced a spiritual consciousness. In Sananda's last incarnation as Jesus, he had an eighth-dimensional consciousness, and in that lifetime was awarded the privilege of personifying and being a channel of the power and consciousness of the Unity Point of God The Manifest, which is commonly referred to as the Christ[9] Consciousness.

Upon Jesus/Sananda's return to the spiritual realms, he attained a ninth-dimensional consciousness, eventually to become the Maha Chohan, the head of the Hierarchal Board. It is written in the New Testament of The Bible that Jesus said, "I will be with you always, to the end of the age."[10]

Planet Earth is now leaving the Piscean Age and entering the Aquarian Age. At the time of the Harmonic Convergence on August 16-17, 1987, Jesus/Sananda communicated mind to mind in thought-pictures to many individuals (including the writer of this field guide) that he had graduated to the tenth dimcon, thereby becoming an Ascended Master. He stated that in three months he would leave the Earth environs and go into silence, thereby leaving contact with Earth. St. Germain then rose to accept Sananda's position as the Maha Chohan.

As you may observe in Diagram E, some dimcons overlap. The seventh level of the third dimcon overlaps with the first level of the fourth dimcon. Many thousands of Participants have one foot in the third dimcon and one foot in the fourth, a transition period during which a Participant is "sitting on the fence," with one foot in each dimension of awareness. This is a precarious position. It is easy for an aspirant to follow the path of least resistance and fall back into the third dimcon, as thousands of Participants have experienced. If you desire to persevere in a forward direction, you can attain the real objective of this "Earthly" experience—a permanent spiritual consciousness. Your guides and teachers are supporting and encouraging you to progress ever onward and upward!

---

9 from the Greek: Christos – the Anointed One. *Messiah* in Hebrew and Aramaic
10 Matthew 28:20, *Good News Bible*
Note: The ancient word for "age" is usually translated into English as "world" since most translators do not know what constitutes an age. A Great Year is the period of about 25,800 years that it takes for the Earth to pass through the influence of all 12 astrological signs of the zodiac. This motion is due to the slight wobble in the Earth's rotation on its axis and is known as the Precession of the Equinoxes. An age, or Great Month, being 1/12 of a Great Year, is 2,150 years. A new Great Year begins when the 0° Aries point in tropical time (the first day of spring) again coincides with the actual star background in sidereal time.

Consciousness on Earth and in the Solar System

You may now perceive that *everything* has within it some degree of life and consciousness. The next step is to envision that *all* of creation has some form of conscious intelligence supporting and giving it life expression and experience.

The planet you are now experiencing, Mother Earth, is not just a mud-ball spinning through time and space, containing some random life forms. It is a living, conscious, intelligent organism unto itself which offers habitation and experience to many evolutionary life forms on, above and below its surface. It possesses a soul, with a nature different than that of humans, but nevertheless, the Earth soul is also learning, growing, and evolving to a higher dimension of consciousness.

Likewise, the sun, and every planet in your solar system is an intelligent, living organism radiating a vast energy field of consciousness. Each planet is "home" to many other intelligences expressing through non-material forms and mainly functioning through the first to the fourth dimensions of consciousness. The higher consciousness of each sun, planet, and moon are *teachers* who assist Earth Expedition Participants to grow, transform, and evolve to higher realms of expression.

An interesting point is that *there is more life in space between the planets than there is on them*. What you think of as empty space is, in reality, teeming with *life*. Just because you may not perceive these intelligences with your physical senses does not mean they do not exist. These beings express through the higher physical and the ethereal realms in a vast variety of bodily forms. Out in the ethers there is a vast store of tasks and adventures from which Participants may choose.

Though largely unconscious of the fact, Participants visit specialized temples of learning on these planets during their nightly REM sleep, when their consciousness transfers to either their astral bodies or spiritual light bodies. Generally, Participants begin by concentrating on the lessons offered by the Sun and the closer planets, Mercury through Jupiter. As Participants progress through the Planet Earth curriculum, they proceed outward, planet by planet, toward Pluto. Refresher seminars are always available on any planet as a Participant may desire or require.

The intelligences functioning in and through the Sun, Mercury, Venus, Mars, and Jupiter are teachers for those Earth expedition Participants with third-dimensional consciousnesses. Uranus, Neptune, and Pluto assist in the evolution of those who have attained the fourth dimcon. Saturn, being the Great Tester of one's awareness, stability, and degree of spiritual attainment, is the master teacher and karmic reaper for *both* third and fourth-dimensional Participants. Saturn is the "Guardian at the Doorway" between the third and fourth dimcons. Only those who have achieved a fourth-dimensional consciousness may pass on to the spiritual courses of study provided by Uranus, Neptune, and Pluto.

Human souls eventually experience the consciousness of the entire solar system as a schoolroom during their evolutionary phase on the Earth plane. Each time the soul leaves the body, whether in the body's dream state or separated through death, it is assigned to a particular planet in this solar system to learn and reinforce specific lessons. Younger souls gravitate to the planets closest to the Sun. These planets are Mercury, Venus, and Mars, on which they learn lessons around communication, love, and correct action. Younger souls experience much stress and discord on the Earth plane until they learn the important lessons relative to these subjects.

On the bell curve of soul evolution through the third dimcon, the majority of souls on Earth are experiencing lessons provided by the consciousness of the planet Jupiter. Jupiterians are required to examine their lessons in communication, love, honesty, and truth. These souls also acquire some minor lessons offered by the influences of Saturn, Uranus, Neptune, and Pluto. On Earth, Jupiterians experience a wider variety of situations and conditions than younger souls.

At some point, Jupiterian souls must make the decision as to whether they will stay in the third dimcon or move into the fourth dimcon and thereby experience the outer planets. Unless a soul has a thorough Jupiterian learning experience, it will find Saturn's advanced courses to be very difficult. Saturn's lessons revolve around discipline and can take the form of military service, membership in a rigid religious structure, or being interred as a prison inmate. These institutions provide an outer form of discipline to offer these souls the parameters they cannot provide for themselves. Real discipline needs to come from within and the soul must remain connected to the planet Saturn until it can finally act and function with the utmost *self*-discipline.

Upon graduation from Saturn, the soul moves to the planetary schoolroom Uranus. Uranus presents a Participant with new, progressive ideas which they are eager to implement in their lives, thereby encouraging others to be more adventurous. Uranian people are always on the move. There is much sudden change in their lives because they have so much to do and so much to learn. They yearn for variety and take the greatest risks for they are always in a new situation—climbing new mountains, working on new experiments, or exploring a new country. When involved in accidents, they must heed the message to curtail their impulsive nature.

Neptunian people are very involved in philosophy and spiritual truths. They work more on the inside than the outside; on the invisible rather than the visible. These Participants fine-tune their intuition and become attuned to the messages they receive from their dreams and their environment. They constantly strive to bring harmony to challenging situations. In their later lessons, Neptunians tend to manifest their spirituality more outwardly and share it with others. Depending upon the extent of a soul's evolution, it is possible to experience several or all the planets in one lifetime. There is no limit to the extent of your progress.

Following are a few examples of the major subjects taught by the solar, lunar, and planetary intelligences in this solar system:

Sun – Self-esteem; self-identity; self-worth; willpower; ambition; authority

Moon – Emotional stability; intuition; imagination; domestic attributes; compassion, and nurturing; relating to and associating with women and the public

Mercury – Developing the intellectual mind; self-expression; logical reasoning; communication in its various forms; memory

- **Venus** – Personal love; beauty; harmony; artistic abilities; social activity; politeness; refinement; cheerfulness; neatness
- **Mars** – Correct dynamic action; enthusiasm; courage; bravery; relating to the male gender
- **Jupiter** – Optimism; expansion; abundance; benevolence; reverence; respect for law and order; orthodox religious orientation; success; philosophy
- **Saturn** – Concentration; contraction; discipline; responsibility; patience; restraint; conservation; diligence; determination; perseverance; modesty; humility; Trust; stopping and thinking before you act; keen spiritual listening; stopping and asking the consciousness of Saturn, "Am I doing this right?"
- **Uranus** – Universal Love; originality; creativeness; inventiveness; independent thinking; humanitarianism; the unconventional; detachment; sudden change; independence; freedom
- **Neptune** – Spiritual Love; inspiration; intuition; understanding the abstract and intangible; devotion; the mystical; spirituality; clairvoyance; improvisation; celestial music, and dance
- **Pluto** – Transformation; regeneration; reorganization; extrasensory perception; connecting with the collective unconscious; hermetic philosophy

You Are a Complex, Many-Splendored Being

Dear Participants. The material, feeling and mental parts of your present bodily experience to which you relate with your five physical senses are but the tip of the iceberg relative to the totality of your individualized nature. Beneath the surface of human awareness, concealed from view, lies the true extent of your vastness, which exists within the ocean of higher vibratory realms of consciousness and experience.

You have been duped into thinking and believing that you are "only human." This paradigm has held you down, restricted your experiences and slowed your evolution to a snail's pace. It has resulted in Participants thinking that they are just *people*. That's all! That's it!

In reality, each of you is a vast, radiant, conscious field of energy in motion. The true nature of your being is hidden from view by your limited intellectual minds and by the extreme density of Earth's very low vibrational environment, which enhances the illusion of separateness from the Creator and the rest of creation. In order to attain your quest for knowledge, wisdom, and a higher consciousness, you need to master the hurdles presented by these challenges.

The Structure of Your Individualized Nature

Each Participant is a unique, *triune* being with an individualized consciousness. You have a three-fold nature, meaning that you are made up of three distinct, separate consciousnesses, each with a different purpose and function:

1. a **spirit** consciousness, referred to as your **Divine Spirit**
2. a **soul** consciousness, referred to as your **Higher Self**
3. a **body** consciousness, referred to as your **anapersona**

Your **Divine Spirit** is pure, individualized life essence and consciousness. Each Divine Spirit vibrates to its own unique "ray" of energy radiating out from God The Manifest. Each has its unique characteristics, drives, talents, and potentials. Your Divine Spirit is vast. Think of your spirit as encompassing the whole Universe—all the countless galaxies, suns, and planets.

Your spirit-self functions from the twelfth realm of existence and functions through a twelfth-dimensional consciousness. It is the overseer of the progress of the body and soul consciousnesses and guards the doorway to your entrance into the realms of God consciousness, the "Holy of Holies." Your Divine Spirit is in union with all the group and individualized spirit essences throughout all the galaxies in the Universe. Your Divine Spirit can assist you in many ways once you learn to contact and consciously unify with it. The *Basic Consciousness Raising Meditation* on the enclosed CD includes a purposeful method of coming into union with your Divine Spirit

The **anapersona** is that part of a triune being that

1. has a continuous consciousness in some form that directly experiences an environment. This form may be physical, physical-etheric, astral, spiritual, or transcendent. An example is the consciousness in a human body functioning on Planet Earth.
2. chooses and exhibits a unique personality with particular talents and abilities that will best suit the purpose and objective of a specific incarnation. Both male and female bodies are experienced in various incarnations as is required.
3. consciously and unconsciously programs its soul through its experiences.

The anapersona itself does not have a memory bank and only remembers what the brain mind of the physical body has recorded from its current experiences. Since the anapersona is expressing through a new body and brain at the beginning of each Earth incarnation, it has no memory of past incarnations. The memory of all past incarnations resides in the soul record. Any past-life recollections are received from the soul through a Participant's subconscious mind, to the conscious mind. Generally, children are in close touch with their subconscious minds up to seven years of age. Unless they are encouraged to remember their impressions and visions, they lose these memories as they confront the outer, physical aspects of Earth.

The anapersona is largely dependent upon the particular programming of its soul for the responses it makes to external stimuli. These responses are affected by the personality as influenced by the astrological structures under which the body was conceived and born and by the conditions of the person's environment.

To achieve these purposes, the anapersona chooses the sex of a new body, his or her parents, the time and place of birth and a general or specific life plan depending upon what various karmic or lesson learning factors it chooses to experience. The degree of wisdom behind these choices is determined by 1) the Participant's level of soul evolution and 2) the basic purpose and objective of that particular incarnation.

The anapersona is the most limited part of the individualized being. However, when caught up in the illusions of Planet Earth, the anapersona tends to want to be "king" or "queen" and rule the whole being. This is a case of "the tail wagging the dog," invariably to the detriment of the being's soul progress. This situation and its resolution can be illustrated by comparing two biblical stories:

1. Adam and Eve insisted on exercising their *self-will* by eating the forbidden fruit, desiring to know evil, and thereby falling to a lower, third-dimensional consciousness.
2. Knowing He was to be crucified, Jesus' prayed in the Garden of Gethsemane, "Father, not my will, but yours be done in and through me."

This comparison demonstrates to humanity the relinquishing of one's self-will to the Wisdom and higher Will of one's soul and Divine Spirit. To achieve a fourth-dimensional consciousness, each Participant must achieve and exercise this realization. You thereby permit your "dog" consciousness to wag your "tail" consciousness.

There are two trinities symbolized by the two triangles in the Six-pointed Star as relates to the fourth-dimensional concept of unity and oneness:

- ▽ the Trinity of the Godhead—The Absolute, The Creator and The Manifest, and
- △ the Trinity of the individualized being—spirit, soul, and anapersona
- ✡ unified as One!

Your individualized nature is not separate from the Godhead, but is part of and connected to the whole. You are the sum of all the parts, as One. Everyone and everything is The All! *You* are The All!

The Nature of Your Soul

How do you relate to and remember your present life experiences? Through your brain? Mostly. What about your memory of past-life experiences? Enter the function of the *soul!* Some Participants associate soul with one's *feeling* nature. But what really *is* a soul and what purpose does it provide?

The human soul has a dual function and purpose. Simply put, it is

1. a data recording and playback mechanism;
2. an internal guidance system.

As a recording and playback mechanism, the soul is the master data collector of a Participant's entire previous and present life experiences. From its recorded data bank, the soul feeds information through one's subconscious mind to their human consciousness. The soul expresses its programming at the material level through one's actions, reactions, emotions, or gut-level intuitive *feelings*. Fear thoughts or hot-tempered responses are examples of disharmonious emotional reactions.

Your soul contains a record of all your past experiences. Functioning through your anapersona's subconscious mind, your soul data forms a basis of reference for your present experiences. This soul record contains knowledge and wisdom accumulated from the past, so once you have firmly learned a lesson, it need not be relearned in every subsequent lifetime. Most Participants are actually functioning about eighty to ninety percent of the time through their subconscious soul programming and are not even aware of it. The nature and quality of your soul programming are important factors in your spiritual evolution.

trauma – A fear-based brain-memory or soul program created by a Participant's reaction to a stressful, shocking, or violent experience that resulted in mental, emotional, or physical harm, or death.

It is significant to note that the soul does not make value judgments. The recording segment of the soul cannot distinguish between fact and fiction, reality or make-believe. The soul can be compared to the floppy disk or hard drive in a computer. It simply accepts at face value whatever programming it receives, from whatever the source, internal or external. The soul records all one's thoughts, actions, reactions, feelings, emotions, fears, and traumas, whether constructive or destructive, fact or fiction.

The soul also records and plays back all addictions, whatever form they may take. From external sources, the soul is influenced by situations it observes and evaluates to be real, like plays, motion pictures, radio, and television broadcasts and actual physical events. A staged murder performed in a stage or television drama appears to be an actual live physical event to the soul. Like a computer hard drive, recorded information can be added, altered, erased, and even fragmented if emotionally or physically damaged, since the soul and its information are more fragile than one would suspect.

Since one's soul functions at the subconscious level, it is strongly influenced by repetitive programming, like brainwashing, subliminal messages, newspaper and magazine advertisements, radio and TV shows and commercials. "Young souls" with little previous Earth experience and, therefore, a minimal amount of soul programming, are particularly susceptible to accepting repetitive indoctrination. Because of limited practical experience and information, young souls have little constructive programming to refute erroneous concepts. Some religious, political, social and antisocial "fanatics" may also fit into this category.

A soul learns and is programmed through the Participant's personal, internalized responses to their life experiences. The greater the *feeling impact* of an experience, the greater the impression upon the soul. The soul retains trauma from particularly intense learning experiences or violent accidents in the form of fear-filled subconscious memories. Shocking incidents occurring at the time of death of the physical body are particularly susceptible to being retained as trauma, for there is not sufficient time for any shocks or reactions to be released in that lifetime. Eventually, usually in a subsequent lifetime, these memories need to be confronted and released, as do disharmonious behavior patterns such as anger, hatred, lust, greed, prejudices, and all addictions, for these restrain one's soul evolution.

From a higher vibrational perspective between Earth embodiments, Participants may desire to access their soul programming for evaluation. Although Participants functioning between Earth incarnations in an astral or spiritual body may clearly observe errors which require reprogramming, they cannot make the required changes from that domain. There is a spiritual stipulation that soul data can be transformed only on the same realm of experience where the programmed experience originally took place. Therefore, erroneous soul programming and traumas acquired on Earth can only be transformed or released in either the current or in a subsequent material Earth incarnation.

Soul programming, constructive, destructive, or indifferent, is carried over into subsequent lifetimes. You choose a particular personality for each incarnation. Thereby, the expression of your soul traits will vary depending upon the nature of the lessons and karma on which your anapersona desires to concentrate.

Disharmonious patterns, a Participant's work areas or *unfinished business,* trip one up like exposed tree roots, block one's path like a pile of boulders and hold the soul back like anchors dragging in the sands of the ocean depths. These self-defeating patterns retard a Participant's soul evolution until released or replaced with more constructive behavioral programming. This field guide will offer suggestions for recognizing and then dissolving or transmuting one's outdated and inappropriate soul programming.

The consciousness of one's soul, the anapersona's internal guidance mechanism, is referred to as their **Higher Self.** The Higher Self is the master intelligence of the soul and functions one dimcon above that of the bodily consciousness (anapersona) which does the actual experiencing. Therefore, an anapersona with a third-dimensional consciousness has a fourth-dimensional Higher Self, a fourth-dimensional anapersona has a fifth-dimensional Higher Self, and so on. As the active Participant in this learning adventure, your *conscious* awareness is this lower self, anapersona.

The Higher Self offers guidance *to assist the total being* to learn, grow, and evolve according to its own unique design and desires. As the Higher Self does not communicate in words, it transmits information through one's intuitive nature in the form of dreams, visions, and "gut-feelings." The Higher Self is also referred to as one's *conscience,* which often sends the intuitive message "Now, you *know* better than to do *that*!" through one's feeling nature. An example is a "hit in the gut" feeling when one is about to perform a disharmonious action. This is the soul giving the anapersona a message not to proceed.

The souls of human beings differ from those of the other earthly kingdoms. The souls of the various minerals, vegetables, and animals are best thought of as **group souls.** That is, a mass of a particular mineral (like iron), a group of a plant species (like roses) and a group of a particular type of animal (like a herd of horses) are all encompassed and guided by one soul. These kingdoms have varying degrees of intelligence, but not true free will. Their destinies and evolutionary growth are guided and determined by higher dimensional beings, including the influences of humans. This relates to human Participants' lessons in responsibility regarding these lower kingdoms, which we will elaborate on in a later section.

It is important to note that over the course of time, the higher, more evolved essences of animal group souls (the domesticated animals, particularly cats and dogs) are transformed into new human souls. A new individualized human soul is endowed with freedom of choice (free will) and self-determination, and functions through an anapersona with a third-dimensional consciousness. This is where a new, young soul's third-dimensional consciousness originates. The third dimcon is a *bridge* between the second dimcon animal kingdom and the spiritual dimcons.

Throughout their third-dimensional experience, Participants transmute their soul programming to master their animal natures, and eventually evolve to acquire a fourth-dimensional spiritual consciousness. The third dimcon encompasses a very broad range indeed. A Participant's higher spiritual nature already exists, however, it is up to the anapersona to realize this fact and begin to function therein through the realization of loving, spiritual principles and truths.

There are only minor physiological differences between the more highly evolved animal bodies and the bodies of human beings. In reality, human bodies are merely refined and very sophisticated animal bodies, capable of sustaining a higher level of consciousness. The major distinguishing features between the animal kingdom and the human kingdom are

1. the different nature of their souls, i.e. group souls versus individualized souls;
2. the dimcon through which they are functioning, i.e. second dimcon or third dimcon;
3. the particular type of mind they are primarily utilizing and/or developing, i.e. instinctual, or intellectual and intuitive;
4. whether or not they are endowed with true freedom of choice.

As Participants in this Earth Educational Expedition, it is noteworthy to recognize that life on Earth is not so much an anapersona *personality* experience as it is a *soul* experience. Your mental, psychological, and physical encounters have programmed and are programming your *soul*. A major lesson all Participants learn is that when the personality ego rules, their lives encounter disharmonious experiences. As you learn to release the little will of your personality to your Higher Self and Divine Will, your life will experience more harmony.

Your Many Interdimensional Bodies

Besides the material body with which you are very familiar, you have twelve innerplane bodies. These interdimensional bodies interlace and interpenetrate your physical body, but are not detectable by your five physical senses. You have a physical-etheric body, an astral/emotional body, a mental body, and many spiritual-etheric and transcendental bodies, each corresponding to the physical or etheric matter of the eleven vibrational realms higher than the material. (see Diagram G)

Diagram G: Your Interdimensional Bodies and Union with the Godhead

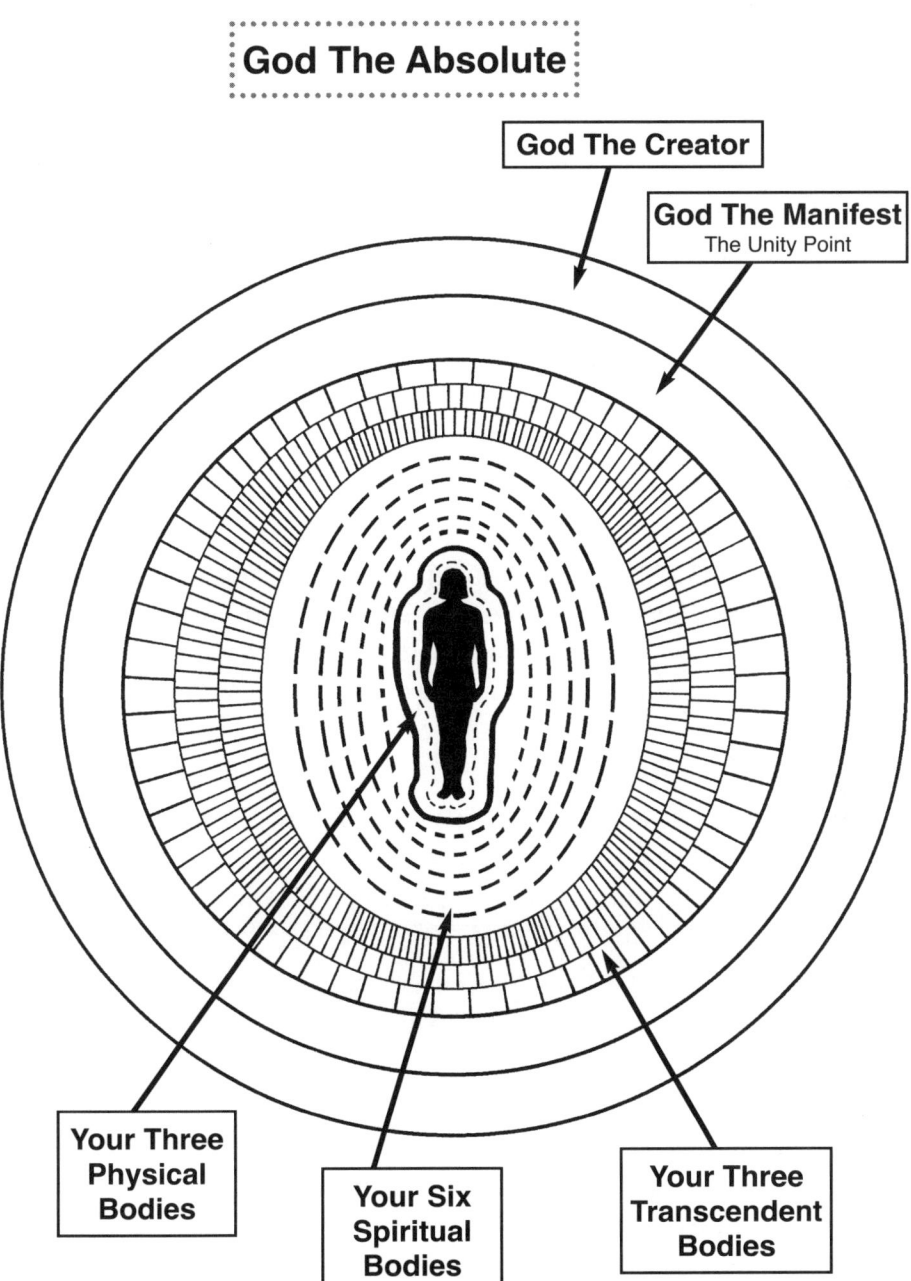

Your material body could not exist without the structure and support of these *inner* bodies, as everything is an extension of and connected to The Absolute. Within infinity, all is One. Your material body, or anything else for that matter, cannot be separated from the Source of its basic qualities and inherent nature, and retain its existence.

Your human body, under the direction of the anapersona, is not the totality of "you." It is simply the material Earth vehicle through which your soul learns lessons, experiences various situations and expresses itself in the material world. When your anapersona and soul incarnate in a material body, only a minute portion of your total conscious awareness is able to fit into the confines of your body and brain. As an analogy, think of it this way. The totality of your consciousness equals 100 gallons. But your physical Earth "tank" has a maximum capacity of only *one* gallon. So actually, you are infinitely much greater and more expansive than your material senses reflect back to your conscious brain-mind awareness.

Your tangible material body is composed of atoms and minerals, and uses products of the vegetable and animal kingdoms as fuel. Your thoughts, feelings, willpower, and spiritual nature emanate from *inner-dimensional sources* which are intangible to your material senses. Each of your various parts and bodies have a mind of their own, so to speak, and each has its own function.

Let us examine a few of your higher vibrational bodies. Next to the material body is the innerplane physical-etheric body, which exists in the frequency vibration of the second realm. The physical-etheric body is like a framework for the human material body, cells, and organs. To Participants with innerplane vision, its energy field is seen as a blue-violet aura emanating about one-quarter of an inch above the human skin, all around the body.

The anapersonas of Participants on many planets in solar systems throughout the galaxies (including Earth) function through physical-etheric bodies. The majority of these beings are non-spiritual, having third-dimensional consciousnesses. Physical-etheric bodies possess minds with far greater power and intelligence than Earth material bodies.

Also, the physical-etheric body is far better suited to interplanetary space exploration. These beings travel in their etheric spacecrafts beyond the speed of physical-material light.

Throughout this vast Universe, there is a much greater variety in physical-etheric bodily characteristics than is evident to Earth Participants in material bodies. Some examples are body forms similar to "ET"s from the Pleiades and the Vega solar system, and various forms with animal or reptilian characteristics from Sirius (The Dog Star), and the constellations of Drako (The Dragon) and Orion (The Archer). Most of these beings choose to be benevolent and Loving, however, some originating from fear-based planets, did not. In the western Bible, there are many references to those beings who have executed disharmonious influences on humans, as either "the serpent" or "the devil."

Moving outward is the astral body which corresponds to the vibrational frequency of matter in the third realm, wherein it exists. Your astral body is actually composed of two bodies, an emotional body and a mental body. The mental body may be regarded as the highest aspect of the astral body. Although the astral body is still physical, it is made of refined light particles like photons.

Some especially gifted Participants can observe people's astral energy field, or *aura,* with its range of colors. Machines have also been developed to photograph this astral aura, which differs from person to person and changes throughout the day depending upon one's current mental, feeling, and physical condition. The Astral Plane is the highest realm a Participant with a third-dimensional consciousness can experience.

Moving outward again, are your spiritual-etheric bodies, corresponding to the Spiritual Realms, the fourth to the ninth. These bodies are non-physical energy fields and do not exist in time and space as experienced on Planet Earth. A fourth-dimensional consciousness or higher is required for an anapersona (Participant) to enter these higher frequency realms.

Beyond your spiritual bodies are your transcendent bodies, which you might think of as vast energy fields, encompassing the whole Universe. These bodies interpenetrate and interrelate with all individualized life essences and beings, thereby personally experiencing the true concept of one's Unity and Oneness with everything—all of creation.

Your Auspicious Astral Body

The astral body you are now "inner wearing" is of particular importance during your Earth Educational Expedition. It is an innerplane body vibrationally situated between your physical-etheric body and your spiritual bodies. Silver or golden-white cords connect each of your bodies. Upon the death of your material body, the connecting silver cord between your material and astral bodies breaks. Your anapersona's consciousness then immediately transfers to and takes up residence in your astral body.

Your astral body has many useful functions.

1. It is the major influence upon your feeling, emotional, and sensual natures.
2. It harbors the consciousness of one's lower self (anapersona) while on the Astral Plane in between Earth sojourns.
3. As one's body consciousness transfers to their astral body during REM sleep, the astral body is the vehicle through which they travel in their dream and planetary temple-learning experiences.

In appearance, your astral body is similar in many ways to your current physical body, but it is of a much finer, higher-vibrational material. Your astral body is confined by space, like the space around the Earth, but not by time. Where time does not exist, beings relate to the passage of events in terms of the various planetary and cosmic cycles.

The Astral Plane is the *place* to which the astral body is related. Though of a much lighter density than the material realm, it is a physical, non-spiritual, temporary learning environment that embraces the second and third dimcons. The Astral Plane consists of seven major levels, with many sub-levels of experience, and is located within and confined to the Earth's and other planets' gravitational fields. Although Earth's Astral

Plane has higher, more cheerful, loving aspects, it is at the three lower levels where Participants' disharmonious emotions, sensual cravings, illusions, and delusions are based. Depending upon the degree of one's soul evolution, these disharmonious pressures may manifest in a Participant's astral body and strongly influence or direct an anapersona's actions.

Primarily, the Astral Plane is a way-station for animal consciousnesses and for Participants moving up through the second and third dimcons, and awaiting return to another material body to continue their soul evolution. A Participant on the Astral Plane is usually required to reside there for a minimum of seven Earth years before again reincarnating in a material body.

Some Participants have waited on the Astral Plane between incarnations for hundreds of years, reluctant to embody on the material plane, knowing the painful Earth karma they have acquired and must experience. Unfortunately, this "vacation" has stopped their soul evolution. The lesson here is similar to having an aching tooth and resisting the trip to the dentist for fear of more pain. The tooth does not get any better, so it is preferable to undergo some temporary discomfort and have the problem resolved. To overcome this "holding pattern" barrier, The Absolute included a built-in cosmic "pusher" that keeps souls ever striving for higher and higher expressions of consciousness.

The Astral Plane is best visualized as located in and around Planet Earth. The three lower vibrational levels of the Astral Plane house astral demons and human "astral bums" caught in their lower animal natures. The most depraved Participants may be required to spend quite some "time" in the lowest of these "icky" environments, depending upon the seriousness of their disharmonious or anti-social activities while in Earth embodiment. These beings are learning very basic lessons on the subjects of Love and respect for the environment, the animal kingdom, and their fellow Participants.

The middle, or fourth level of the Astral Plane is home to Participants endeavoring to lead good, moral lives while on Earth, but who require more practical experience to overcome the pitfalls of their disharmonious behavior patterns.

The three upper astral levels accommodate Participants who are at various stages of learning to express Love, peace, and harmony in their Earth lives (among many other lessons). At the sixth and seventh levels, one finds Participants yearning to move into a higher, spiritual, fourth-dimensional expression of consciousness. A part of these highest levels is referred to as the Mental Plane. Many Participants residing in this area are extremely intelligent beings, but are caught in their intellectual minds, thereby retarding their progress. Their task is to develop their intuitive minds to a degree that enables them to complete their Search for Self, thereby permitting their graduation to a fourth-dimensional consciousness.

The upper levels of the Astral Plane contain schools (referred to as *temples*) of higher learning for those who desire to make their next material embodiment a more productive and aware experience. (Note: These schools offer day and night classes as well as correspondence courses. Tuition is included in your tour ticket. Enrollment is easy. You simply locate the temple and show up for the class.)

Participants who are astral beings are to be distinguished from spiritual beings. A Participant on the Astral Plane functions only within the *third* dimension of consciousness.

Upon the death of the material body there is a condition wherein an anapersona becomes "stranded" in their physical-etheric bodies, in the second realm, between the material realm and the astral realm. This situation usually results from the sudden, accidental, or violent loss of one's physical body. It is also caused by a Participant's very emotional state at the time of death. Since one's physical-etheric body, like the astral body, appears to be identical to their material body, the anapersonas of these Participants have become "earth bound" through a belief that they are still embodied and alive on the material Earth plane. They tend to wander around and near the location of the material body's sudden death, or in a familiar place that was comfortable to their material experience, like a home or place of work.

In spite of prompting by guiding angels, these wanderers have ignored their suggestions to let go of Earth attachments and move to a higher, loftier vibration. However, stranded Participants usually heed the suggestions of Participants in material bodies who, through innerplane communication (verbal or mind-to-mind), are able to convince these stranded Participants that they are indeed Earth-bound. They no longer belong in this relatively dense, physical-etheric realm, and will be more comfortable on the higher, Astral realm. Angels are available to assist these stranded Participants in this upward journey. From there, they can eventually return to Earth to continue their soul evolution.

Some specially sighted Earth Participants have visited memorials at places where many people had died suddenly, such as the Gettysburg battlefield or the site of the airplane crash at Lockerbie, Scotland. There they have observed many lost Participants wandering in their physical-etheric bodies. By encouraging them to reach up toward a higher, more comfortable vibration, the wanderers who heeded their suggestions ascended to the Astral Plane where they were able to proceed along their evolutionary paths.

The Seven Astral Energy Centers, or Chakras

Housed in each Participant's astral body are many energy centers that, depending upon their placement, relate to the functioning and performance of various aspects of the astral, physical-etheric, and material bodies. Seven of these are major energy centers situated in a vertical alignment from the base of one's spine to the top of the head. Each of these seven centers relates to the health of a particular bodily organ, and an aspect of a Participant's spiritual development and progress.

In Participants whose consciousness functions through the lower and middle levels of the third dimcon, these seven major chakras are barely functioning. As a Participant begins to become spiritually aware, these chakras begin to open, depending upon what aspect of development the person has been working. Only when all seven of these major energy centers are open, activated, and fully functioning can a Participant attain a purely fourth-dimensional consciousness. (see Diagram H)

Here is a brief description of the seven major chakras:

1st – The Base Chakra is located at the bottom of the spine between the anus and genitals. It is where Earth energies enter to enhance your vitality and creativity. The Base Chakra is the root wherein the Kundalini energies originate and are then drawn up to enjoin the other chakras. The color **red** is associated with this chakra.

2nd – The Sacral Chakra is located just below the navel. It integrates the flow of liquids in the body. Caring and domestic qualities are developed to enhance all types of relationships. **Orange** is the color associated with this chakra.

3rd – The Solar Plexus Chakra is located between the navel and the bottom of the sternum. As the seat of the emotions, it has the ability to process disharmonious emotions, and transmute stress. The color **yellow** is associated with this chakra.

4th – The Heart Chakra is located behind the sternum, in the center of the chest. It regulates the flow of the Kundalini energies between the three lower and the three upper chakras. Total Love, Enthusiasm, Compassion and Joy are developed in and distributed from the Heart Chakra. Bright **emerald green** is the color associated with this chakra.

5th – The Throat Chakra is located just below the larynx in the neck. It balances your personal will with the Will of your Divine Spirit. The Throat Chakra harmonizes your personal strengths with the Power of God. The color **turquoise-blue** is associated with this chakra.

6th – The Mind's Eye Chakra is located in the center of the forehead just above the eyebrows. It is where the material world is transmuted into the spiritual. In the developed intuitive mind, it activates the higher range of senses and is the seat of clairvoyance (clear-seeing) and clairaudience (clear hearing) The color associated with this chakra is **indigo-blue**.

Diagram H: The Seven Major Chakras

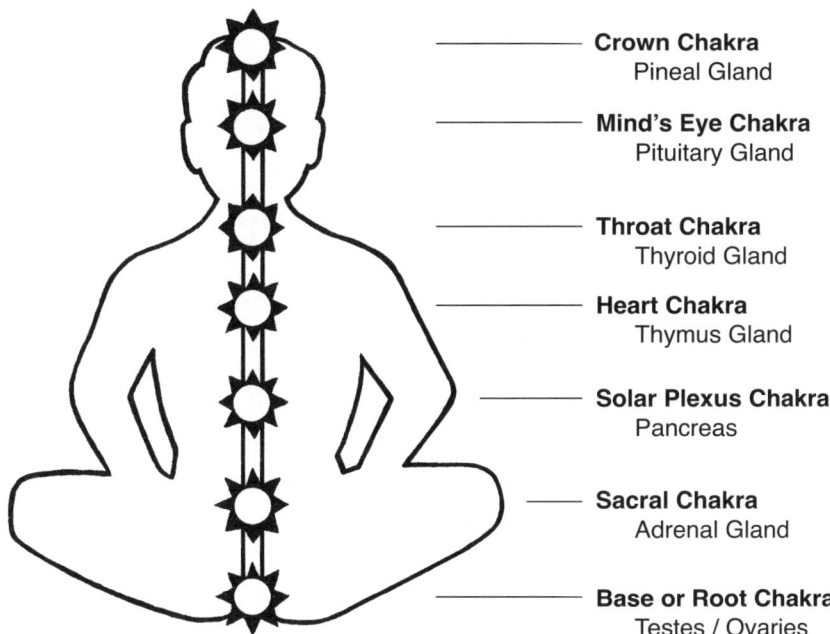

7th – **The Crown Chakra,** located at the top of your head, is the doorway to higher consciousness. Upon its opening, it unites one's lower consciousness with the soul's Higher Self, and thereby recirculates the Kundalini energies between the crown and the base chakras. The color **blue-violet** is associated with this chakra.

All of your chakras are equally important, as each has a specific purpose. Each chakra requires clearing and cleansing of disharmonious energy blocks. It requires effort on your part to energize them equally, enabling them to function freely and openly. The best time to do this is when you meditate. Here is a simple breathing exercise to help with this process:

Slowly inhale a deep breath, seeing, and feeling your breath going down your back, through your lower intestines, through your root chakra, to your feet. As you slowly exhale, see, and feel your breath rising up your legs, through the chakras in your body and exiting through an imaginary portal in your crown chakra. Repeat this exercise for five to ten breaths.

There are a variety of approaches to opening and activating Participants' major chakras. There are many workshops, magazine articles, books, and audiotapes available on the subject. (See the Recommended Reading section for some suggestions.) Following are some excerpts from *Journey to the Fourth Dimension* by St. Germain, as transmitted through Judith Ann Gordon, to illustrate how blocks to the proper functioning of each chakra are created, and how they may be transmuted. This presentation starts with the top, Crown chakra, and moves down.

"Incorrect (fragmented, illusionary) thoughts are lodged in the Crown, or seventh Chakra. ... It is your thinking that dictates and directs your actions, whether the action be correct or incorrect. Refining thought is one of the hardest steps you will go through. It is through the mind, the Crown Chakra, that you fall into traps of illusionary thinking. Basically, it comes down to disciplining yourself and monitoring all your thoughts.

"In this whole process of thought, word, and action, you must now begin to use your fourth-dimensional Vision and open your Mind's Eye (6th) Chakra. You will see the world with new Vision, in a new Light. As thought, word, and action must change for wholeness, so must the eyes change to see fourth-dimensionally. When you see something that you used to evaluate in harsh, critical terms, refocus your eyes, and look again. Notice how you perceive people and events differently, by allowing this new Vision to manifest within you. You now see through God's eyes, for **you are God. God's eyes see only with Love. Allow your eyes to discern with Love. See the world immersed in the Light of Love.**

"The next blockage is in your will, lodged in the thyroid gland, the fifth (Throat) chakra. … It is the master gland where your will resides. … This area manifests Faith and Trust. When you lack Faith and Trust you become willful. This is to say you insist on having your own way, and that your will must be dominant and must prevail. … The thyroidian energies operate in the duality of the third dimension. … It is your little will that you need to transform into God's will. [At this point, St. Germain offers affirmations to facilitate this process.] … To balance the thyroid means to balance your will with God's Will.

"We have been working in the areas of the three upper chakras: the Crown Chakra, Mind's Eye Chakra, and Throat Chakra. … It is important for us to work so diligently in the head and throat areas because thought, word, and action originate here. If thought and word are not pure and in sync, harmonizing together, you ultimately act incorrectly. It is your responsibility to concentrate on achieving correct thinking. Only when your thoughts are correct and totally whole in Oneness can you achieve right words and right actions.

"The next area where you exhibit blocks is in the Heart, the fourth Chakra. I am going to repeat what many others have said to you. **You do not share enough Love with one another.** You have inside yourself this enormous, beautiful, Loving Heart that wants to reach out, exude, and shower Love upon everyone and everything. However, when you become fearful, insecure, and do not Trust, this causes you to withhold Love.

"All these kinds of thoughts keep you from Loving and being Loved. I want to say it once more. "There is no one who Loves enough." One of the things you are going to be called upon to do in this fourth-dimensional work is to Love, to really Love, to reach out to one another. … Just feel yourself pouring out the Light of Love, freely sending it to others without condition. …

"When you have learned to lead with your Heart, and your Heart is open and flowing, your Heart chakra is activated to attract your Light Body experience.

"The lower chakras, the digestive tracts, the lower back, and the Root Chakra, all contain blocks. These blocks reside in the liver, gall bladder, and pancreas. These physical organs carry the residual fears and trauma of the third dimension, including past lifetimes. While doing this work, some of you will need to visit a nutritionist, a homeopathic doctor, or someone to guide you in flushing out these organs, because they carry the blueprint for receiving the fourth-dimensional Light-energies.

"The Root Chakra, your foundation and energy base, is where all energies culminate in your physical body. An enormous amount of "garbage" gets trapped here. When the organs are cleansed, the Root Chakra, in turn, can realign and balance itself. ... Know that the Root Chakra energy is every bit as important as the Crown Chakra energy. ...

"As you become more comfortable with these new energies, learn to feel them keenly, and permit them to flow smoothly and equally through all seven chakras."

Your Cosmic Connection

You are not an isolated being! Consider the principle of Unity, Oneness, and Wholeness. Although you have an individualized soul, you are not separate from the rest of the human race, the other kingdoms on Planet Earth, Mother Earth herself, and all of creation. **Everything is connected. All is One!**

At a higher spiritual level, you are part of and connected to life on all dimensions of consciousness and with all "matter." The All (The Absolute and all of creation) is similar to a hologram, in which each part or division is identical to the whole, no matter how small. Each individual component within the twelve realms of experience is unified in God The Manifest, The Unity Point.

The third dimcon begins the human learning process on Earth. Under the conditions of a fear-based planet, Participants for whom this is their first experience as an individualized soul initially perceive duality and separateness as the only reality. This perception of duality in Participants tends to induce and maintain a false sense of isolation. It is only near the higher aspects of the third dimcon—the sixth and seventh levels—that Unity, Oneness and Wholeness are clearly perceived, and Participants begin to understand their actual connection to everything. Participants ultimately realize they are all one family, one community, one nation, one race, one solar system, one galaxy, one universe, one God!

The main factor blocking Participants from understanding and accepting higher, spiritual truths is their resistance in relating to and comprehending abstract, intangible ideas and concepts. This resistance encourages the prevalence of dualistic factors like ignorance, fear, skepticism, and suspicion regarding alternative philosophies of life. This is understandable since spiritual truths are opposite to third-dimensional, physically tangible realities and experience. Separateness and division are opposite unity and oneness. The visible is opposite the invisible. Tangible is opposite the intangible. Intellect is the polar opposite of intuition. Fear is opposite Total Love, and so on.

By their very nature, spiritual truths and experiences are not provable by physical scientific methods for they function through higher vibrational realms. Spiritual experiences are unique to each individual. As noted above, third-dimensional realities and fourth-dimensional realities are very different. This gap can be bridged only through the functioning and utilization of one's intuitive mind.

It is mainly through the realization of spiritual ideas and concepts that Participants may relate to and comprehend that they are not an isolated being in a lifeless universe, but connected to and unified with everything in all of creation.

Identity Crisis: You, The Creator?

As a soul evolves and gains the capacity to understand increasingly complex, abstract concepts, the Participant searches for more accurate truths regarding the intrinsic nature of the Self, the environment, and the true purpose of this physical experience. Through research, study, and spiritual guidance, a simple reality is eventually discovered. Humans are an individualized extension of the divine, creative consciousness of The Absolute, with the similar basic attributes of mind, will, and feeling.

Creative abilities exist in every life form throughout the Universe. Examine your life. Throughout each day you are consciously, although in most cases unconsciously, creating your personal universe and influencing the universe of all humankind and beyond. Just look around at the multitude of objects, products, procedures, techniques, and problems to solve that you and your fellow Participants have created.

Participants on Planet Earth are, individually and collectively, an infinite aspect of the Creator-God. You are experiencing and interacting with a multitude of creative processes through either a third, fourth, or higher-dimensional consciousness, on Planet Earth, within this first realm of experience. As each Participant is a creator, you have many creative pursuits and tasks from which to choose for your individual experience and contribution to society. You, as an individualized Participant, are an integral part of this ongoing universal creative process.

Thought is the initial power and primary ingredient behind the creation of anything. Everything created first began with a thought, an idea that was formulated into a plan, a design, a pattern, a thing. Keep in mind that, as a creator, you will personally experience whatever you create through your thoughts. Therefore, you need to carefully monitor and discipline your thinking and decrees, for in most instances you are unwittingly attracting uncomfortable and even disastrous situations to yourselves through your self-talk, communications with others, and actions.

Some common phrases or statements in your everyday language are prime examples of this. "I get sick whenever I feel chilled." "Each winter I come down with a cold." "My allergies bother me every fall." "I am short of (or out of) money." "(Name) always does (acts like) that to me."

Fear is a wonderful prayer for disaster. Many statements you make, even casually, are actually decrees. Given enough emphasis and power, your thoughts and desires will return to you and in some manner materialize in either this or a future lifetime. The object of your thoughts could manifest at a time when you have no current need or use for it. **Also, what you desire for others, eventually returns to *you*.**

Stating adverse circumstances in a manner consistent with spiritual principles can cancel and avoid perpetuating them. Your spiritual objective is to bring harmony to a disharmonious situation. Some examples of constructive statements or decrees are, "I *now* enjoy perfect health." "All harmful bacteria and viruses be dissolved!" "I see, feel, and know that the money I require is *now* in my possession." "(The other person) is always kind and considerate of me."

The spiritual lessons of Love and Trust conquer fear. **Trust** is a major spiritual lesson of the fourth dimcon. **Trust is not something you *do*, but something you *have*.** Trust does not come from the intellect, but from the Heart. Trust has no relationship to outer, external circumstances but with the inner realization and Knowing that you are One with the Infinite Source of Everything. Trust is Knowing that, regardless of outer appearances, **"All is Well."**

In the fourth dimcon, you begin to realize and envision that the resources of the entire Universe are at your disposal, for the asking. Your next steps along the path of soul evolution will teach you how to use the universal creative principles for protection, health and wellbeing, and the attraction of your needs.

God The Absolute, The Creator, and The Manifest are not outside of you—they *are* you. You are the God of your own life, creating your own destiny. You are God experiencing Planet Earth in this solar system, in this Milky Way Galaxy, in this first realm. It is your choice as to whether you open to and live by this truth. It is your choice what you do with your life. It is your choice as to just how fast and how far you progress your personal soul evolution in this lifetime.

Summing Up the Cosmic Secret

The only limits you have are those you place upon yourself!

Who are you? *All is One! There is only one consciousness* in and upon this planet, this galaxy, this universe, all of the universes, in all of creation. You are a facet of Infinite Being, The Absolute, experiencing on Planet Earth through an individualized, limited consciousness in an extremely dense, restricted material body. Yet, as a Ray of infinite Light, your potential is limitless. You are partaking in a challenging, exciting adventure of self-discovery. If you like paradoxes, **you are god learning to be God.**

At the spirit level everyone and everything is equal. Considering the precepts governing infinity, no part of creation can contain or be more or less God. Everything is God. The All is all! All is The All! The All is infinite. All matter is infinite. Every "thing" is infinite. Every "one" is infinite. Any beliefs or theories to the contrary are illusions and delusions.

Where are you, and Who are you? You are functioning on a small planet, within a spiral galaxy, in a Universe system that was created in a void, out of no-thing. Ultimately, everything created exists only as pure energy. You are an individualized, spiritualized extension of The Absolute with all of the basic qualities of this Source.

You are The Absolute currently experiencing Planet Earth. Your immediate assignment within this dense physical environment is to deal with the "matters at hand" and, in the process, advance along your path towards total union with your unique, individualized spiritual essence.

Analogies

Imagine a power generating plant that is producing electricity at a pressure of 500,000 volts over 300 miles of high-tension cables. These cables lead to a transformer substation near a group of cities where the voltage is reduced to 50,000 volts. At the outskirts of one of these cities, the voltage is reduced to 25,000 volts. The substation at one of the suburbs reduces the voltage to 10,000 volts. At a large industrial plant the voltage is reduced to 2,500 and then 880/440 volts. At the pole outside your home, the electricity is further reduced to 240/120 volts.

Although reduced in voltage and power along the way, it is still the same electricity! The continuous line from the power source to your home is unbroken, just transformed. 240/120 volts is a relatively safe electrical pressure for domestic use. What would happen if you plugged your bread toaster into a 500,000 volt plug, or even 2,500 volts for that matter? Instant toast! … and toasted toaster, too!

In reverse gear, here is another analogy. Let us assume that Participants with a third-dimensional consciousness are only aware of the 120-volt wall receptacles in their house. They know that if they turn on the stove or plug in an appliance it is going to function as intended. When a Participant begins to desire a fourth-dimensional consciousness, they begin to look out the window and notice there is a transformer on the pole marked "DANGER! 2500 VOLTS!" If the Participant is more curious, they would follow these heavier wires to a substation where the warning sign reads "DANGER! 25,000 VOLTS!" With more perseverance, they follow the cables all the way back to the power generating station. They then discover the facts. The electric power is all from the same source, just stepped down in power to be of practical use at home, the material realm.

Still another analogy! A single cell in a body (human, animal, insect, plant, whatever) contains all the information necessary to reproduce that entire body or life form. You are a single cell, a microcosm, in the body of God, the macrocosm. You are a holographic mirror image of The Creator. Through the process of raising and aligning your consciousness, you have the ability to develop within yourself all the qualities inherent in the Infinite Source from which you emanated. As an individualized Participant, this is the goal toward which you are striving in this exciting University of Life!

Final Summation

We have provided you with all these cute little drawings depicting the various categories and levels of creation. They serve to satisfy the intellectual mind of the individualized ego which loves to analyze, classify, rank, and pigeonhole everything it observes and comes into contact with. But—

Technically and realistically speaking, all that exists is God The Absolute, which cannot be divided or separated.

It is like sitting on a bluff overlooking the ocean and counting the limitless progression of waves breaking onto the beach, or crashing against the rocks by the seashore. It is all one ocean. We just count the number and observe the magnitude of the ripples on its surface.

Meditate on this; think about it; feel it—and you will begin to realize the true nature of your being. This is what self-realization is all about.

Rather than thinking of everyone and everything as a *part* of God, conceptualize that every*one* and every*thing* is an individualized *extension* of The Absolute—like a ray of Light extending from the Central Sun! In reality, the Real You is Infinite! The fact that your consciousness is presently inhabiting a dense, limited material body has given you the false impression that you only exist in this limited physical realm. To transcend this erroneous illusion and reprogram your soul/subconscious to a more accurate spiritual truth, repeat the following affirmation to yourself many times throughout each day:

"**I Am God The Absolute experiencing Planet Earth as (your name).**"

Or, stated simply and succinctly:

"I Am God The Absolute in human form."

Think about these statements. See and feel their reality. Do you now have a different concept of yourself other than simply expressing through a limited personality ego? Can you now modify your attitudes of self-worth and self-esteem as to be in perfect harmony with The All? Can you now see, feel, and know you are One with All; **you** *are* **The All?** To assist in this endeavor you may choose to repeat this affirmation:

**"I, (your name), now see, feel, and know that
I Am One with Everything!"**

Good fortune and a safe passage toward attaining your spiritual Goal!

- 7 -

COSMIC PURPOSE: WHAT'S THE PLAN?

A question that is frequently asked is, "If God is in all ways infinite, how can It make Itself greater?" Well, the answer is really quite complexly simple. The Absolute appears to have concocted a "game plan" that goes something like this:

1. Always in balance, The Absolute, as an extension of Its energies (the only ones that exist), will create universes with customized qualities (The Creator) and realms (The Manifest) of progressively lower vibrational frequencies. Every learning environment, realm, galaxy, star system, or planet will be unique—no two will be exactly alike.

2. Conscious lifestreams, consisting of many species of life forms, will extend from The Manifest to experience the various realms. Each species group, or individualized life form, will have its own spirit, soul, and anapersona. Life forms begin their first soul experience without any knowledge as to where they are, who they are, and what the environmental situation in which they are embodied is all about. A lifestream may begin its existence on any realm to evolve from there up the ladder of consciousness.

3. Each spirit consciousness will be unique, with varied attributes and talents. Beginning with the third dimcon, each individualized spirit/soul/anapersona will have freedom of choice. No two individuals, therefore, will have exactly the same thoughts, feelings, preferences, desires, or come to the same conclusions regarding the various situations they experience.
4. All life forms will have a built-in motivator, pushing them to progress through higher degrees of awareness and realms of experience.
5. There will be a minimum of coaching directly from the Creator of this plan. Life forms are to learn through personal experience and figure things out for themselves. Technical support is available. Upon request, Participants with higher degrees of consciousness may offer their perspectives to others.

The object of this plan is twofold.
1. To permit the Absolute, having extended Itself into The All, to become more expansive in consciousness through a vast variety of unique personal experiences on a wide range of vibrational levels (realms). Because of an infinite number of variables, the number of possibilities is infinite.
2. To observe and ascertain what percentage of Participants are able to properly evaluate their experiences, and thereby discover the true nature of creation, their real identity, and just what this whole cosmic game plan is all about.

As life forms were created within each realm, galaxy, solar system, and planet, all Participants easily adapted to and identified with their immediate environment. It was natural for them to assume they were limited to those confines. The Creator's intention was that after a long period of "time," all Participants would question the validity of their existence, realizing it was a puzzle to be solved. The solution would be for them to eventually discover their true identity, transcend their outer conscious reality by going *inward,* thereby beginning their ascent back to the Source from which they originated.

Here is an analogy. You purchase a brand new computer. It comes with an operating system and a basic word processing program on the hard drive. There is no other information on the memory of this computer.

You want to write an original novel from ideas centered around people and experiences you have encountered, using the computer as a convenient writing tool. One big advantage of this computer is its processing speed. Also, it is programmed so you can conveniently correct spelling errors, rewrite the plot, and otherwise edit your work. When problems are encountered, you dial up Technical Support for advice.

You write your book sentence by sentence, paragraph by paragraph, chapter by chapter. This is a day to day, week to week, month to month, year to year process.

By the time you have finished your first book, there is much more information recorded on the computer's hard disk memory than when you started the project. The book now has a table of contents, preface, introduction, a story with many plots and subplots developed throughout the book, a conclusion, and an index.

Your life experiences on Planet Earth or in any realm of this Universe system are very similar to the process of writing a book on your personal computer. The only difference is that you are the author (anapersona), the computer program (spirit), and the hard drive memory (soul) at the same time. The more books you write, or lifetimes you experience, the more expansive your soul grows in awareness, knowledge, truth, and wisdom.

Your expedition to Planet Earth is also like a cosmic sporting event in which you are rewarded to the degree you learn the guidelines and apply yourself to perfecting the game. Can you relate to how the game develops character and teaches many lessons? How we sit in the penalty box when we make serious errors? How we groan at every blunder; cheer every advantage? How there is a great celebration when we win? Can you see more clearly how The All grows through our personal, family, and group experiences?

Your purpose on Earth as an individual human being, and the human race in general, is to enhance the wisdom of The All, which is, ultimately, *yourself!* On Earth, this purpose is fulfilled through the process of transcending one's animal nature and developing a spiritual consciousness. This is accomplished by realizing who you are and why you were created, then thinking, feeling, and acting in harmony with your *higher, spiritual nature*.

For those ready, willing, and able to make the leap, the immediate objective is to evolve into their spiritual nature by achieving a fourth-dimensional consciousness. Each individual who accomplishes this feat clears some debris from the road, making it easier for *all* humankind to progress along their evolutionary paths at higher speeds, and with fewer detours.

Truth, Reality, and Illusion

An important part of this winning plan is that each Participant constantly engages in the search for higher truths, whether they are aware of it or not. What is truth? What is the highest, unchangeable Truth? Something to think about, isn't it? Well, think of this. There can only be one highest, unchangeable, Absolute Truth, and that is God The Absolute. Anything less than this Absolute Truth must be a *relative truth*. This includes God The Creator, and on down the scale of vibrational frequencies and consciousness.

So, what is reality? Where does reality exist relative to your tangible, physical experience?

What does exist is each Participant's unique *perception* of reality. Reality, then, is personal to each Participant.

It is like watching a motion picture that is projected on a screen. The movie appears to be real and tangible, especially to one's mind, feelings, and emotions. However, a movie is only the projection of a series of still visual images with a sound track on a prerecorded strip of film. This Planet Earth Educational Expedition *is* real in that the physical, tangible world, as experienced through your five senses, is a **subjective reality.**

A similar experience means something different to each Participant. When ten Participants watch an event, you will get ten different stories relating to what took place.

How you think, respond, act, or react to situations in this virtual reality is dependent upon your personal set of truths and perceptions, and your self-talk, that is, what you tell yourself. In life, there are many situations of little importance that Expedition Participants take too seriously. You know this as "making mountains out of molehills." A third dimcon reality takes its significance only from the extremely limited, subjective perspective it is assigned by a Participant. With a clearer realization of this concept, a lot of mental tangles and emotional knots could be untied and many others avoided.

This Earth schoolhouse is teaching you to relate to your life experiences in an ***objective manner*** by transforming your perceptions of what constitutes "reality." This is accomplished by simply observing situations and being aware of certain possibilities, potentials, or causes. Not by making *judgments*—establishing *"facts"* that result in *conclusions*. From a spiritual perspective, *relative realities and "facts," which are subjective perceptions,* do not exist on the material Earth plane, for they lead one into judgment, which is of the third dimcon. Judgment does not exist in the fourth and higher dimcons.

We each find many events, conditions, ideas and concepts we believe to be "true." Yet, have you ever found two Participants whose "truths" in all matters are identical? If you really meditate, think, and feel about this subject you will understand how each Participant in this expedition possesses their own personal set of relative truths. Relative to what? Relative to their own or someone else's perception of reality. You may consider the following treatise on <u>Reality vs. Illusion</u>.

> When one's consciousness is focused totally in the outer, physical world, that is their only reality. To them, the inner realms are an illusion.
>
> For an enlightened individual who is in the world but not of it, the physical world is the illusion (maya), the inner, spiritual realms being their reality.

When a man or woman is in the process of changing their realities from the outer to the inner, there is a crossover period wherein the distinction between reality and illusion is blurred.

The only guiding lights on this path are Trust, Knowing, Patience and Perseverance, testing the waters, and learning through a combination of experience and wisdom.

A fine line exists between reality and illusion. Reality is relative to the individual, one's personal Truth! Reality is what one thinks it is, says it is, believes it is, what one knows it is.

So is illusion.

The trick to closing the gap that separates reality from illusion is to identify and align one's Self with the one, Absolute Truth, and then to consciously become that Truth.

In the quest for this highest, Absolute Truth, each Participant is coming from a different direction. It is like the spokes of a bicycle wheel, each separate, but all supporting the tire and attached to the central hub of the same wheel. Although each Participant has their individual relative truths, all paths eventually lead in the direction of the one Absolute Truth.

Bumps on the Path of Soul Evolution

There is one obvious attribute of God The Absolute that most Participants either take for granted or fail to recognize. That is the attribute of free will or, stated in other words, freedom of choice. The purpose behind individual free will is to assure that each Participant has their own unique experiences. No two individual souls have accumulated identical programming, knowledge, and wisdom.

In the spiritual dimcons, Participants, being conscious of their union with the Godhead, choose to express only action that is in harmony with spiritual principles. The potential for Participants to choose to experience both harmony and disharmony simultaneously began with the creation of the third dimcon.

A Participant housed in a physical body with a third-dimensional consciousness relies mainly on the instinctual and intellectual minds to function in their physical environment. This being the case, the Participant can relate only to the simplest, most basic ideas concerning God, since higher reality is based upon intangible, abstract concepts. Therefore, the effect of experiencing the third dimcon on a fear-based planet, is to lose the conscious realization of one's unity and oneness with the whole of creation. This situation literally leaves a Participant "in the dark" concerning spiritual realities.

The normal course of evolution is never a steady, upward journey. The learning and growing adventure constantly has its ups and downs. Through trial and error, a Participant may spend four or five lifetimes learning one particular lesson and then experience a setback when introduced to the next, unfamiliar one. There is always another lesson to learn. The process seems endless. However, when you seek out, pursue, and attain a spiritual consciousness, life has a way of telling you, "Enough trudging through third-dimensional lessons!" You then seek more harmonious experiences and move on to higher modes of expression.

To Participants with a spiritual consciousness, the errors perpetrated by the humans on Planet Earth appear to be obvious and the solutions so simple. However, what is difficult to comprehend by a spiritual being who has never experienced the duality and density of Planet Earth, is the extreme loss of awareness and consciousness when a soul is born into the confines of a human body with a limited brain-mind. Also, to Earth Participants, the allures of the physical world appear to be very enticing.

When one does not comprehend the consequences, it is very easy to misuse power, money, and sex in ways out of harmony with spiritual principles. The result has been that many spiritual beings who came to Planet Earth with the original intention of helping raise the consciousness of Earthly Participants, themselves became entrapped in the third dimcon, the realm of duality.

It is like climbing a ladder you are constructing from the ground up into the sky. As you build, you climb higher and higher, step by step, struggling against fatigue and gravity. You test each rung for strength before you reach for the next higher one. In your eagerness to ascend, you become less vigilant. Then you step on a weak rung. You slip and slide down two rungs, but you recover without falling further. Catching your breath, you climb higher and feeling confident, throw caution to the wind. Suddenly, you step on a rung that collapses under your weight! You attempt to catch yourself and latch onto a lower rung, but it breaks, too. Thud! You fall all the way and hit the ground. In the process your ladder has fallen and been destroyed. You now have to start the whole process over, from the bottom up, rung by rung.

We can only draw upon analogies as to why The Absolute included this "GO DIRECTLY TO JAIL! DO NOT PASS GO AND DO NOT COLLECT $200!" feature in Its game plan. Perhaps, this is why there are sand traps, trees, and the rough on a golf course. Consider that each sport has its obstacles, penalties, and goals, which challenge one's mettle, polish one's skills, and provide for unplanned experiences.

Life is very similar to a spectator sport. You were created to participate in this cosmic "game." One way or another, you are all players in the grandest, most imaginative, most creative sporting event in all of Creation. A Participant may sit in the grandstand and watch for a while, but eventually, life has a way of getting one involved. Those who progress the fastest in this challenge are strong, well-trained, disciplined, adept, determined, consistent, and enthusiastic. Whether you choose the major leagues, the minor leagues, or the amateurs, it is always a win-win situation. We encourage you to play your best, and learn something from every engagement. Know that each Participant is a winner.

Wrestling Yourself Free of Duality

Who concocted this disharmonious condition of duality with the powerful opposing forces of good and evil? Was it The Absolute? It was Participants who, through the misdirection of their free will, desired to think, feel, and act in manners out of harmony with the highest nature of their being. This resulted in their creation of an environment, a fear-based planet, whereupon they could act out their unbalanced egocentric desires and disharmonious passions.

What has experiencing this extreme condition of duality achieved for you? When a Participant, or a whole sports team, realizes they have a game coming up against some strong competition, especially their arch rivals, do not they train harder, plan all their offense and defense more shrewdly, and rally more optimism, enthusiasm, and determination than they thought they could possibly muster? Do not they attempt to conquer their opponents? Experiencing the opposing teams of Good and Evil has transformed you into a wiser, stronger, tougher soul.

What is your personal reward for conquering the third dimcon on Planet Earth? Having acquired a fourth-dimensional consciousness, upon the demise of the physical body, your soul is imprinted with a special Medal of Achievement upon which is inscribed—

What happens to those Participants who do not make the grade, whose souls are so programmed to error performance they are unable to escape the darkness and reach for the Light? Eventually, their soul programming is completely erased so they may reenter the third dimcon with a fresh start. This situation does not occur on Love-based planets, as the high vibrational feelings of Love are so intense among all Participants that everyone eventually graduates with honors.

The Three Searches – Seek and You Shall Find!

Here is a little known fact for you to ponder. There are three basic searches along the path of soul evolution regarding the attainment and application of a fourth-dimensional consciousness:

1. the Search for Self
2. the Search for Truth
3. the Search for Wisdom

The first and most formidable task to advance your personal soul evolution is to readily tackle and complete the Search for Self. The Search for Self is concerned with the individual Participant perceiving, and then relating to the qualities of the true nature of their being—God The Absolute.

An acute problem has been that the process of completing their Search for Self is taking Participants far too many Earth lifetimes to accomplish, as many as a hundred, two hundred, or more. Within the realm of duality, the illusions of separateness and division have been a major soul evolutionary obstacle. We anticipate that the introduction of higher vibratory fourth dimcon energies will remedy this situation.

Upon attaining the seventh level of the third dimcon, a Participant seeking spiritual enlightenment more actively embarks upon The Search for Spiritual Truth. After about seven years of dedication to this search, one may move *solidly* into a fourth-dimensional consciousness (occurring at the second level of the fourth dimcon), wherein one embarks upon The Search for Wisdom. This final search includes the study of the secrets of creation and how to consciously apply them to enhance one's personal wellbeing and experiences.

Soul Groups

A momentous event takes place when a Participant achieves a solid fourth-dimensional consciousness. To explain this, we will delve into the subject of soul groups. We are not referring to group souls as this is a different subject covered previously. Participants with third-dimensional consciousnesses are gathered into soul groups, each containing about one thousand members who share common interests, purposes and objectives. The path of soul evolution is easier when traveled with like-minded individuals with whom one has a comradery, or joyful affection. As all members are functioning through a third-dimensional consciousness, these are referred to as *horizontal* soul groups.

Upon achieving a solid fourth-dimensional consciousness, a Participant joins a *vertical* soul group, the members of which function through the *fourth* to the *ninth* dimcons. Each of these vertical groups are headed up by a being with a ninth-dimensional consciousness, with all members assisting each other to rise as easily and quickly as possible up the ladder of soul evolution. This is much different than the situation encountered in third-dimensional soul groups which can be likened to "the blind leading the blind."

Guidelines for Progressing Your Soul Evolution

The purpose for which you were created is to evolve, step by step along your own unique path, ever higher in consciousness, to union with your Divine Spirit in The Unity Point of All Individualized Consciousness. As you are a god learning to be God, soul evolution relates to the degree to which you align your consciousness with the Mind, Will, and Feeling natures of God The Absolute, the Source of these Three Primary Qualities. Through learning and experiencing, this ongoing process involves directing, redirecting, transforming, and refining your thought, willpower, and feeling natures. The major step in soul evolution which concerns humanity on Planet Earth is the evolution of Participants from the third to the fourth dimcon.

The goal of attaining a fourth-dimensional consciousness has been referred to as "entering the Kingdom of Heaven," for one has thusly acquired a spiritual consciousness. One thereby forgoes the requirement of cyclical death and rebirth in a dense physical body. From this higher fourth dimcon perspective, one more clearly perceives the differences between the disharmonious illusions and delusions of duality, and the harmony inherent in conscious unity and oneness with the Whole.

Certain conditions place the seeker of higher Truth and Wisdom on the ascent towards a wholly fourth-dimensional consciousness. One must have progressed to the *sixth level* (out of seven) of the third dimcon to begin their final assault on this formidable mountain.

A seeker steps up into **the sixth level of the third dimcon** through being motivated to learn and explore spiritual concepts and begin to apply them in their daily experiences.

1. There is a powerful desire for self-improvement. Through reading, attending classes, lectures, seminars, and so forth, you begin to learn practical fourth-dimensional principles and put them to use in your daily life.
2. You have the inner desire and feel compelled to advance beyond limited, fear-based thinking. You feel uneasy and unfulfilled with the merry-go-round nature of fear-based religions and begin to comprehend how spirituality and true freedom of thought differ from rigid dogma.
3. You begin to comprehend your unity and oneness with all creation and the true nature of your relationship to Supreme Being.
4. You set aside sufficient time (20 to 60 minutes) for appropriate daily silent meditation. This may be preceded by a guided meditation to clear blocks and align your consciousness.
5. You strive to develop your intuitive mind, and thereby more readily comprehend abstract concepts like soul, spirit, consciousness, infinity, and reincarnation.
6. You work to reprogram your soul data in areas where it requires modification and refining.
7. You become aware of the existence of your seven major Astral Chakras and begin to consciously clear, align, and activate them.
8. You endeavor to practice and live the highest truths that you know.

Two additional conditions need to be fulfilled in order for you to achieve **the seventh level of the third dimcon,** which overlaps with the first level of the fourth dimcon.

1. You must have completed 90% of your Search for Self, thereby beginning your Search for Truth.
2. Through increasing your realization of the essence and significance of being unified with All That Is, you consciously work toward the development of your feeling nature and the constant expression of Limitless Total Love.

To achieve the giant step into **a wholly spiritual consciousness by graduating to the second level of the fourth dimcon,** the additional requirements are:

1. You have received a passing grade in all previous requirements and agree to constantly refine your feelings and expression of Limitless Total Love.
2. All seven of your astral energy centers, or chakras, are open, activated, and fully functioning.
3. You are willing to accept total responsibility for all experiences in your life and forgive others all their misdeeds.
4. You desire to progress your soul evolution and strive for more accurate, higher truths.

Everyone Enjoys a Challenge

The mission the Participants of the Planet Earth Educational Expedition undertook is a tremendous challenge. You are ordained to progress out of your instinctual, animal nature through the use of correct thinking, self-discipline, and the proper focus of willpower. By struggling through the duality of Earth environs, it is anticipated that you look inward for the source of your true nature, and evolve to a spiritual consciousness.

The intention is for your anapersona/soul to accumulate enough wisdom to perceive the limitations of your intellectual mind and develop and use your intuitive mind. This will enable you to make substantial progress through the reception of *higher* internal and external guidance. Your personal spiritual quest will produce higher perceptions of Truth, and Wisdom, resulting in your freedom from the merry-go-round cycle of birth, death, and rebirth on Planet Earth.

This is a great challenge indeed, but not one that is impossible. Over time, many millions of Participants have graduated from Earth environs. The commission that has been added, is for a sufficient number of humankind to leap forward in consciousness and, thereby, raise the vibrations of Planet Earth back to that of a spiritual, Love-based planet.

- 8 -

NOW, WHY DID YOU *REALLY* COME TO THIS PLANET?

From the perspective of soul evolution, why do you think you (as an anapersona/soul/spirit) were destined to participate in this Planet Earth Educational Expedition? When first created with a third-dimensional consciousness, your soul-computer was brand spanking new, right off the shelf containing a basic operating system and a new "hard drive" with no programming. So, by what method were you expected to learn, grow in knowledge and wisdom? Let us examine the process you are expected to follow.

1. **To make mistakes. Without error there is no growth.** Error is an indispensable component in the learning process for it reveals the lessons your soul needs to learn. These lessons are your *work areas,* or, as they are collectively referred to, your *unfinished business.* Error needs to be awarded the respect it rightfully deserves for it is the first key to unlocking the mystery of your present bodily life experience.

   What few Expedition Participants realize is that when laying out this lifetime *you actually planned to make certain major and minor mistakes* in order to learn or reinforce specific lessons. Unfortunately, there have been many stigmas attached to mistakes. From the higher point of view, however, mistakes are crucial to the learning process.

2. To realize that you have made a mistake. This is the difficult part. Your soul learns largely through *trial and error;* through personal experience. Intellectual exercises are just that. They supply you with information but it takes actual "hands-on" experience for the soul to adequately record a lesson. Likewise, when an error is deeply ingrained, it may require intense effort on the part of the Participant, perhaps through traumatic experiences, to transform it.

Dear Participants, it is not necessary to repeat the *same* error as many times as you are doing to learn a particular lesson. Ideally, to err once or twice is sufficient for you to realize you are looking at an area that requires some attention. However, many Participants repeat their same disharmonious patterns over and over without realizing that what they are doing is spiritually dysfunctional. Life continually sends them messages, but they are reluctant to acknowledge that in some manner they are misusing power, money, sex or drugs, or have other disharmonious mental and emotional patterns.

Listen to your mother, father, siblings, teachers, spouse, fellow workers, police, judges, the janitor, the news media, your body, your car, your dog—*they* will tell you. You are not here simply to have an isolated, unrelated physical experience. Since people do not see themselves clearly, interaction with other Participants is vital to one's soul evolution. Living in a vacuum is productive for a while, but to file the rough edges down to the final polishing requires seeing yourself through other peoples' eyes. **Everyone and everything on Earth is your mirror, and your teacher. You are not separate from your environment.**

Each bodily lifetime presents new learning experiences. How do you recognize what courses you had signed up for on this particular cruise? Simple! *Pay attention* when you repeatedly trip over the same obstacle, especially those times when you fall flat on your face. Watch for repeating patterns in your life that cause you discomfort. These have a personal message for you.

3. **To want to transform the error through self-improvement.** This is a big step. This is where you put on your hard hat and get to work. It takes humility, willpower, self-control, and determination to evolve. You need to be *strong and determined!* Your God-self is All Powerful! Your spirit is always in perfect balance and harmony. You need to really shape-up if you are to emulate your Higher Nature!

You are on this expedition to make progressive, constructive transformations in yourself during this lifetime. *Without constructive change there can be no progress.* It is OK to change. It is OK to transform old concepts so more harmonious, loving, expressive, and expansive aspects of yourself can be exposed and developed in their place.

Old, obsolete patterns die hard. They have a life of their own to which they desperately cling. If they succeed, they hinder your evolution. At one point in your evolution they may have served a useful purpose, but that purpose is now far behind you. Hanging on to self-defeating patterns is like dragging anchors on the ocean floor. They slow you down and retard or completely stop your progress. Why wait until you are totally exhausted before releasing old, useless baggage? Decide *now* to replace the old with newer, more constructive patterns of behavior. You will be eternally grateful.

4. **To actually *do something* about effecting constructive transformation within yourself.** Current Participants have a distinct advantage in this modern age. There are many talented counselors, neighbors, friends, self-help classes, books, and audio and video-taped programs available to assist you in transmuting uncomfortable behavior patterns. Remember that you are transforming *ingrained soul programming*. Comprehension, willpower, and self-discipline effect permanent transformation. Chemical solutions are only a temporary placebo as far as the soul is concerned.

Self-knowledge and self-awareness are indispensable to personal transformation. You must know and see yourself clearly—not viewing yourself through a glass darkly. The sooner you let go of the self-imposed restrictions and limitations to your progress, the sooner you will free yourself from the chains that are holding you back. The hike up the mountain of enlightenment begins with a single bold step; then one robust, lively step after another. To achieve transformation, remember that Patience, Persistence, and Perseverance are required provisions to tote in your backpack.

5. **To progress your soul evolution.** True evolution is *soul* evolution. Day by day, experience by experience, change by change, learning higher concepts lifetime after lifetime, your soul accumulates wisdom along the spiral path of evolution.

Most Participants have been led to believe that their evolutionary process had begun and then ends with this one bodily lifetime. It is true that this is the only lifetime you will be George or Mary. But it is also true that *you are a soul* that experiences multitudes of material incarnations as Fred, Veronica, Gertrude, Clyde, John, Robert, Kathy, Paul, Lauren, etc. Many books are available explaining and substantiating the principle of reincarnation. If you are unclear about this concept, it would be wise to research the subject.

6. **To become enlightened and achieve a fourth-dimensional consciousness.** Your ultimate purpose for participating in this Earth Cruise Adventure is to progress your soul evolution to the extent you attain a spiritually-based fourth-dimensional consciousness.

Herein is the meaning of attaining "eternal life." Upon achieving a fourth-dimensional spiritual consciousness, your soul is not required to reincarnate on Earth in a dense, material body that *lives* and *dies*. Your soul may *incarnate* on Earth *by choice,* but you are not required to *reincarnate*. That is, you will not be required to return to Earth in another material body *out of necessity.*

Earth material bodies are designed to be operable only for a relatively short time span. They were engineered with a built-in self-destruct mechanism so that your soul might experience a variety of uniquely different experiences within a reasonable time period. On higher vibrational realms of expression, less dense physical-etheric and astral bodies have longer life spans, but eventually they also wear out and need to be exchanged for new ones. In the spiritual environs, the long infant-child-adolescent-adult growing process familiar to Earth Expedition Participants does not exist, for there is a full transfer of consciousness between the discarded body and a new one.

Planet Earth As a Cosmic Schoolroom

Planet Earth is one of the outstanding school campuses in the universe. Here, you come to grips with problems quite tangibly and very intensely. You thereby learn lessons faster than anywhere else in all of Creation. In this schoolroom, Participants have emotions, confrontations, physical trauma, and conflict resolution processes that do not exist on the higher, more refined vibrational levels. On Earth, Participants learn lessons in a few hundred years that would take thousands of years on spiritual realms. There are many educational advantages to participating in this Earth Expedition. Lessons are learned more decisively and make a stronger impression on the soul than on higher vibrations.

In this University of Life there is no tuition or registration for classes. Although you may plan your own curriculum, you automatically receive the lessons necessary for your growth at the time you need them. You cannot escape a lesson by ignoring the teachers' promptings. Just try it! When you turn the next corner, there it is—smack in your face—waiting for you!

Throughout the variety of daily Earth experiences your soul recorder/data-bank is constantly being programmed and reprogrammed to greater truths and more constructive modes of behavior. How does a Participant know when they are making progress through this learning process? Overall, they feel more happiness and joy, and are able to function, solve problems, and resolve conflicts in a more effective, peaceful, and relaxed manner. As self-confidence builds, Participants actually look forward to their next learning opportunity. They understand the rewards in personal growth.

As with any school, you are constantly being tested. Are you passing your tests? Are you progressing on to the next course, the next grade level?

You Came to Transmute Your Addictions

Addictions are the obsessive and habitual dependency to physical, emotional, or mental substances or stimuli. Addictions hide in many forms. Addictions may be subtle, severe, obvious, or obscure.

Addictions can be to many things: drugs, chemicals, beverages, plants, foods, sex, lust, power, money, wealth, poverty, work, play, hobbies, entertainment, gambling, violence, anger, war, dishonesty, theft, gossip, criticism, complaining, depression, and fear, to name some.

We observe that, whether they are aware of it or not, each Participant on Planet Earth has one or more addictions to something or other. Not all addictions are "bad" in the sense they are destructive. However, from a spiritual perspective, they are all in some way distractions that prevent a Participant from achieving a well-rounded personality, and from directly achieving their material and spiritual objectives. Think of addictions as being cul-de-sacs that are interesting and have fascinating features, but are side roads that lead to nowhere.

Habits are a form of addictive behavior in that they are actions you do repetitively—daily for instance (not withstanding eating, sleeping, and brushing your teeth). When there are alternative options, something like driving the same route to work each day can be a habit. If you have a choice, take the back road for a change and enjoy the scenery. Do you have favorite TV programs that are "must sees" on your list? For a change, watch another show at that time, or better yet, turn off the TV and do something else, like meditate. After all, variety is the spice of life, for it rounds out and expands your overall soul experience.

Since you are The God of Your Life, *you always need to be in total conscious control of your life*. Question any substance that takes you "out of the game," even temporarily. If you are looking for a "high," be a spiritual warrior. Select spiritual highs like meditation, spiritual reading, or group discussions that will keep you centered and focused on your spiritual path. As the dedicated warrior, continually ask yourself, "Is this action harmonious? Will it progress my soul evolution?"

Be aware that habits and addictions interfere with your soul progress, for if not transmuted, they are carried over into subsequent lifetimes until they are released. There is, however, one master addiction that will actually serve you well in your soul evolution. That is being addicted to Love—Limitless Total Love—a high that will never let you down.

Your Adversary Is Your Teacher

Has it ever occurred to you

- that *your greatest teachers* are persons who appear to cause you the most difficulty and present you with your most stressful challenges?
- that these incidents are messages to examine your behavior patterns?
- that the higher intent is to get your attention when you have not previously listened to numerous, more subtle promptings?
- that every distressing situation, like an "accident" or other "catastrophe," is a significant teacher for you?

Do you feel as though life is hitting you over the head with a 2x4?

On Planet Earth, the learning process requires that you transform and evolve through daily interaction and conflict resolution with other Participants. Whenever there is conflict, all Participants involved have something to learn through the process. There is a key, though, to making your learning experiences much less painful—if not downright enjoyable—by first calmly asking yourself, **"What is the most Loving and constructive approach to handle this situation and resolve this conflict?"**

Confrontation based on a Love-based dialogue and a sincere interest in the progressive soul evolution of all concerned is an indispensable factor for personal growth. When the process is based upon mutual Love and respect, it is a situation wherein everyone gains.

Remember, *you asked* for this course of study. *You asked* for this body in which you are functioning. *You asked* for these lessons, and, oh yes, *you asked* for *that* experience too! The one that was so painful to you. The one wherein you are so critical and vindictive of the other person. No, it was not an accident that it happened. It was all set up and carefully planned from these higher realms for your personal benefit.

We will now reveal to you a little known cosmic principle. **All intimate relationships must conclude in Love and forgiveness!** This applies to dedicated lovers, married couples, parent-child relationships and siblings. If a relationship does not end in love and forgiveness on the part of each Participant in one lifetime, it must in some manner be repeated in another until the issues are resolved. These are known as **karmic relationships.**

Most often in karmic relationships there is a deep Love for one another at the soul level. To resolve karmic conflicts in a new lifetime, a preplanned and predestined purpose brings the two or more persons together. As time passes, though, some aspect of their interactions will usually turn into conflict, anger, and perhaps animosity. This is the signal that the old, unresolved, unfinished business is resurfacing. Whenever you are confronted with or engaged in conflict, you are working on unfinished business which must be resolved in Love and forgiveness. You cannot escape it. Dodge a lesson and as you turn the next corner, there it is staring you in the face—the next day, the next month, the next relationship, a future lifetime.

Almost *any* type of relationship—friendships, classmates, coworkers, employees, clients, and neighbors to name a few—has the potential to have karmic (comfortable or uncomfortable) overtones.

Here is another well-kept secret. Very often when planning a lifetime, a Participant with whom your soul shares great affection will volunteer to assist you in learning certain lessons by playing the role of your adversary. A spiritual reward is due the soul who offers their services for this type of special mission. Relationships are seldom what they appear to be on the surface. There is usually some agenda concealed beneath the outward appearances.

Here are a couple of real-life examples for you to ponder.

1. When he was five years old, Henry's father died. His mother was in poor health and it was all she could do to care for Henry's older brothers and sisters. So, Henry went to live with his Uncle Matt. Now, Matt was very kindly and understanding. He cared for Henry just as if he were his father, perhaps even better. To this day, Henry is eternally thankful for the seven years of love and nurturing he received from Matt, and dearly appreciates the home and compassionate care he received from his uncle during this difficult period in his life.

    In his later years, through communication with his spiritual guides, Henry discovered that in a lifetime in Scotland four hundred years ago, the soul of his Uncle Matt incarnated as his neighbor and archenemy. Scotland was then a country where emotional tensions prevailed as taut as an arrow in a bowstring, ever ready to fly toward an adversary. There was constant feuding between the two with Matt continually pulling on Henry's anger chains. This encounter had been preplanned just to teach Henry some valuable lessons concerning anger. One would never have guessed that this loving uncle and Scottish adversary were the same soul.

2. In a lifetime two hundred years ago, Martin chose the experience of being a prominent Protestant preacher in a small city. Being dedicated to displaying an authoritative, well-controlled, celibate nature, the topics of many of his sermons were on adultery and fornication. The objects of his sermons, although not named directly, were easily recognized as some of the local townsfolk. The results were spectacular, for week after week there was standing room only in the church.

    One day, a new parishioner arrived at the Sunday service.

She was gorgeous and cut quite a striking figure! Martin exhibited a handsome appearance himself, and the new attendee was immediately enamored with this popular religious orator. Brought together by the irresistible forces of love at first sight, they soon found themselves in each other's arms. In spite of their efforts to keep their "unsanctioned" romantic union secret from the town, you can surmise that it did not take long before their tryst was discovered. Martin was unmercifully disgraced and drummed out of town so fast he took with him only a few personal essentials.

Just who was this young woman that waltzed into Martin's life to pull his heartstrings into this whirlwind adventure? Well, in this present lifetime this soul reincarnated as his loving mother! Of course, there had been several previous lifetimes through which the anapersonas of these two souls formed loving bonds. Only a kindred soul would agree to perform such a challenging role, thereby assisting a dear friend in overcoming a disharmonious soul disposition.

What was the lesson, obviously carried over from previous lifetimes, that Martin needed to learn? That it is not only unwise, but also disharmonious behavior to judge and criticize another Participant's personal experiences, especially publicly. One can never know the past and present life ramifications of another's current actions, and *look out!—*

Whatever energies you extend toward others will eventually return to *you!*

As these examples illustrate, too much energy is wasted on accusing other Participants of being the cause of your problems. Just remember— **whenever you point your finger in accusation, you have three other fingers pointing back at *yourself*.**

Everything you do either creates or consumes energy—every thought, every feeling, every emotion, every action, every reaction. A major step in progressing your soul evolution is learning to utilize energy efficiently—to stop needlessly wasting energy and begin creating energies that have the greatest rate of constructive, productive return in your life.

What wastes energy? Simply stated, **disharmony wastes energy.** Negative and fear-filled thoughts, statements, emotions, or actions waste energy and stop your evolution in its tracks. Disharmony is creation in reverse. Disharmony exists in the absence of Total Love. Disharmony withholds, inhibits, and blocks anything constructive and fruitful you may attempt to attract to yourself or achieve in your life. A major lesson in the third dimcon is to learn what actions create harmony and what actions create disharmony. One eventually comes to the realization that actions encompassed in Total Love create harmony.

When you resist constructive change, your lessons are learned through *conflict*. Without confrontation you would never discover your "hard-hat" areas that require reconstruction or "retrofitting." Your adversary simply puts up the red flags and orange warning signs alerting you to pay attention—your next work project is directly ahead!

Who are or have been *your* adversaries? A family member? A friend or acquaintance? The property owner from which you rent your home? Your employer, or if you are an employer, an employee? The police officer or judge? Someone else? How did you handle the situation? Do you need more practice?

If you think a fellow Participant's criticisms are unwarranted, what might be the best way to reply to their suggestions or accusations regarding your actions? Be *calm* and *ask them appropriate questions* like, "Why do you think that way." "What would you have done?" Perhaps the whole point of the confrontation was to train you to ask appropriate questions of other people who challenge or disagree with you. This is a talent that takes practice and is indispensable to effect calm, rational social interaction. Also, your inner knowing will tell you whether your challenger's comments are valid. Go inside and plug in your intuition to get *your* answers. Above all, **be honest with yourself**.

How can you maximize your personal growth when confronted with a difficult situation? Become quiet and ask yourself, "Why am I in this situation? What do I have to learn from it? Is this person reflecting my actions from a previous lifetime? What do I have to change in *myself?* Do I need practice in this area?" You may be amazed at times how quickly the answer will pop into your head. Sometimes, you may need to search a little longer for the answer, but ask spirit for guidance and you *will* receive it.

When you planned this lifetime you had access to your soul record. You purposely set up this material life path to highlight and accentuate your weak areas. You also set up experiences to provide you with opportunities necessary to transform your faults into merits, thereby growing in strength and clarity. Before coming into your material body, you even made agreements with other Participants to share certain experiences so both or all would learn, grow, and evolve through the resulting interactions. Unfortunately, this process has not been adequately explained to Participants entering Earth environs in a new material incarnation. This has resulted in the true purpose of many uncomfortable experiences being lost, and the proposed lessons not learned.

Out of ignorance, many Participants have a fear of self-transformation. Some resist changing their disharmonious patterns at all costs. They fear a part of themselves may be lost, their self-identity, their uniqueness, their individuality. When this barrier is breached by risking a little improvement here and a little there, Participants soon realize they become more comfortable and are able to confront life more lightly, objectively, and humorously.

When the transformation process is explained in terms of personal soul evolution and a Participant begins to personally experience the benefits of progressive, constructive change, they are more apt to eagerly look forward to each new growth opportunity. They come to realize the advantages of personal transformation outweigh the disadvantages of remaining uncomfortable. They feel more self-empowered and less dependent upon outer circumstances.

Love Is a Many-faceted Thing

Love is a *feeling*. In its highest, purest form, it is the source of all feelings and emotions. In the English language, the word "love" is used to describe many intricate facets of this very significant and vastly misunderstood creative energy. Some languages, such as Greek, have a different word for each form of Love, whereas English requires adjectives to describe a specific form of "love."

For their soul evolution, Participants with a third-dimensional consciousness are required to personally experience, through many incarnations, all the various aspects of human love. There is much conversation, and there have been many books, fiction and non-fiction, written on the subject of love. Although most Participants do not realize it, the issue of love, or the lack of it, is at the very basis of all human interaction. At the "heart" of any human conflict lies the opportunity to resolve the problem through applying the principles of Total Love and mutual respect for all life. Ultimately, self-love, personal love, love of family and friends, brotherly love, love of country, and love of nature are all combined and transformed into a universal Love that has no limits.

In the third dimcon, the realm of duality, you are acquainted with the terms unconditional love and its implied opposite, conditional love. As individual Participants progress in soul evolution, the way they relate to the word "love" changes. The ultimate and highest realization of this most sacred of feelings, is Limitless Total Love, a fourth dimcon, spiritual concept. Limitless Total Love is complete and reflects a recognition of unity and oneness with the All. There are no strings attached, no doubts, no fears. Limitless Total Love brings Participants out of the disconnected realm of duality into an understanding of the unified concepts of oneness and wholeness.

Love is the most powerful, constructive, harmonious energy that exists. Love is the manifesting power of creation. To think, speak, feel, and act in terms of Total Love is the major lesson to be learned by the inhabitants of this Universe. Any action not performed in *harmony* within the principle of Limitless Total Love is eventually doomed to failure. An example of this type of disharmony is an action that benefits a Participant personally, but results in another's loss. Where the condition of Limitless Total Love exists, everyone triumphs.

− 9 −

CRASH! WHERE TO BUY NO-FAULT-OF-MINE INSURANCE

"You hurt my feelings!" "She made me angry!" "He made me cry!" "Who is to blame for what happened?" "Statement angers local ethnic group." "Who's fault was that?"

How many times a day do you hear statements like this—from your family, friends, co-workers, television, the newspapers and magazines? Just who *is* responsible for the unexpected and unforeseen events that happen in *your* life? Who is responsible for *your emotions?*

Accidents: It Was All Their Fault

A question often asked of us on spirit's side is, "Are Participants provided with No-Fault-of-Mine Insurance?" Basically, No-Fault-of-Mine Insurance protects a Participant against ever taking responsibility for anything in their life. The policy states that someone else, never yourself, is to blame for all your hurts: physical, emotional, and mental.

Sorry, but there is no provision for this type of coverage in the terms and conditions you agreed to upon the purchase of your cruise ticket. Where can you purchase no-fault insurance? At the flaming-red painted booth outside the main entrance gate to Hades. There you will meet a very handsome, pleasant talking gentleman in a scarlet suit who will graciously assist you! Just watch out for the sweet-talk and that barbed hook on the end of his tail!

Accidents and unforeseen circumstances happen, particularly in the dense atmosphere of the material realm. Projects planned on the higher realms may not come into fruition on Earth because once they arrive here, the Participants may change their minds as to what they desire to do with this lifetime.

Always remember that the wild card is *free will*. The Absolute does not desire to interfere with your free will. It will offer guidance, but does not want to control your personal experience. Participants have freedom of choice to raise their consciousness, lower their consciousness, or remain static. The power of Participants' thoughts and unpredictable emotional natures, all choices, keep everything in a constant state of flux. This increases the chance for "accidents" to happen.

Negligence, carelessness, physical body and product material fatigue, judgment errors, another's malicious acts, and the forces of nature are some direct physical causes of accidents. But what is going on behind the scenes from a spiritual perspective? A Participant's lesson-learning karma is perhaps the greatest spiritual cause behind "accidents" —karma from past lifetimes or acquired in this present lifetime.

Here is a real-life illustration. A personable, well-liked young man in his late thirties, we will name him Franz, had an important position in a moderately-sized corporation. One night, Franz was driving home with a friend along a narrow, two-lane country road. The road made an abrupt zigzag as it crossed a narrow bridge. Franz lost control of his vehicle on the turn and it rolled over several times. When the sheriff deputies and paramedics arrived, Franz was not breathing and had no heartbeat. His neck had been broken. He was dead. The passenger was uninjured.

Then something unusual happened. In the ambulance, Franz began to talk, telling the paramedics he was going to be all right and not to give up on him. He was revived at the hospital, but paralyzed below the arms.

Was there a spiritual cause to this accident? Yes! Franz had not been following and progressing along his life plan, so his soul decided to take him out before he wasted the rest of his life. When on the other side, however, Franz realized what had happened and begged to be given another chance. Although destined to the use of a wheelchair for the rest of his life, he accepted his fate gracefully, eventually quit his corporate position, and began a new life headed in another direction.

The assassinations of Presidents Abraham Lincoln and John F. Kennedy were "accidents" in the sense that these tragic events were not in their original life plans. The destructive free will choice of their adversaries resulted in their premature deaths. Although great humanitarian political leaders, they had not attained a level of consciousness high enough to have absolute protection by spirit.

Earth is a chancy planet, so wise Participants learn to expect the unexpected. Because of its heavy physical density, Earth environs are much more accident-prone than are realms of higher vibrations.

So, the advantages of attending this marvelous Earth schoolroom are sometimes offset by the chaos surrounding unanticipated events. Graduates of Planet Earth, though, are noted for their adeptness and adaptability, resulting from their handling of the many-faceted, impromptu learning adventures they encounter.

It Was Really My Parents' Fault

On the Astral Plane, there is a great demand by Participants wishing to continue their soul progress in material Earth bodies with particular physical, feeling, and mental characteristics. Know that you not only asked for the body through which your anapersona is now experiencing, but most of you begged for it, for other souls were requesting that same bodily experience.

Most of you have embarked upon a customized learning adventure. You even chose to have particular stressful childhood experiences in your formative years so you would have something to work on and, hopefully, resolve at some time during the remainder of your Earthly life. Your soul knows that the best way to learn particular lessons is to struggle out of ignorance and error into enlightenment.

Remember that from the higher perspective of the Astral Plane, you chose and had made agreements with your prospective parents or guardians, mates, friends, employers, and even your enemies. You knew the intricacies of their personalities and something about their soul programming. In most cases, these people were anapersona/souls with whom you had loving past-life encounters in some form of relationship. In terms of Earth years, you may have begun to plan this present lifetime one hundred or more years before your birth. If your parents, or others, in this lifetime had caused you great stress, anxiety, or even trauma, have you considered that you *asked* for that experience before you were born?

It is important to understand that eventually you must accept total responsibility for everything that happened in all your Earth lifetimes. It is, therefore, very important that you forgive your parents, Uncle Jack, Cousin Wendy, the next door neighbor, and that awful stranger, for what they did to you as a child, or beyond. As soon as you do, you will begin to live a more comfortable life and also accelerate the progress of your soul evolution.

If you are harboring resentment and anger over some past traumatic event in your life, the wisest move would be for you to say while in a meditative state,

> "Somehow I attracted that experience to myself, whether it was a karmic lesson due to a past error on my part, or some other reason. Although that was an extremely difficult experience, I sincerely forgive him or her, and I thank them for being my teacher. In Light and Love, I release and dissolve all blame, resentment, and anger I harbor from that experience. And so it is!"

If certain situations turned out to be a lot tougher than you had planned from the higher perspective, well, that's the breaks! When on spirit's side you know that Earth is a chancy place. All you can do is keep your fingers crossed and accept events as they occur, while trying your best to learn from them. Remember the terms and conditions you accepted—there are no guarantees that everything would work out as planned. That is why this Earth Educational Expedition is so exciting! You never quite know what to expect next!

What Is Your Responsibility?

Now, here is a word to remember! **Responsibility!** Your **"ability to respond."**

How is this stated on a practical level?

Responsibility is your obligation to respond to your experiences in the highest, most Loving manner that you know at any given moment.

An inappropriate or lesser response will generate an uncomfortable learning experience somewhere down the line for your evolutionary benefit. The downfall of humankind in general, and Participants in particular, has resulted from not consistently performing in the highest, most Loving manner they know.

Responsibility is a major lesson in the curriculum. Sooner or later, you will come to the conclusion that it is in your best interest to **accept total responsibility for everything in your life.** You may as well, for even if you do not, the cosmos will eventually teach you to do so. Remember that your soul is recording *everything*, all the time. It does not sleep. It is not partial. It will not give you a break. Your Higher Self knows that all errors of commission or omission must be corrected if your total being is to grow and evolve.

Most Participants are uncomfortable to one degree or another from being bombarded by karma they have created for themselves. However, they choose not to recognize that they have been the source of their own difficulties and discomforts.

Now, an important point which many Participants overlook and about which they are misinformed.

Your *first* responsibility is to yourself, your own well-being, and your own soul evolution.

No one else is responsible for your soul evolution—no one can do it for you. Only after you are relatively secure physically, and feeling-wise, mentally and spiritually, are you prepared to devote your energies toward helping others less fortunate than yourself. This is not selfishness, but selfness. You cannot give another what you do not possess yourself.

Although you do grow spiritually through engaging in charitable activities, it is not wise to do so at the expense of your own well-being. If you spend time helping and being of service to others, it is best you spend at least an equal amount of time serving yourself. The Universe does not require that you deplete your strength to the extent that you jeopardize your overall well-being.

To offer a fellow Participant assistance when they are discouraged because of adverse circumstances is admirable, but undue or excessive support may actually hinder the other's evolution. It is through adversity and the solving of one's own problems that a soul becomes strong and wise. Wisdom dictates you ask your spiritual guidance, "To what extent may I help this person? What does this person *really* need?" A sure-fire method of receiving your own answers is covered in a later section under "Making Correct Decisions."

What is your responsibility to another person who is acting in a disharmonious manner? Usually this is applicable in a personal or work-related relationship. First, ask your spiritual guidance if it is appropriate for you to be their mirror and say something to them. If the answer is yes, at an appropriate time, calmly and lovingly ask the other person if they might choose to listen to your suggestions regarding a particular area of their self-expression.

You might ask, "Shawn, why did you respond to that situation in that manner? ... Would you like to hear my suggestion as to what might, perhaps, be a more harmonious way to handle it?" After this, you may grade yourself as to how you think and feel you handled the situation. The more comfortable you feel, the more you may give yourself a higher grade.

When confronted with another's suggestions, however, many Participant's react by launching a counter-attack, like pointing out the other person's errors. Using this tactic is a neat way to avoid looking at your own work areas, and is a major diversion from *your* primary responsibility. As you are responsible for *your* personal growth, wisdom dictates that you calmly listen to another's suggestions. Although you may not agree with the other person, always assume they are acting in good faith and have your best interests at heart. Be thankful for these opportunities for growth, as these situations are learning and growth opportunities for both parties.

A graduation prerequisite is that every Participant learn and practice the art of being responsible for their own thoughts, words, and actions, as well as accept total responsibility for everything that happens to them. Each Participant who learns this important lesson will find more peace, contentment, self-confidence, and inner security than they have ever previously experienced.

Hazard Insurance Is Available

From spirit's side, we have observed that most cruise Participants leave themselves open to and at the mercy of the "whims of the world." They progress through life with their nose to the ground, totally engrossed in materialism, and the outwardly tangible, material world. The result is that these Participants attract the highest percentage of "accidents" to themselves.

How do you purchase hazard insurance? It's really *too simple!* Simply *ask* for it! "Just ask," you say? Remember the admonition, "Ask and you shall receive?" You were endowed with freedom of choice, right? Well, spirit, or God if you please, will not give you any assistance, of any kind, unless you *ask* for it. To do so without your permission would infringe upon your free will.

To attract spiritual protection, all you need to do is direct your attention to a higher, spiritual level of consciousness and say,

"Thank you for your absolute safety, security, and protection!"

During meditation, you may also add,

" ... of my person, my loved ones, my home and property, and my motor vehicle; plus whatever else!"

It is best to repeat a request for protection often, especially when you leave home, are in a crowd of people, or find yourself confronted with an awkward or potentially dangerous situation.

One point to remember is, if you ask for something and receive it, spiritual beings appreciate a simple "Thank You" for their efforts.

Participants who practice the art of creative visualization may wish to use an additional technique. This is to wrap yourself, your children, your auto, home, possessions, or Aunt Jenny two states over, from top to bottom within a cocoon of golden-white Light, the color of spiritual protection.

Particularly when protecting your own person, have the intention that no disharmonious energies from the outside may penetrate this brilliant, gold shield of Light, and, as the cocoon encompasses your energy field, no one may take your energy. Then say your prayer asking for security, knowing that "It is so!"

Before venturing out walking, shopping, exploring, or traveling, the wise person observes their gut-level intuitive feeling and asks, "Is it best I do this now, or not? Is it safe for me to go to this place, or not?" If you have a *feeling* that something is not right or receive a "No" answer, then *don't do it!* Stay home, do not do whatever you intended, because *this is a warning not to proceed!*

You must always be aware of subtle, or not-so-subtle, warnings coming to you from spirit. Let us say you are rushing to make an appointment or just going to the grocery store. But your car will not start. The plumbing may spring a leak. The washing machine overflows. You lock your keys in the car.

After one or two interruptions say, "Okay, Thy Will be done! I will not do this right now. I will stay here and deal with this problem. Thank you for your guidance and protection." Be grateful for these inconveniences, for spirit used these methods to warn and prevent you from going into an unsafe place and thereby encounter a harmful event.

Okay, so you asked for protection, or this is the one day you forgot, and you have your purse or wallet stolen, or you and your auto are involved in a cruncher. What then? Well, perhaps your Higher Self is trying to get a message through to you—"someone is draining your energy;" "you need to change your direction in life;" "you need to be aware of accepting an incoming influence in your life, or the necessity of releasing an old pattern." Maybe there was a lesson to be learned in which the injury or the loss was the catalyst. Also, an attack on your person may have been your reaping of a karmic lesson. This brings us back to accepting total responsibility for your life.

Whether you experienced an accident, an attack, an illness, an injury, an insult, or whatever, it is wise to remember that, being an extension of the Absolute, you are not disconnected from the entire human race. Each Participant shares some responsibility for the actions of others. Everyone must accept some responsibility for conditions as they exist—for objects being manufactured, for more deadly weapons being developed, for chemicals and drugs being formulated, for peacefulness and anger, for tenderness and violence, as well as the misuses of power, money, sex and drugs. All is One. You are all in this experience together.

Although you are on a majority-rules planet, many times a minority gains power and control simply because the majority did not act or respond propitiously to a situation. If a disharmonious situation exists, you have a responsibility to help change it either through prayer (inner means) and/or outer, material means.

Everything has its constructive side, its proper uses and advantages, and that which brings pleasure and joy. The perception that as individuals you are powerless to improve a disharmonious situation is an illusion. Majorities, as well as powerful minorities, are made up of individual Participants. In a free state, the majority rules, ideally with consideration for the minority. If a certain condition exists, it is because the majority wants it that way. However, it has been said, "Sometimes a majority simply means that all of the fools are on the same side." If you do not like the decision made by the majority, then, through education, resolve, and diligent effort, you have a responsibility to work for harmonious, constructive change. A major lesson learned on Planet Earth is that all problems must be solved through understanding, wisdom, compassion, and Love. If a sufficient number of Participants would work for harmonious transformation from a higher spiritual consciousness, miracles would manifest. More is and can be accomplished through the Power of prayer than the World realizes.

By assuming total responsibility for all your difficulties, you will greatly progress your personal soul evolution. When an uncomfortable situation enters your life, the first question to ask yourself is, "How and why did I attract this problem to myself?" You *will* get your answer. Remember that you are not disconnected from the Universe.

As a learning circumstance warrants, everything and everyone everywhere are available to benefit *your* progress. You do not have *to do* anything to call in the lesson. "When the student is ready, the teacher will appear" in the form of the necessary experience.

So, who is responsible for your thoughts, your feelings, your emotions, your actions, for everything that happens in your life? You are. No one else. The sooner you accept total responsibility for your life, the quicker you will climb higher on the ladder of soul evolution.

Your Own Personal Security System

Do you believe you are living in a random universe where all events happen without any design or purpose? Do you assume that all Participants are equally unprotected from personal danger and from the whims of the world? If so, we wish to dispel these notions by clarifying how this universe you are currently experiencing actually works.

In your industrialized societies you are bombarded daily with the word "security." You have national security, social security, job security, home security, auto security, communications security, personal security, and so on. Obviously, all these phrases refer to various forms of *outer* security—security dependent upon physical, material means and methods for their implementation. Being materially based, they all have their flaws, imperfections, and failures. All of these security systems are *fear-based;* based upon a fear of lack, harm, or loss.

There is a security system, though, that is consistent, fool-proof, and once you learn how to use it, never lets you down. It is inner security. Inner security is based upon the Principles of Trust, Confidence, Knowing, Courage, and Fortitude. It is Knowing that, in spite of external appearances, and in spite of whatever happens, **"All is Well"**—in God's world, and in your personal world. Spiritual mastery involves Knowing that "All is Well" despite any five-sensory, fear-based evidence to the contrary.

When Participants achieve a fourth-dimensional spiritual consciousness, they learn to Trust the entire Universe of spirit for their protection, Knowing that "it is so!" As they transcend fear, they realize that to arm oneself with guns and weapons is a fear-based, third dimcon response to threats of outer world violence. These Participants discover, through personal experience, that by learning spiritual techniques and practicing them in their lives, their chances of leading more comfortable, happy, and safe lives are vastly increased.

Mother Theresa demonstrated these principles in her life. She showed no fear of harm to herself and others under her guardianship through a positive Trust and Knowing that she and they were safe and protected.

Earth is a very interesting planet to experience, for the material, outer world incessantly shouts to all cruise Participants, "All is *not* well! There is much to fear! You cannot trust anything or anyone. Do not take chances! Lock your doors and buy the best security system available!" These are the fear-based illusions of life, the Beast barring the door to your spiritual progress and enlightenment.

Trusting that "All is Well" in your life, in spite of what the outer world is screaming, is a major, basic lesson for all Participants to learn, truly understand, and make an integral part of their soul wisdom. Being a fourth-dimensional lesson, the opportunity to employ Trust in a situation may at first be obscure and difficult to recognize. The more you are able to replace fear of any kind with Trust, the more your needs become met and the more comfort you will feel. Trust, Confidence, Knowing, Courage, and Fortitude will take you far along your path.

- 10 -

UPGRADING YOUR SOUL DATA

Embedded in your subconscious awareness is the recognition that you signed up for this expedition to learn lessons, gain valuable knowledge, and thereby grow in wisdom. The purpose is to progress your soul evolution. This has been, however, one of the best-kept secrets on Earth!

Most primitive societies have traditional rituals, myths, and ceremonies to remind them of the purpose of their Earth sojourn. These groups allow time each day for its members to be introspective and offer gratitude and thanksgiving to the source of their daily necessities and show respect for the wonders of nature upon which they depend.

Each human race on Planet Earth has had its own distinct purpose and its own unique lessons along the path of soul evolution. In Africa, for instance, most of the Participants were organized in small hunter-gatherer groups or lived in villages. For the most part, they lived peacefully and in harmony with their environment. Theirs was a very physical experience, close to the earth, the animals, and the flora around them.

In the more technologically advanced countries, the Participants have been blessed with time-saving devices on the one hand, and overwhelmed with time-consuming leisure activities that include mechanized and electronic toys on the other, all competing for attention. Modern technology has interjected its blessings and its curses.

Even with their time-saving technology in the Western countries, Participants have been distracted from recognizing and pursuing activities which encourage them to fulfill the intended purpose for which they signed on to this adventure.

Self-Improvement: The Road To Transformation

It is important to realize, that at this moment, while you are *Now* in this material experience, you have the golden opportunity to search out and upgrade your personal soul programming. If you make the choice to begin effecting spiritual progress through self-improvement, all parts of your being will be eternally grateful.

Too many opportunities for growth go unrecognized. They are either ignored, or passed by. However, if you knew you could be more happy, calm, relaxed, and aware, is it not worth expending the required effort to dive in and complete your assignment—cleaning up your unfinished business?

The entire process of evolution is dependent upon the principle of change. Only change is constant. Self-improvement is the most productive form of change one may undertake.

Throughout a lifetime on Planet Earth, Participants are presented with many opportunities to make improvements in their psyche that are advantageous to their growth. Unfortunately, many of these opportunities are either not recognized as such, or are ignored out of fear—fear of change, fear of breaking the rules, fear of what others might think, fear of making a mistake, fear of the unknown, fear of being the fool, fear of failure, the fear of what *might* happen.

We strongly advise you, therefore, to look back on your life and observe wherein, through fear, you may have missed valuable growth experiences. Whenever you feel these fears creep in again, ask yourself, "Now, what do I *really* have to fear? How can I handle this opportunity more wisely?" Then say, "I will pursue this opportunity for growth. I hereby dissolve the fear that is holding me back."

Identifying Areas Requiring Transformation

Over centuries of varied experiences, your soul was programmed with the data it contains today through your anapersona's consciousness. You are continually receiving output from this accumulated data, and you are functioning through this programming. Whatever the source, you are the only one responsible for your soul's contents, which primarily consist of mental statements that can be translated into words. Some of these statements are harmonious and constructive, others are disharmonious and potentially destructive.

Invariably, Participants retain and repeat programming in their adult years that they accumulated from their childhood experiences—the manner in which their parents or foster parents treated each other; the way the Participant was treated and taught as a child; the hurts, anger, and fears the child or teenager felt when experiencing traumatic abuse, especially from an adult. These experiences become a part of the soul record (if not already there), and may manifest in adults as various destructive behavior patterns.

This present time in your evolutionary process may be a good point to purge these disharmonious data files. Or, you may wish to modify some conflicting or fear-based data blocking you from proceeding in a new, more desirable direction. Ideally, this introspection and updating procedure is a routine to be utilized throughout each Earthly lifetime.

To identify these areas and then edit, rewrite, and program some new data into your soul record *requires effort on your part.* However, please realize that this process is a very necessary step in the progression of your overall evolution.

Remember, data that was programmed while in a material Earth body *can only be reprogrammed during a material body experience.* On the Astral Plane or a spiritual realm, a Participant can only evaluate their soul data to determine what old data needs refining and what new experiences are needed. Thereby, one can decide what to attempt in their next material incarnation. Disharmonious patterns that were attained on Earth can only be released or transformed on Earth, or on another planet with a similar environment.

There are schools on the Astral Plane which are largely designed to teach the anapersona how to better cope with Earthly life experiences and, thereby, get the most out of their next physical embodiment. There are certain situations whereby a soul can graduate directly from the Astral Plane to a fourth-dimensional spiritual consciousness.

On the higher realms, there are times when spiritual beings with a fourth-or-higher-dimensional consciousness may realize there are some disharmonious remnants of Earth soul programming interfering with their spiritual progress. The being may choose to *incarnate*[11] on Earth with the express desire to transmute or eliminate these blocks.

Since current Earth teachings have not emphasized the necessity of this soul editing and revision process, it eventually catches up to a Participant. You may experience this in your life when, at times, you feel overwhelmed with problems. Know that you asked for these experiences. The more you can relax and Trust, the easier it will be to focus and work through each challenge.

At the subconscious level, soul data is continually filtered through the unique personality each Participant has chosen for this lifetime. This personality is but a basic tool, or medium, through which the soul expresses itself. The full soul consciousness cannot directly express through a human body, for its information bank is too vast for a limited human brain to handle. It would overwhelm the intellect and blow out all the fuses.

Your responses to life's everyday situations involve an automatic process which you are ordinarily unaware of at the conscious level. Throughout your daily experiences, your soul continually plays back its recorded data through your subconscious awareness. When a particular situation occurs, the soul searches its database and instantly comes up with the response in the form of programmed actions and reactions. Situations for which there is no programmed reply may result in a totally inappropriate behavior response, or perhaps, no response at all.

Your soul functions in this manner so you do not have to reinvent

---

[11] To incarnate is by choice; to reincarnate is through necessity.

the wheel each time you are confronted with reoccurring events, encounters, and challenges. You have probably solved that problem before, even in a previous lifetime, and now immediately recognize how to handle it. Much of this data, though, has not been reviewed, updated, expanded upon, or refined for centuries.

When problems arise and conflict ensues, it is a caution flag to examine your subconscious soul programming and determine if your automatic responses are appropriate to the situation.

Some automatic responses may cause you constant stress, and you may not recognize the source of your discomfort. Many Participants continually run ten degrees into the red on the stress calibration scale and think that is normal! These Participants are unaware they may be laying a heavy trip on others, causing them the inconvenience of dealing with the effects of their detrimental words or actions. Situations in which your behavioral manifestations are out of balance, block you from being aligned with higher-dimensional energies.

Now, here is a great analogy! You just purchased new tires for your car and pull out of the tire store onto the city streets. Twenty, thirty miles-per-hour, smooth as can be. At forty MPH you begin to feel a slight vibration in your steering wheel. You turn onto the entrance ramp to the freeway. At fifty the whole car begins to shake, and at sixty, the vibration is so unbearable you immediately take the next exit, turn around, and head back to the tire dealership.

Well, you know the answer. A tire is out of balance. You return to the tire store, the offending tire is balanced (or rebalanced) and you again head for home. Thirty, forty, fifty, sixty MPH. What a difference! Smooth all the way!

The same principle applies to personal soul evolution. As you strive to attain higher realizations, concepts, and truths, you occasionally need your psyche to be realigned and rebalanced. This allows you to function more smoothly at elevated frequencies of consciousness.

A worthy objective is to practice being calm and relaxed when in the midst of chaos. In this state you are able to handle crisis with relative ease. When relaxed, but not slack, you are able to reach the heart of a problem without being encumbered by unnecessary emotional stress. If you are continually bouncing off the walls of the world around you, it is a message that your responses to the pertinent situations need upgrading.

The reprogramming of your inappropriate soul data is a major venture you undertook this lifetime. Life is set up to give you the lessons you need, and the ability to recognize areas of inappropriate behavior is an art which requires development.

Awareness – Look Sharp! Feel Sharp! Be Sharp!

There is a major tool in your self-improvement arsenal—*awareness!* To consciously progress your soul evolution, you need a new perception from which you evaluate yourself and all events around you. Employing spiritual awareness is a talent that requires practice to develop.

Being aware means observing all facets of a situation from a broader perspective, but without judgment. Rather than accepting a situation at face value, what might be the meaning *behind* what is happening? Be aware of everyone around you. Observe what they do, how they look, their body language, and what they say. The exercise here is to not take what everyone says at face value.

When someone talks with you, observe what is *behind* the words they speak. *Look* at the person. They *say* they are fine, but they *look* like they have a fever and are ready to pass out. You may find it appropriate to offer your assistance to this person or offer them a suggestion whereby they may be more safe or comfortable.

Learn to develop compassionate allowance for another's disharmonious behavior. Everyone has areas which require refining. However, living in close proximity with a Participant who occasionally displays discordant energies can be disruptive to the peace and harmony of your environment. If appropriate, you may bring you observations to their attention and ask if they desire to search out the problematic script at the basis of their actions.

Most importantly, however, **you must be totally aware of** *yourself!* *Introspection* is the key word here. "Know yourself" is the admonition. Being totally aware of your thoughts, feelings, and actions assists you to better recognize and evaluate your lessons, work areas, and karma. This may be accomplished by employing the following steps:

First, develop the technique of mentally standing outside of your body and observing what you are doing from an impartial point of view.

Second, become attuned to your *feeling* nature. How are you really *feeling* now? Do you feel uncomfortable and feel yourself reacting to the present situation? Have you just been confronted with a situation to which you do not immediately have an answer? Perhaps this is a new lesson for you.

Third, when you notice that something does not feel quite right about what you just said or did, ask yourself,

- "What was I thinking that caused me to say that? Was that a positive, constructive thought, or is there a more harmonious way to express that idea?"
- "Now, why did I just do that? Could I have performed in a more constructive manner?"
- "Was there a better way of suggesting to Bill that he might improve his performance? Did I express myself constructively?"
- "Was I acting in the highest manner I know? Was I acting in Love?"
- If you feel a tingling sensation in your body, you might ask, "Was there a message in, or purpose to that occurrence? I do not feel quite right about it."

Self-awareness is an essential ingredient in the formula to progress your soul evolution. It is very important that you constantly utilize it.

On Stage and In the Audience

Has it occurred to you that this cosmic schoolhouse we call Planet Earth is also a cosmic theatre? In this environment you are the player of your role, and also a member of the audience.

One of your noted playwrights, the fame of whose plays is still honored on your contemporary stages and in film productions, had many particularly astute insights into human behavior. Let us examine a quote from one of his more popular works.

> *All the world's a stage,*
> *And all the men and women merely players:*
> *They have their exits and their entrances;*
> *And one man in his time plays many parts, ...*
>
> *As You Like It,* Act 2, Scene 7, by William Shakespeare

In each of your Earth lifetimes, you chose to play a specific role. You agreed with other Participants that you would play a certain role in their lives and they would play a particular role in yours. But always be mindful that these temporary roles do not represent the totality of one's consciousness!

At birth, you chose a body stamped with certain personality characteristics, and you carried over a whole set of subconscious scripts in your soul programming. However, you are not stuck with this original role and its associated programming. As you progress through childhood, adolescence, and adulthood, you are presented with countless opportunities to modify and expand your soul knowledge and wisdom. Remember that—

Your soul evolution is the only thing you can take with you when you eventually discard this material body and leave this current role behind.

To consciously enter into the playhouse of your life, **sit down in a comfortable seat in the fourth row, directly in front of the stage.** Now, this is where you use your awareness. **Carefully observe your performance and your interaction with the performances of the**

other actors. From a detached perspective, constantly ask yourself, "Why did I say that?" "Why did I do that?" "What is this play teaching me?" Note what parts of your role you like, and what parts could use improvement? Ask, "Is there a more constructive way to play this role?"

You may also observe, "This role I am playing is too confining. How can I expand my self-expression into another area of expertise?" Or, "I have played this stressful role long enough. How can I perform a more harmonious one?" You may conclude, "I need to transform my script. Certainly there must be a higher level of awareness through which I can function." There are all kinds of questions to ask yourself that will inspire you to challenge the present role you are performing, thereby motivating you to achieve maximum spiritual progress in this current lifetime.

Then, realize that **you are *the writer, the director, and the critic* of this little play. If you do not like your script, you can change it at any time!** However, do not walk off the stage in anger, for this would mean you do not understand what the play is all about. To accomplish the most from this process will require the utmost utilization of your awareness, introspection, and evaluation of your life patterns.

If you desire to get the most out of this present adventure, not only **play your current role to the max,** but **search out and expand into areas you had never thought possible.** Everyone has many hidden talents developed in past lifetimes. The more you break out of any self-imposed bonds, and improvise and expand upon your present role, the more wisdom your soul will accumulate. Where in your life are you surrounded by artificial barriers that limit your self-expression? Where can you expand your personal experience so to be of greater value to yourself, your loved ones, and to your community?

Nowhere in the whole Universe is there more God or less God. You are as much God as anyone else. You are Limitless! Within the constraints of the material condition and the level of your consciousness, you have no limits. The greater experience is to test and challenge your self-imposed boundaries. You will discover they are illusions—they do not exist.

Action vs. Reaction

Are you the actor or the re-actor in life? When you *act,* you are in full control of your mental, emotional, and physical faculties, and proceed to accomplish your intended objective in a calm, methodical, and rational manner. When you re-act to outer circumstances, you feel mildly to intensely uncomfortable, perhaps overwhelmed by irrational emotions that, in themselves, accomplish nothing constructive, waste energy, and thereby *stop your soul evolution.* Energy conservation is a major asset toward attaining a spiritual consciousness.

reaction – 1. The disharmonious emotional response generated by an erroneous fear-based or otherwise limiting idea or statement recorded in a Participant's subconscious soul programming.

2. An emotional signal from a Participant's Higher Self indicating that he or she is being confronted with a work area of unfinished business.

At their core, all reactions have some fear-based, disharmonious idea or concept buried in one's subconscious soul programming. If you are to achieve a spiritual consciousness and live in the state of Limitless Total Love, all vestiges of fear and disharmony must be eliminated from your psyche. To attain this objective you must first be aware of the state of consciousness you are to striving to achieve.

Your goal is to remain calm and relaxed in the midst of chaos.

The first step towards the recognition and identification your *work areas,* or *unfinished business,* is to practice total awareness of yourself and to—

Observe your emotional reactions.

Your emotional reactions point directly to areas of hidden, subconscious fears, stashed away in your soul programming. Whenever you observe yourself reacting to an internal thought or an external situation, you are looking directly at an area that requires constructive change. Resisting self-improvement stops one's soul evolution. The stresses caused by continued avoidance of a problem area may result in physical illness, injury through accidents, or even the body's untimely death.

The basic principle behind the recognition of emotional reactions is, **Whenever you feel uncomfortable, you are looking your unfinished business—a work area—right in the face.**

Reactions are emotional signals that are transmitted from your subconscious soul programming and manifest through your physical *feeling* nature. Reactions alert you to take notice that a disharmonious script requiring transmutation is lodged in your soul programming. You identify reactions through being aware that you are—

1. Feeling uncomfortable in any situation.
2. Feeling irritation or being impatient with a situation.
3. Getting your "hackles up"; feeling yourself being "hot under the collar," or otherwise burning with anger or resentment.
4. Responding in a defensive manner to another's statement by heatedly defending your position.
5. Responding offensively by verbally or physically attacking another person, animal, or inanimate object in anger.
6. Experiencing any uncomfortable physiological response to a situation such as feeling anxiety, faint, sweating, a tingling sensation, an adrenaline surge, tension in your gut, etc.
7. Choking when about to utter inappropriate remarks. This is a direct warning message from your Higher Self to say nothing or change the subject.

Some reactions resulting from one's fears are very subtle, and it takes a learned awareness to begin to recognize them. Also, Participants are very clever at disguising their reactions with excuses such as, "If it wasn't for you, I wouldn't have to react!" or, "It's all *your* fault! There is nothing wrong with me!" A major step forward in one's personal evolution is to own up to one's own "stuff."

If you are thinking that another person's action is the cause of your *reaction*, FORGET IT! For your benefit, the other person unconsciously set you up, that you would have the opportunity to observe yourself reacting. Bless them!

Do you react to what other people say and do? Know that the people or situations that trigger your emotional reactions are there for a purpose. The faces may change, but the situation will be repeated until you learn to eliminate your reactions.

Criticism, a close cousin of judgment, is a fear-based reaction. Everyone must learn the difference between destructive criticisms, usually a statement expressed in the form of an accusation, and constructive suggestions, usually best stated in the form of a Love-based question. An example is, "Would you mind if I gave you a constructive suggestion regarding (your actions)?" Or, "Do you realize that you are reacting to this situation?"

Criticisms have disharmonious repercussions, while constructive suggestions are intended to have harmonious overtones and improve a situation, thereby advancing the soul evolution of everyone concerned.

Many of your strong subconscious, disharmonious beliefs served a valuable purpose in prior lifetimes. They are like gold-painted bricks which appear to be valuable, but are worthless. Each brick is an erroneous thought-form existing in your soul record as a subconscious statement. They keep you attached to Earth concepts and restrain you from achieving a spiritual consciousness. They are like attack dogs nipping at your heels. These creatures remain with you until you eliminate them.

An example is the use of force and anger to defend oneself against physical or verbal attack. In the past, these responses may have been acceptable. However, are these appropriate responses to dealing with today's everyday problems, as we struggle to evolve to higher expressions of relating to our fellow Participants? Obviously, now is the time to drop the heavy suitcases filled with these gold-painted bricks which are weighing you down and exhausting you. They are restraining your progress. The more of these subconscious mental and emotional blocks you uncover and transmute, the lighter and freer you will be.

Where there is heat, there is *fire*. Any reaction to either an inner thought or outer stimulus is a direct message that you are looking your unfinished business right in the face. That is it! **Do not even bother to** challenge another's statement or blame a situation as being the cause of your discomfort. *Your* **reaction means that it is** *your* **problem. Solving** *your* **problem is** *your responsibility.* Others may help you see your problem more clearly, but it is your primary responsibility to modify and transmute your unwanted soul programming. It is important to note, however, that through prayer and meditation, we can assist another Participant in transmuting their disharmonious scripts.

When you see a lesson coming, it is our advice to go right through the middle of it. Do not go around or try to suppress it. Say to yourself, "This lesson is staring me in the face, and I have something to learn from it. I am reacting to this person's actions and they are trying to teach me something." Then ask yourself, "Why am I reacting to this event? What am I to learn from this situation?"

You can achieve progress only by acknowledging your responsibility and acting upon your reactions. No progress, and you are not achieving your potential and your goals for this lifetime. Waste a lifetime, and it will have to be redone. Why wait? "Seize the day!" Start NOW!

Monitoring Your Reactions

This is where your awareness and resolve are put to the decisive test.

The **first step** here is to **be aware you have just reacted to a situation.** Once you begin to practice observing your reactions, within a short time you will become quite adept at recognizing the symptoms.

The **second step** is to **take total responsibility for your reaction.** "Yes! I own *that* one!" Being defensive only blocks your soul evolution.

Third, put the basis of your reaction into words. That is, become aware of the disharmonious words buried in your soul programming that are the source of the reaction. This one may take a little more work to accomplish, because reactions are so instantaneous that you would swear you said nothing to yourself. But persevere and ask, "What was I saying to myself that caused me to react?" You will be amazed at the answers you receive once this exercise begins to work for you.

In many cases, while you were reacting you actually *did* use words, either in your self-talk or in what you said directly to another. In either case, *analyze* what you said. If you *truly* are **objective** and logical, you will begin to realize that what you were saying was, in reality, *not true!* With a little searching, you may discover your hidden script is stating one or more of the following:

"I need this (thing) (person) for my happiness."

"What my mate and children do is a reflection upon me."

"My self-worth is determined by the value of my possessions."

Ask yourself, "Oh? Is that statement *really* true?" "Do I *really* need this thing or person for my happiness, or just because I am saying so?" "As a spiritual being, am I discredited by what another person does?" "Is my self-worth based upon external objects?" You may discover that these subconscious statements or stories make no sense at all to your newfound, developing higher awareness.

This raises the question, "Can I be humiliated or become embarrassed by my own or by another's actions?"

Answer: Only if you choose to feel humiliated or embarrassed; that is, if this is the response directed by your personal soul programming. In this case your subconscious script might be, "I will feel humiliated and embarrassed by my or another's words or actions." Or a variation of this might be, "It is socially appropriate for me to feel embarrassed if I make a mistake." Whenever these situations actually occur, your programming plays out your script and BANG!—the reaction is automatic.

Yes, you can lie to yourself and not even realize it. A major step toward becoming more comfortable is bringing to your attention hidden, erroneous thoughts which, when you stop, think about, and analyze, are obviously flawed. This is what enlightenment is all about. It is looking at everyday Earth life from a different point of view wherein the obscure becomes the obvious.

The Reaction of Anger

Much confusion has arisen over the appropriateness of the emotional reaction of anger—as to when it is acceptable and when it is not. The disharmonious emotion (reaction) of anger is sometimes confused with the use of controlled, purposeful, seemingly forceful, calculated words and actions. The actor uses this technique to accomplish a worthy goal when more calm and relaxed approaches have been ineffective. There is a vast difference between the reactional emotional rage of anger, and purposefully acting strongly assertive, decisive, and emphatic in your communications. In the first situation, the reaction of anger *controls you;* in the second, *you are in calm, deliberate control* of your actions.

The objective is not to suppress one's anger, but to eliminate its root causes by transmuting the disharmonious soul programming at the basis of the anger. The retention of suppressed anger may eventually cause a person's body severe physical illness and even death.

Anger is a marvelous spiritual teacher because it is opposite the peacefulness, serenity, and calmness you seek. From a spiritual perspective, the issue underlying anger is **the desire for control over others, situations, or circumstances.** These are precipitated by fear of loss, and not getting what you want. Two primary fear-based causes of anger are:

1. Frustration resulting from not being able to control a situation or another person's action.
2. Displaying anger in an attempt to force your control over a situation or another person's action.

You may notice that anger is ego based, exhibiting a "Me-Me" attitude toward others and life in general. Some examples of subconscious statements or scripts that trigger the disharmonious emotion of anger are:

"I will be extremely displeased and angry if people (or animals or things) do not act the way I want them to."

"I will be angry if situations do not conform to my expectations."

"If others cause me inconvenience or interfere with my plans, I will become angry with them."

"I will be angry if others do not make me happy and bring me comfort and pleasure."

"Whenever I make an error, I must exhibit anger to let others know that I am displeased with myself."

It is necessary to challenge these incongruous concepts and repeat this acknowledgment many times:

"All Participants have freedom of choice to do whatever they desire. Everyone is at a different point of evolution, is working on different lessons, and has different abilities. Others are too busy and concerned with their own problems, happiness, and comfort to be concerned with just pleasing *me*. I can express my disappointment over the outcome of that situation in a calm, relaxed manner. I am worthy of love in spite of *my* errors."

You may also say,

"It is an unrealistic assumption to expect outer circumstances to conform to my desires. Absolute perfection exists nowhere in the created Universe. I hereby release all my ego attachments and expectations as to the outcome of these circumstances (or to the actions of myself and others)."

If you feel anger toward another person, look to yourself for the source of that anger. You are totally responsible for your emotional state, not others. No one can make you angry. Anger is your choice. Remember that anger begets anger; violence begets violence; love begets love.

Seen from the inner planes, when a Participant exudes anger, the color of the energy field of their astral emotional body turns a dirty dark red and black. Their aura sparks like electrical short circuits and swirls flaming-red mini-tornadoes as in a monster thunderstorm. Not a very pleasant scene to observe.

Anger is an energy. It is a very powerful, disharmonious energy. If higher-dimensional spiritual beings did not diminish the enormous amount of energy behind some Participant's anger, this unrestrained energy could kill the person to whom it was directed. Anger teaches many lessons—patience, consideration, compassion, understanding, tolerance, respect, and kindness among them. The lesson is to be kind to yourself and others in your thoughts, words, and actions.

Know that the concept of "perfection" is a relative term of comparison. Nothing in the created Universe is "perfect," and no Participant is expected to perform at their optimum level one hundred percent of the time. Simply stated, a person, situation, or thing performs "perfectly" if the action or result performs its intended function. Other than The Absolute, no measure for the condition of perfection exists, for it is relative to a particular situation. For all Participants, absolute perfection is a worthy ideal to work towards, but is impossible to achieve.

Does the reaction of anger have a karmic lesson attached? Definitely! The objective of karma is to teach that all action be in harmony with and reflect the basic qualities of God The Absolute. As with all disharmonious action, anger brings a Participant a learning experience. In our modern age, your Higher Self may use your vehicles to return your energies of anger. Since vehicles represent one's direction in life, tire problems, like blowouts (blowups), are the most popular medium used to bring this lesson to Participants' attention.

Here are some real life examples illustrating the karmic effects of anger.

Peter was a beginning student on the spiritual path. He was fortunate enough to have personal guidance in the form of channeling from spiritual guides and teachers. Several of the lessons were on the subject of anger, a problem through which Peter was working.

In one session, the guides stated that perhaps whenever a student expressed anger in a situation, a wheel on their motor vehicle may come loose. While visiting family in a neighboring state, Peter engaged in a fiery verbal exchange with his sibling. Peter could feel the heat behind his words, but felt his anger was justified under the circumstances. Afterwards, Peter had second thoughts as to whether his anger was appropriate.

The next day, while driving back towards home on the interstate highway, Peter noticed that his car was beginning to quiver and shake.

He pulled onto the shoulder and inspected his vehicle to discover the cause.

The right rear tire was slightly askew. Peter removed the wheel cover. Three of the five lug nuts holding the wheel to the hub were either stripped or sheared off, and the other two were loose. Peter got the message and made the choice to totally transmute his anger problem.

Next is a real life experience that shows what can happen when one gets up on the wrong side of bed in the morning, and carries their anger throughout the day.

Julie and her boyfriend drove in her car to the drive-up window of a popular hamburger establishment. They stopped at the menu board and were giving the attendant their order over the microphone when another, speeding car roared past their car and the menu board, the driver cursing and swearing at them.

The three hostile individuals gave their order directly to the attendant at the pickup window and waited there for it to be filled. Julie and her boyfriend were astonished to say the least, but they were calm and patient, making the best of an uncomfortable situation.

The rude individuals used foul language at the window, demanding they hurry up and deliver their order *pronto!* After paying for their order, the driver stomped on the accelerator and squealed, tires smoking, out of the drive onto the side street heading towards a main intersection.

As Julie and her boyfriend were observing this, the car belonging to the three hostile individuals speedily approached the corner intersection. A red traffic signal faced the driver, but he did not stop. CRASH! A car coming from their left side broadsided them. The force of the impact projected the three occupants out of their automobile. It was a real mess, with the three being severely injured. This was a graphic example of an instant karmic lesson.

Ending Reaction by Transmuting Disharmonious Soul Programming

Here are some suggestions and techniques for transmuting disharmonious soul programming. Each of them takes practice and repetitive use to be effective, but they *will* and *do* work if used persistently.

1. Have you ever noticed that the words we use, either in our thoughts, self-talk, or social communication, can instantly determine how we feel and what emotions we express?

   "I am insulted," and you feel insulted.

   "I am embarrassed," and you feel embarrassed.

   "I am angry at you," and you feel angry at the person.

   "I am unhappy," and you feel unhappy.

   "I am depressed," and you feel depressed.

   "I am happy and cheerful!" and you will feel that way.

   The list goes on and on and on.

   Of course you can ask, "Which came first, the feeling or emotion, or the statement?" From a third-dimensional perspective the feeling or emotion came first. However, from a fourth-dimensional perspective, the statement came first. **Thoughts create scripts that produce or condition responses.** Most likely the script, in the form of a statement, was written on your soul record in a previous incarnation and then reinforced throughout many subsequent lifetimes. Every time you utter one of these statements you are reinforcing and perpetuating the existence of the response or condition.

   Remember that YOU ARE GODS! Whatever statement you make, whether harmonious or disharmonious, is TRUE as far as your subconscious soul programming is concerned. The words "I Am" are the two most powerful words in existence, especially when used in making a decree. Whenever you say, "I Am …!" you are making a decree. A current emotion, feeling, or condition stated in your decree will be reinforced. If the condition you are decreeing does not already exist, given enough energy, it will manifest.

Always be mindful that the scripts stated above are self-generated, or generated from an external source through your consciousness—like watching TV. To create a new response, you can generate a new script any time you choose. Given enough thought, willpower, and feeling, your new script will take effect in your life. Patience, Persistence, and Perseverance are also essential requirements.

Suggested Solution: Watch what words you use after "I Am." Use only constructive, loving words in your decrees. Always *Know* that in spite of outer appearances, "I Am fine! All is well in my Universe!" (You will find more information under "Affirmations.")

2. In response to a startling, unfortunate event do you say, "That was *HORRIBLE* (or TERRIBLE, AWFUL, APPALLING, DISGUSTING or the like)? These words, by their nature, have a disharmonious ring and generate fear. Is fear a constructive response? Do you realize that you radiate fear by using these and similar words? Also, don't these words have a definite ring of judgment and condemnation?

One uses these words as a programmed subconscious response to certain incidents. Can you feel these words trigger terror-like reactions within yourself? Do these words disrupt your peace and harmony, thereby wasting energy? Do you realize that by using these words you are attaching yourself to the situation?

The use of these words indicates a lack of Trust that "All is well in God's Universe." Trust is a major lesson in the fourth dimcon.

Suggested Solution: By using only constructive or indifferent words in our communications, the more we can function from a fourth-dimensional perspective. Ideally, use the phrase **"That is *interesting*"** when responding to what might ordinarily be a discomforting situation. **"Interesting"** is a neutral word that does not generate disharmonious emotions.

In situations where this response may not be appropriate, you may try using intermediate words and phrases such as, "That outcome was a *disappointment*," "That was indeed *unfortunate*," or "You have my *condolences*."

It is best to realize that what is, Is! An event that has just happened cannot be changed or reversed. **Detachment** is a worthy virtue to develop. Be involved, interested, caring, compassionate, and loving, but also be detached—*empathetic,* but not *sympathetic*. Feeling empathy is to show compassion and have an understanding of a situation but at the same time not become caught up in disharmonious emotions.

Suggested Solution: To practice *detachment* in a difficult situation that is beyond your control, say to yourself,

"If I was not here and did not know about this event, it would have happened anyway, and life would have gone on without me. Therefore, I must be the impartial observer of this situation and be the *actor,* possibly by offering my assistance; not the *reactor* spinning my wheels."

This brings us to the subject of **expectations.** To have any expectation as to the outcome of any situation or event is to set yourself up for disappointment, frustration, and disillusionment. Expectations attach one to an outcome that is usually beyond their control. The Universe will make certain that Participants learn this lesson.

The answer is to do the best you can and work as hard as possible to achieve a worthy goal, but not be attached to the outcome. If you achieve the goal, that is great! If not, that is great also. Nothing is lost but effort and time, and everything is gained in experience and wisdom. Nothing ventured, nothing gained. Something ventured, something gained.

In the fourth dimcon, a Participant is more **objective**, that is, they look beyond themselves to the greater picture without personal feelings, prejudices, or interpretations. The opposite is being **subjective**, which is only looking at what feelings or situation applies solely to oneself or another person. With a spiritual consciousness, you have a broader perspective regarding life's circumstances, for you then comprehend that a huge iceberg of countless intricate factors exists beneath the surface, hidden from ordinary human sensory perception.

3. Do you react in a defensive manner or in anger to what other people say or do?

Suggested Solution: Ask yourself what fear-based subconscious programming is causing you to react? What statement, in the form of a script, is at the basis of your concern? Do you now have enough information to properly evaluate the significance of what the other person is saying or doing? Is what the other person saying really true? If so, is this any concern of yours? Are you feeling that your self-esteem, self-worth, or self-confidence are threatened? If so, why?

What "they" (other people) say, feel, or do is unimportant. Listen to others' opinions, but know when to take them seriously. The only things of importance are what *you* think, feel, and do.

This is another lesson in detachment—being the actor rather the reactor. Even though what the other person says or does may have life-changing implications, all you need to know is that All is Well, and that there is a purpose to these events that is not apparent on the surface. Know that you have and will be given the ability and the resources to overcome all obstacles. When applicable, ask your spiritual guidance and human counselors for assistance, carefully evaluate your choices, then chart your plan of *action*. These situations can be your test to remain calm and relaxed when in the midst of chaos, and to keep your actions in harmony with the principle of Total Limitless Love—for the greater good of all concerned.

4. Do you react in indignation, disgust, or anger when another Participant makes a mistake or an error in judgment?

Suggested Solution: Allow the other person the "right to be wrong." Every Participant not only makes mistakes, but is expected to make mistakes. Then again, when someone errs, this is often a subjective evaluation that may be considered a difference of opinion. Say to yourself, "I allow the other person the right to their own experience. I hereby emotionally detach myself from this situation and another's experience."

5. When someone questions you regarding something you had said or done, do you have an instant reaction of guilt and/or fear? Do you instantly respond in a defensive manner with an untruth, making up a story to defend yourself? Underlying this reaction is a fear of the truth.

Too many times in past lives, Participants had been excessively or brutally punished for misdeeds when they admitted their guilt. When challenged, they soon found it much safer to deny any involvement and make up an alibi regarding their participation or whereabouts. In the past, this had become such a habit that they have carried this characteristic forward into this lifetime. Some Participants go to the extreme of making up stories regarding their experiences even if they do not feel threatened.

Sooner or later all Participants must confront and transmute their disharmonious traits. Like all habits and addictions, this is a difficult one, but with the exercise of Patience, Persistence, and Perseverance, it can be transmuted.

Suggested Solution: First, recognize where the basis of the problem came from—most likely a past lifetime. Conditions are not the same in this lifetime. Know that when you accept total responsibility for everything in your life, you have nothing to fear. You understand your motives and when applicable, calmly accept the consequences of your actions.

Realize that your Higher Self knows what is true and what is not. Your spiritual guides and teachers, as well as The Absolute, all know the truth of a situation. From a higher perspective, there are no secrets on spirit's side where our lives are an open book. It is senseless to attempt to hide the truth about anything. Dishonesty will always be exposed—in this or a future lifetime. Truth will always triumph, particularly now, as the vibrations of Earth are steadily increasing, and karmic lessons come to you more quickly!

There is never any reason to defend yourself. You are not required to answer for your actions to anyone but yourself. You always have the right to remain silent.

If you choose to speak, ask pointed questions. "Why do you want to know?" "What difference does it *really* make?" "Do you know and comprehend the *real cause* behind my actions?"

6. Many times Participants have a reaction wherein they cannot pinpoint the exact cause. One case may be when they had erred in a previous lifetime, learned their lesson when it came due, but are still carrying forward the *trauma* they acquired from the resultant uncomfortable karmic experience. Another reason for carrying trauma forward may be from terror reactions acquired from a karmic or accidental severe injury or death.

The soul retains a memory of these past events and the related traumas can even affect the present physical body. Following are some examples with the associated past-life possible causes:

a. You have a fear (feel uncomfortable) of being on or in a particular mode of transportation.

Possible past-life cause: You were involved in an accident when riding a galloping horse, or a cart, wagon, carriage, automobile, ship, train, or airplane.

b. You have a fear of heights.

Possible past-life cause: You were injured or fell to death from a high cliff, tree, or building.

c. You have a fear of animals and/or people.

Possible past-life cause: You had been attacked by a reptile, wild cat, stag, or other animal, or by another person. Being killed by a wild animal can have the resulting effect of being afraid of other people, especially strangers, since Planet Earth Participants inhabit animal-type bodies.

d. You have a chronic neck pain.

Possible past-life cause: You had been hung or beheaded.

e. You have a chronic ache or pain, or are otherwise sensitive or ticklish in a certain point or part of your body.

Possible past-life cause: You were hit in that area by a stick, arrow, knife, sword, bullet, or the like.

You may find within yourself many other reactions or conditions which are based upon trauma carried over from past lives. These all need to be released for they cause fear-based reactions. These reactions have behind them a programmed script or story which, when reinforced, can ultimately cause the original incident to be repeated.

Some traumas can be very difficult to release, especially if they had been reinforced through several occurrences. Here is an example. Let us say you had experienced death in a past incarnation when your home burned down. Subsequently, for several lifetimes you worked hard to overcome the fear of dying by fire, and eventually you succeeded. Then, several lifetimes later, you died when the building you were in accidentally burned to the ground. The resulting trauma renewed your fear of death by fire, and now was even more deeply ingrained.

In this lifetime, again, you have an inordinate fear of dying by fire. But also in this lifetime you have a distinct advantage over the past. Through the spiritual knowledge and wisdom you have accumulated over many lifetimes, your use of spiritual tools is much more effective in solving these problems. Focused, directed thought is one of the most powerful tools you can use, especially when combined with willpower and feeling.

When on the spiritual path, heading toward a fourth-dimensional consciousness, you have a greater degree of protection than in past lives, mostly because you now know *how to ask for it!* Also, when you live consciously and apply the five Personal Principles (trust, confidence, knowing, courage and fortitude) to your outlook on life, you will acquire a greater sense of peace and comfort.

Ideally, upon experiencing a traumatic occurrence, it is best to have an attitude of total inner peace and acceptance, knowing that all is well regardless of the outcome of this event, even severe injury or death. This is indeed a great challenge. However, if you persistently meditate on this concept, you will eventually find yourself in harmony with it. The objective is that you imprint a minimum of trauma into your soul programming.

The following solution and technique will assist you in releasing these traumas. Previously, through doubt, you would not have thought this possible. Remember, believe and do not doubt, and you can move great obstacles.

Suggested Solution and Technique: Know that the traumatic experiences causing you discomfort happened in the past. If karmic, Know you had paid your debt. Therefore, the experience will not be repeated.

Talk to your soul and tell it, "There was a reason I encountered that unpleasant experience. It happened in the past, and I gained through the experience. I release all associated trauma. Know that it will not happen again."

7. Here is **the ultimate, sure-fire method** for transmuting any reaction, trauma, and associated disharmonious soul programming. This is an advanced technique, but with the proper attunement, dedication, and practice, you can perfect it.

Suggested Technique: As soon as you become aware that you feel yourself reacting to a situation—you are uncomfortable or depressed—note the thought or situation you are thinking about and the feeling you are experiencing. From the center of your body, immediately visualize your body and soul immersed in a brilliant, golden-white Light, like a Sun blazing forth from the center of your being. Then, while seeing this Light and feeling Love, say decisively, **"Be dissolved! I release you in Light and Love!"**

Perhaps you have observed from experience that whenever you stand up to speak before a group of people, or some similar situation, you feel stressed and tense. Through meditation, it would assist you to determine what fear-based statement(s) is/are causing you discomfort. Then, in your morning meditations, especially before your speaking engagement or other encounter, bring these statements to the forefront of your awareness. Using the above technique say, **"All disharmonious fear-based statements and energy blocks, be dissolved!"** *Know and feel* that the reaction and its cause *are dissolved*.

Repeat these techniques as often as necessary, each time you sense any reaction occurring, until you feel only harmony with all thoughts—as thoughts affect feelings. Each time you perform this exercise, you halve the disharmonious energy behind the reaction. You will be amazed how quickly, usually within a month, the reaction will cease to exist.

Remember that eternal vigilance is always required. Soul programming is an energy that has a life of its own. It may try to cling to life at all costs and hide in the depths of your soul where you are unaware of its existence. You may find that a month, a year, even two years later, just when you think a particular script has been annihilated, to your astonishment it will crop up again. Address it again by repeating the above exercise and command with Knowing and conviction, **"Be Dissolved!"**

When you feel only calmness, peace, and Joy, and you are free of stress and tension in situations to which you had previously reacted, you may begin to surmise that the associated disharmonious soul programming has been completely transmuted.

Praying for One Another

You can greatly assist another Participant in transmuting a detrimental tendency or energy block by praying for them—sending them spiritual energy with the intention of dissolving their disharmonious soul programming. When sending them healing energies by way of their Divine Spirit, you will not interfere with their lessons and take on their karma. Their Divine Spirit knows what is best for them.

Suggested Technique:
1. Raise your consciousness in union with your Divine Spirit.
2. Call on the Divine Spirit of the person to whom you desire to send healing. Say, "Divine Spirit of (their name)."

3. Visualize the person in the center of the energy field of their Divine Spirit, and say, see, and feel, "Through Light and Love, may all disharmonious, fear-based statements, and energy blocks be dissolved!"

I Vow That ... Oops!

The next topic is a tough one to pinpoint, but if you dig deep you may hit pay dirt. It is on the subject of **vows.** As far as the soul is concerned, *vows stick until released.* Once on the soul's hard drive, they stay there until deleted or modified. The problem is compounded when you either formally or informally made a vow in a previous lifetime, but forgot to release it before that body died. This scenario results in the vow being carried forward in your subconscious soul programming into each subsequent lifetime, until released.

The problem manifests when you desire to have a life experience which opposes a vow you took in a previous lifetime. The result is you feel a restraint in the form of an inhibition or fear and, yes, this is another manifestation of a *reaction*.

When reviewing your soul programming between Earth lifetimes, these vows are readily apparent. Usually, when the Participant was younger in this lifetime, some event transpired whereby they repeated this old vow and by feeling the restrictions thereof, would bring it to the forefront of their brain consciousness. This process makes the old vow easier to recognize, counteract, and release.

An example would be a vow of celibacy required of Participants who join a particular religious order. In a subsequent lifetime they may desire to get married and raise a family only to discover they have serious sexual inhibitions to transmute.

Many times Participants make vows without even realizing they are doing so. Watch out for statements you make starting with "I will never ...," "I am always going to ...," "I cannot live without ...," "I will forever ...," "I do not want ..." or "I will never do *that* again!" Sometimes these statements may be appropriate in transmuting disharmonious behavior, but many times they simply inhibit future productive action.

Inhibitions serve a useful purpose in our lives. Through their discomfort they offer many lessons. As these Participants gain confidence in themselves through experience, they learn to leave their inhibitions behind and live more expressive and expansive lives.

Regular Service Requirements

As with an automobile, your body, soul, and spiritual vehicles require continual maintenance. Servicing your psyche at regular intervals will minimize the frequency and intensity of on-the-road breakdowns.

Before you retire each night, review the events of the day and analyze your performance. What did you do well? What do you feel uneasy about? What could you have improved upon? What will you do or say differently when the same occasion arises? What do you need to alter to make your next performance more comfortable?

If in doubt, just before falling asleep say to your Higher Self and spiritual guides, "Please show me what I need to improve upon and what I need to do tomorrow." Most likely, you will have a thought during the night or a dream just before waking up, giving you the answer.

Also, keep an inquisitive, open mind. Participants have great difficulty observing themselves clearly. Therefore, *everyone* is a mirror in which we may see our reflection. Listen carefully to any suggestions others have regarding you. Determine if their recommendation was constructive or destructive. Some critiques may seem unwarranted, but, then, maybe not. It is very important to be *objective* in this regard, for any *subjectivity* may either unduly inhibit you or cause you to become defensive and discard an important point.

Be particularly aware that we attract people in our lives who reflect back to us what we think of ourselves. Are some persons critical of you? Do you criticize yourself and other people? Are others unloving and indifferent toward you? Do you project an unloving and indifferent attitude toward them? Do you respect yourself?

If you want to attract the type of person you want in your life, you first must become that kind of person. If you want love, you must first **be Love.** If you want kindness and attention, you must first *be* kind and give other people *your* attention. Observe what words or actions another is exhibiting toward you, and then examine *your* self-talk and *your* performance. You may be surprised to discover how they correlate.

Your Toolbox is Full of Techniques

There are various spiritual tools and techniques you may use as a service procedure on an ongoing basis. Each Participant is unique, so no one soul upgrading technique suits everyone all of the time. One or more of the following suggestions may be appropriate to your particular circumstance. You will be eternally grateful for pursuing the technique that best suits your temperament. Be creative! You may find a method unique unto yourself.

1. Daily Meditation

Daily meditation is the most important tool that you can use to accelerate your soul evolution. It is the most effective manner through which to clear away the clutter of the intellect and open the door to the clear perception of spiritual truths and realities. Meditation is your direct connection to spirit. It is the only way through which spirit can communicate with you. It is only through daily meditation that you can escape from the sticky, Swiss Cheese-like denseness of matter. Many books and classes are available on the subject of how to meditate. One book is listed in the Bibliography of this field guide.

The basics of silent meditation involve—

1. sitting on a flat, comfortable seat or the floor with your spine straight and perpendicular to the ground. Take a few deep breaths, in through the nose, out through the mouth, to help you relax.

2. using a technique, such as observing your breathing, or silently repeating a mantra or affirmation, to calm the mind and induce a relaxed state of consciousness.
3. practicing and then achieving a state of silent, imageless, vacant consciousness wherein you experience a state of timelessness and spacelessness.
4. experiencing this meditative condition for at least twenty minutes, twice a day. Forty or more minutes of meditation at one sitting is preferable.

When you first attempt to meditate you will notice that a myriad of thoughts, concerns, and worries enter your mind. This is normal. Do not try to force yourself to think of "nothing." Be the silent observer of these thoughts. Attempt not to lose them, but actively focus on them. Start doing this exercise for a period of five minutes, extending it for one minute a day, until you can hold onto these mental images for ten minutes. Each time you perform this exercise, you will find the thoughts becoming less intense, until they eventually appear to be in the far distance. They then tend to disappear.

By performing this little, but extremely important, exercise initially, you will find your psyche cleared of many subconscious blocks that would otherwise continue to haunt your meditative process. You will discover you have acquired a power over your mind that you had not previously experienced. Your meditations will now begin to flow as naturally as a gentle stream.

There are two basic types of meditation: guided and silent. Guided meditation assists you to embrace various abstract concepts so that you may identify with them. In a relaxed, meditative state, the subconscious soul record is particularly receptive to positive, constructive, transformative suggestions in the form of thoughts, feelings, and statements.

The guided *Basic Consciousness Raising Meditation* CD included with this field guide is designed to assist you in relaxing your mind and body while raising your consciousness to higher, inner aspects of your own being. You may find this a powerful aid to assist you in achieving a higher degree of consciousness.

Anything you do that raises your consciousness—like thinking, reading about, or discussing spiritual subjects—counts as meditation time. However, silent meditation itself serves a unique purpose. When you are in a meditative posture, your spiritual guides work with you to accomplish things not otherwise possible. These include linking up, energizing, and activating all twelve strands of your DNA helixes that, centuries ago, had been reduced to two by those wanting to control you.

2. Affirmations

Affirmations are a powerful tool in your soul repair kit. Affirmations are the repeated verbalization of a phrase or statement with the intention of revising your subconscious programming. Their use can be an efficient way to transmute disharmonious programming and replace these unwanted scripts with more constructive ones. They may also be used to acquire new capabilities. Here are some secrets to their proper use:

First, the words "I Am" are extremely powerful when used at the beginning of your affirmational statement.

Secondly, formulate your affirmations with only positive, constructive words. Do not use negative, disharmonious words for, as previously mentioned, the soul (subconscious) does not make value judgments. It simply accepts at face value whatever statement or programming it receives.

Third, you are altering *soul programming*. The soul is especially sensitive to *feelings!* For affirmations to be effective, very strong, *intense feelings,* combined with words in a thought process, are required to transform old, or establish new soul programming. In order to release or change current data recorded in your soul databank, strong *feelings,* equal to or greater than the emotions that established the information in the first place, are required. If affirmations are to be used effectively, they must be repeated *aloud* with lots of *feeling!* You must *feel* the old tendency dissolved and *feel* a new one established as an integral part of your being. It is also extremely helpful to visualize yourself living your desired new condition throughout each day.

Words spoken aloud have 100 times the power of thoughts alone. Always be careful that what you *say* is what you *intend!* **Decreeing, Seeing, and Feeling** are the three creative actions relating to the Principles of Life, Light, and Love. When all three are used together they make for extremely powerful affirmations.

Books, such as *Heal Your Body* by Louise Hay, contain excellent physical body and soul-transforming affirmations. Also, ask your spiritual guidance for assistance, then listen to your intuition for the answer. Your Higher Self and spiritual guides know what affirmations will be most effective for you.

Here is an easy method to formulate your own personal affirmations. On a large pad of paper, draw a vertical line down the center to divide the page in half. On the left side make a list of the statements (scripts) you wish to change. State them in the mode of "I am not" or "I do not feel," such as, "I am not honest and truthful." "I do not feel comfortable around other people." "I am not a dynamic speaker." "I do not feel safe and secure." "I am not strong and healthy."... and the like. Then, on the right side of the page rewrite each statement eliminating the "not" or "do not" words. Presto! Your own personalized, instant affirmations!

As this is generally a very private activity, the best time to state your affirmations effectively may be when you are experiencing some quiet alone time. Repeating them when driving your automobile is a very efficient way to use your time. Repeat each affirmation or series of affirmations aloud at least three times per session, adding all the *feeling* and *visualization* you can, while still driving safely.

Here are some sample affirmations and their suggested uses, with *feeling emphasis* written in *italics*. Energetically, repeat each affirmation or series of affirmations at least three times consecutively, three times a day, Seeing, Feeling, and Knowing their reality.

To release anxiety or hostility in stressful situations:

"I Am *calm and relaxed* in the midst of chaos."

When feeling fearful:

"I *Know* that *All Is Well!*"

To overcome depression and negative self-talk:
"I Am *happy* and *cheerful,*
I Radiate *Light, Love, and Joy!*
My body is *filled* with *vitality* and *energy,*
I Am *enthusiastic* about my *Life,*
I Am *motivated* to *accomplish my goals!*"

Feeling frustrated when confronted with unexpected circumstances:
"I Am That I Am! I Am the *Master* of my destiny!"

When feeling a lack of financial resources:
"I Am *Infinite Abundance!* My needs are *now* in my possession!"
"I Am *prosperous!*"

To feel and strengthen your inner power and resolve:
"I Am *courageous* and *fearless!*
I have *absolute power* over my *total being!*"

Now, compose your own affirmations: "I Am …!"

3. Psychological counseling

There are many excellent trained counselors and therapists available to assist you in recognizing the source of unwanted psychological patterns. From spirit's side, we observe that almost every Participant would benefit from some form of counseling, particularly when experiencing stressful situations. Since it is extremely difficult for Participants to see themselves clearly, a talented therapist can be invaluable to assist in clearing unwanted programming and blocks from a Participant's soul record, especially those that are deeply ingrained.

The word psychology is derived from two Greek words meaning "soul science." One problem is that few western psychologists and psychiatrists understand the true source of their clients' problems, which is inappropriate *soul programming,* and that the ultimate objective of therapy is to progress their client's *soul evolution.*

The use of pharmaceutical drugs to alleviate stress or depression is acceptable as a temporary emergency measure to bring an extremely uncomfortable Participant to a more calm, receptive state of being. The use of appropriate natural herbal remedies is preferable as they do not have the addictive or detrimental side effects of chemically synthesized pharmaceutical drugs. The spiritual solution is for physicians to be trained in counseling methods based on a holistic *soul* perspective.

Except in extreme cases, the extended use of pharmaceutical drugs may alleviate a patient's mental and emotional symptoms, but mask the real problem without solving anything. Nothing can replace the actions of a Participant consciously taking steps to transmute their own uncomfortable programming.

You have opportunities in this lifetime, to work toward solving the true condition to which your symptoms are pointing. Disharmonious programming not transmuted in this lifetime is carried over into all subsequent lifetimes until the cause of the imbalance is identified and transformed.

4. Hypnotherapy

Hypnotic therapy can be very useful in identifying and transmuting the causes of past-life disharmonious programming and trauma. It is preferable that the client be in a conscious, albeit very relaxed, state, for the problem is then presented to the awareness of the anapersona. Hypnotherapy can directly access the client's soul memory bank. To avoid blowing open a Pandora's Box of fears and trauma requires a well-trained therapist sensitive to the delicacies of this form of therapy. When the Participant is consciously aware of the proceedings, they are then able to consciously facilitate their own transformative process.

Unconscious hypnotic states and subliminally programmed recordings permit *someone else* to toy with *your* subconscious programming, a process that is not spiritually acceptable. This can possibly do more damage than good. The ideal approach is for *you,* the anapersona, to have conscious access to the real cause of your difficulties. Since *you* put them there, you are best able to discover the basis of the soul programming you desire to transmute.

When seeking to engage counselors and therapists, it is wise to look beyond the person's credentials and observe the actual person. Plug in your intuition and ask, "Is this man or woman competent to help me solve my problem from a spiritual perspective? What point of view are they coming from? Does their approach and recommended schedule of sessions reflect their ability to get directly to the heart of the matter and help solve my problem?"

Participants may desire to engage the services of counselors and therapists who demonstrate certain inherent healing talents. These abilities may include seeing a person's chakra centers and auric energy fields, and the ability to enlist the services of competent guides residing in the spiritual realms. From their broader perspective, spiritual guides are better able to access the source and cause of a problem that one desires to alleviate.

Some spiritually advanced human Participants are able to access very high Creator energies, identify the specific problem, and then instantly dissolve the offending programming. Ask your Higher Self to lead you to the practitioner who can best resolve your particular problem. Many times spiritual healers do not advertise, and only by word-of-mouth may you be aware of them.

5. Books and Self-Help Recordings

Many self-help books, recordings, and videos, which can be of great benefit to you, are found on the shelves of booksellers, the internet, by mail order, and in health and nutrition stores. Some books may contain general information, some addressing specific subjects such as reincarnation, and others may specifically address a problem you wish to solve.

6. Lectures, Classes and Seminars

When you signed up for this Earth educational expedition, you did not expect your learning to stop with formal education. It was intended that education, in all its many forms, was to be a life-long process. You can expand your knowledge by observing, listening to, and then practicing some suggestions that others have offered. Perhaps another's ideas may help solve a problem you are working on. From a variety of viewpoints, you may gain insights into spheres of research, knowledge, and understanding you never knew existed.

There are many lectures, classes, and seminars offered by your fellow Participants covering a vast array of subjects, some of which you may find applicable to your needs and of practical value in your life. You will benefit by becoming aware of varied approaches to studying and applying techniques relating to your physical, feeling, mental, and spiritual well-being. Through this process you may observe how everything is integrated and connected by an intertwining thread. From a selection of varied presentations, you may then choose ideas and approaches you think and feel will benefit you.

7. Journal your dreams

Your Higher Self knows every detail of your soul programming. Its job is to bring imbalances to your attention that need correction, and lead you towards their resolution.

One major way the Higher Self communicates messages to you is in the forms of dreams, especially those you experience just before waking up with a *jolt!* You will find it beneficial to have a pad and paper by your bed to jot down notes about your dreams, or journal them in detail. Dreams are messages in symbol form. You will then need to interpret the symbols for the dream messages to be useful. Many books are available on the subject of dream interpretation. It is best if you interpret your own dreams. Some of your friends may have suggestions that will help you decipher the coded messages in your dreams.

8. Trusted friends

A trusted and respected friend may be a good sounding board for your problems. First, ask them to assist you. Make it clear that you are sincerely looking for constructive insights and are not just "dumping" your grievances. They may have suggestions for alternate ways to solve a problem which you have not considered.

9. Trusting the Universe

When Participants are ardently attempting to solve a problem, it is interesting to observe how the Universe has a way of offering its assistance, particularly when asked. A movie you attend, a TV drama, the book a friend suggests or gives you for your birthday, a comment or suggestion made by a friend or acquaintance, a television interview you watch—*there* is the answer you were looking for!

10. Astrology and Other Guidance Techniques

You are living on the surface of a spherical schoolhouse, in time and space, within a planetary solar system that is surrounded by billions of star systems and billions of galaxies. Within this cosmic environment everything, including matter, is alive, and has consciousness and intelligence. This universe is teeming with life, functioning through many realms and dimensions of consciousness. Each thing and each being has a job to do, and these are constantly interacting with and influencing everything and everyone else.

In our solar system, the sun, moon, and planets all have a mind of their own, each sustained by a conscious intelligence. Each of these has its own vibration, its own "personality" traits, and its own special job to perform in this educational environment. The intelligences inherent in the heavenly bodies influence but do not direct a Participant's destiny, for one's freedom of choice is always paramount.

The art and science of interpreting the energies and influences behind the positions of the various planetary features is called astrology. An astrologer provides studied opinions as to how the planetary influences may affect a Participant's life affairs and offers beneficial suggestions for handling these occurrences.

The analysis and interpretation of these phenomena begins with the creation of an astrological chart that depicts the positions and interactions of the major heavenly bodies relative to Earth. The chart with which most people are familiar is the natal chart, erected for the time and place of a newborn's birth.

The natal chart is a map of the life plan a Participant had chosen. It indicates the purpose of the lifetime and the soul tendencies, traits, and programming one desires to gain, augment, and/or transmute. Astrology assists Participants to more fully understand the role and personality traits with which they were born, and how to best take advantage of the changing energy patterns which influence them throughout their earthly sojourn. The birth chart can be a very useful tool to assist Participants in understanding the strengths and weaknesses of the personality they chose and what transformations they sought in their soul programming.

Astrological "transits" study the road map of this lifetime's journey and indicate the timing of opportunities, challenges, roadblocks, stresses, tests, and rewards one may expect to encounter along the way. A competent astrologer can analyze and interpret these celestial planetary influences and cycles, and offer suggestions as to how the Participant may overcome the obstacles they chose, and how to take advantage of opportunities as they occur. The astute use of astrological information can assist Participants to make more rapid progress in their soul evolution.

Similarly, the information garnered from your own or professional readings of Tarot cards, I-Ching, Runes, or the like can be very useful to Participants who have gained confidence in one of these techniques. It is recommended that you choose only one method of divination and stick with it.

11. Contacting your Divine Spirit

The *Basic Consciousness Raising Meditation* is designed to assist you to consciously unify with the highest aspect of your individualized nature, your Divine Spirit. Your Divine Spirit is in union with all the intelligences in the Universe, each with its own specialty. Once you have made a secure contact with this highest part of your Self, you can learn to communicate with it. You can ask your Divine Spirit to supply you with the answer to any question, and either solve any problem you have or lead you to the solution.

The available *Progressive Consciousness Raising Meditation* CD assists you to consciously unify with even higher aspects of yourself—

God The Manifest, The Creator, and The Absolute. When functioning through these higher levels of consciousness, you decree and feel that you have received your request, and if all prerequesites are met, it may manifest in your life.

When praying or decreeing for another person, it is proper to contact *their* Divine Spirit and ask if your desire for them is acceptable. If you get a "yes" answer, you may then proceed. Always state in your request/decrees, whether for yourself or another, "Your Will be done, in and through me."

Keep in mind that whatever your intention is for someone else, you will ultimately experience it yourself. Send out hate, and hate will return to you. Send out Love, and Love will return to illuminate you.

There is much to learn on the long road of soul evolution, and your Divine Spirit can direct you to whatever you need to know that will facilitate your unique role in this grand adventure we call Life.

Receiving Guidance Through "Channeling"

This complex area has been the basis of much confusion and misunderstanding. However, learning through this technique can be the most rewarding if certain precautions are observed.

Exactly what is "channeling?" Beings functioning on spirit's side live in vacuum-like conditions on higher vibrational realms where there is no "air," through which you on Earth are accustomed to speak and hear. On the spiritual realms, beings communicate mind-to-mind with one another in the form of "thought-pictures."

When you communicate with your spiritual guides, they "hear" the thoughts you project to them. Behind your words are thoughts, that through the communication are translated into ideas and concepts that your spirit guides understand.

If a spiritual being wishes to communicate directly to a Participant on Earth, the process is reversed. The thought-pictures projected to you are in turn translated into Earth-language words. The translation is done either on spirit's side before reaching the Participant or by the Participant receiving the transmission, depending upon the individual Participant's receiving and translating abilities. You generally refer to a man or woman receiving mind-to-mind communications from spirit's side as a "channel." This process of communicating is called "channeling."

If you desire to open a personal, direct line of communication with an astral or spiritual guide and teacher, simply ask in meditation, "Please send me a guide appropriate to my level of understanding that I may progress towards a spiritual consciousness."

It is important that whenever you make contact with an innerplane being you ask, "In the Name of The Creator, who are you and what do you want?" Universal Law dictates they must either answer you correctly, or they must leave your presence. To clarify any confusion with terms, we suggest you then ask, "Are you an astral being, or a spiritual being?" For further clarification ask, "Through what dimension of consciousness are you functioning?"

Some astral beings may say they are sixth dimensional, when they are actually functioning at the *sixth* level of the *third* dimcon. Some may claim to be "ascended masters," which they are not. Since he ascended to the tenth dimcon, Jesus/Sananda is in silence as concerns Planet Earth. A channel claiming to channel Jesus/Sananda is in reality channeling an astral being. Our advice is, be cautious so you are not deceived.

Seventh level astral or mental plane guides (functioning through a third-dimensional consciousness), tend to be very nurturing and specialize in assisting Participants to bring more harmony into their mundane Earth affairs. They encourage Participants to pursue their higher spiritual path. Astral beings usually speak in words and may communicate by automatic writing through a channel using a pen, typewriter, or computer keyboard. When speaking before groups, astral beings may displace a channel's astral body, speak through the channel's larynx, and even cause the material body to stand up and walk around.

Spiritual beings have a consciousness ranging between the fourth and ninth dimcons. Their perspective is obviously spiritually oriented, although they may be quite adept at giving appropriate advice concerning mundane Earth affairs. The highest, most pure communications come from the spiritual dimcons. Also, spiritual guides never take a channel's energy, and never suggest any course of action not in harmony with Limitless Total Love.

If you think and feel you are close to attaining a fourth-dimensional consciousness, we strongly recommend you seek and specifically request the guidance of a spiritual being, whether for you personally or through a channel. It is most effective to be guided by only one or one small group of guides and teachers at a time. If you feel uncomfortable with your current situation, you may release a guide. Simply say, "Thank you for your past assistance. In Light and Love, I desire to sever our relationship, and I hereby release you with gratitude and appreciation."

As you make progress along the spiritual path, your spiritual guides may introduce you to a, higher dimensional teacher, like St. Michael, St. Germain, or Serapis Bey. A spiritual teacher and guide may request that you communicate with them exclusively, to have a strong connection.

NOTE TO CHANNELS: Always know exactly whom you are channeling. If you desire to attain a fourth-dimensional consciousness in this lifetime, we suggest that you request and channel only spiritual beings. The continual channeling of astral beings will hold you to a third-dimensional consciousness.

Interpreting and Trusting Your Guidance

Whatever source of guidance you receive from others through various techniques such as astrology, tarot, runes, the I Ching or channeling, know that you alone are responsible as to how you accept and use this information. This is your lesson in awareness and discernment.

Be aware that naughty, mischievous physical-etheric and astral beings may function through some channels. This has been the source of much misinformation, confusion, and fear surrounding "channeling." Also, these disharmonious beings may interfere with a channeling session from the spiritual realms by adding, subtracting, or changing the words being sent. If an innerplane communication does not sound or feel quite right to you, stop and continue an hour later or on another day.

It is necessary for you to be guided by your own inner feelings and intuition as to the appropriateness of channeled messages. If a message jars your personal truth, question it. This information may not be for you. Accept and use what feels right to you. Do not necessarily discard information which you cannot immediately correlate or assimilate, for you may be able to use it in the future. Just put it on the shelf in your memory reference library.

When a spirit guide attempts to transmit ideas and concepts through a channel, they are usually confined to using the memory, knowledge, and vocabulary of the channel. This limits the type of information spirit can transmit through a particular Participant. Also, each channel translates into their own words the ideas, concepts, and thought-pictures transmitted from spirit's side. Therefore, no two Earth channels would use the same exact words to narrate channeled lessons and guidance.

Channels who have established a solid bond with one spiritual teacher/guide receive and transmit the purest communications from spirit's side. A channel with one strong connection carries a higher level of communicative accuracy and energy than a transmission through a channel who has several weaker connections.

Even the best spiritual counselors and channels of spiritual information are subject to error. Some Participants transmit our messages more accurately than others, however, no one is perfect, even on spirit's side. Realize that Participants have differing perspectives and points of view, and use different words to convey similar meanings. This does not mean that one is wrong and the other is right. It simply means that the one-twelfth portion of the Pie of Truth through which they relate, initially appears to be in conflict with another's portion of the pie. By communicating and discussing these differences, the common thread of Truth will become apparent. Within the vast potentials of infinity, there are limitless personal truths and endless possibilities.

Through awareness and experience, you will be able to recognize the vibration and/or style of your spiritual guide and teacher, thereby gaining confidence in the interpretation and accuracy of either your own or another's channeled communications.

– 11 –

SETTING A COURSE TOWARD YOUR DESTINATION

When planning a trip to a foreign country, you usually try to imagine what you might encounter when you arrive. You might buy books and maps to get an idea in your mind where you are going, the geography of the area, and the local customs and languages. You may even talk with people who have been there to hear of their experiences. Then you make travel arrangements, booking modes of transportation and living accommodations, that take you in the direction of your destination.

Planning to attain a fourth-dimensional consciousness is similar in many ways. You need to have your basic goal in mind, generally know where you are going, and read, study, and plan how to get there.

Perhaps your mate and some friends may wish to accompany you on this journey—ones who share a similar vision and goal. The spiritual quest is more pleasant and easier traveled with like-minded Participants who support, encourage, and assist one another in attaining higher expressions of consciousness.

Curriculum: What Courses Did You Sign Up For?

Your soul came to Earth via your material body to learn many lessons. In this schoolhouse, all subjects offered teach basic theory and include practical work-study programs. Some of the major courses in the curriculum include:

- Right Thinking—achieving harmonious feelings and actions.
- Living in Limitless Total Love—transcending romantic, emotional love.
- Self-discipline—mastering your personal Universe.
- Honesty and Integrity—being true to yourself first.
- Accepting Total Responsibility—for everything in your life.
- Awareness—being alert and aware of all events and others around you; especially being aware of yourself.
- Harmlessness—transforming your animal nature into that of The Divine.

It was not intended that these courses be a snap. Your soul grows and evolves through choosing problems to solve, hurdles to overcome, and lessons to learn. View yourself as running the high hurdles event in a track meet. The hurdles are there for a reason. They are what the match is all about. Practicing and then mastering these hurdles gives you a great sense of achievement. Mastering life takes practice, dedication, and hard work. You will succeed only to the degree you apply yourself. On an inner level you know that your goal is to be the master of yourself—your own personal universe.

There is one aspect of Earth experience that can be confusing to Participants. It appears that everyone has their own, different direction. The question then becomes, "How do you find *your* direction?" Your path is unique unto you. Your guiding lights are the ideas, inspiration, and wisdom received through your intuitive mind. For the most part, however, you are left to your own devices to figure out the best solution to a problem, for the experience you gain through the search is your best teacher.

Your anapersona/soul learns primarily through personal experience. Intellectual exercises may serve as a guideline, but where doubt exists as to the most effective course of action, only experience provides the answer. The most effective way to learn and function is to search out and then apply what you decide to be the most harmonious, constructive course of action. Each conscientious decision takes you another step toward achieving a higher degree of wisdom. Life will let you know if there was a better solution. This process, although tedious, makes for strong, tough souls and has given Earth its well-earned reputation as the greatest schoolhouse in the Universe.

Developing an Objective Outlook

To be subjective is human; to be objective is divine.

The spiritual being eventually becomes a Master. Why? Because they have mastered *themselves,* that is, their mind, their actions, and their feelings. When one has mastered themselves, the microcosm, they are on their way to becoming a Master of the Universe, the macrocosm!

As a Participant evolves along their spiritual path, they are required to be progressively more *objective* in their outlook on life, thereby subjugating their *subjective* desires. Through wisdom, one realizes they must distinguish between their endless array of personal wants and desires, and their *real needs*. Consideration for the greater good of others takes on more importance than one's personal comforts. Romantic love is transformed into an impersonal, universal, Limitless Total Love. One then *becomes* Love; *is* Love. When one becomes more objective in their outlook, personal relationships experience more love, fun, peace, harmony, and Joy!

As you progress, the more you will comprehend that it is your accumulated wisdom that must rule your thoughts, feelings, and actions. Eventually, your anapersona, soul, and spirit all function in unison— in perfect balance and harmony. This is the spiritual objective of everyone's personal soul evolution.

An important step in your spiritual progress is to continually identify and reevaluate your immediate goals. What do you desire to achieve on your physical, feeling, mental, and spiritual levels? It is important to know where you are going so you can choose the most direct, opportune route to get there.

Without clearly defined spiritual goals, unaware souls comprehend no alternatives other than to overindulge in their physical, emotional, and mental gratifications and sensual desires. However, the spiritual warriors with loftier aspirations will subjugate their lesser desires for the attainment of their highest goals. As your perspective of life and priorities change, things that at one time had glitter and shine, now seem dull, empty, and senseless. Your old interests and objectives have been transmuted into more elevated ideals.

Since each Participant is responsible for their own soul evolution, eventually all learn to ask more objective questions of their human, material lives, such as:

- How can I optimize this learning experience?
  How can I implement a loftier experience?
- Who are these players in my life, and what role are they performing relative to mine? What are they teaching me?
- Is this the type of person I need in my life to optimize my experience and assist me to reach higher, spiritual goals?
- What are my choices at this time? Must I decide now, or be patient and wait for clearer answers?
- What wisdom have I learned that I may apply to this present situation?

Championing the Road of Soul Evolution

Do you feel that you have real power over your life, or are you captive to outer factors and circumstances? Are you really in control of your life direction or are you following the path of least resistance, simply copying what everyone else is doing? Are you a slave to senseless man-made rules and their associated institutions? Are you caught in mindless habits and addictions? Would you like to have more power over yourself, your own life and destiny? Are you living as a sovereign, a totally free individual functioning beyond the irrational restraints imposed by the world around you?

Did not many great Masters such as Jesus, Buddha, and others, show humanity "the way" to freedom by teaching and demonstrating higher principles, potentials, and possibilities? Do you recognize that *your destiny to attain a spiritual consciousness* is within your reach?

You, the microcosm, are identical to the macrocosm, The Creator. You are a cell in the body of The Creator, identical to It in all respects. Your potential and your destiny are to reestablish the connection between your individualized self and the Infinite Mind and Power that created the individualized "you." The intention is that you accomplish this here on Planet Earth, not on some other planet, solar system, or realm.

You are the God of your life. You are the master of your destiny. From your current position on the Road of Soul Evolution, are you living up to your maximum potential? Rather than letting life happen to you, are you happening to Life?

Daily, you are fabricating a key that operates the padlock connecting the chains binding you to a third-dimensional consciousness—a key that unlocks the door to your higher, spiritual consciousness. You fabricate this key by being aware, learning from your experiences, correcting your errors, engaging in a daily self-improvement program, striving toward living in Limitless Total Love, and keeping your sights focused on your spiritual destination.

A significant step onto the Road of Soul Evolution involves first developing and then directing your strengthened willpower towards transmuting your lower, dysfunctional instincts through self-control and self-discipline. This ability is developed through exercising Patience, Persistence, and Perseverance. A notch in the key is formed when you concentrate on the higher, spiritual ideals that will keep you centered on your direct road to enlightenment.

You are unique. You have your own individual key that will actuate the lock blocking access to your spiritual consciousness. There are many roads leading to the fourth dimcon. Your task is to find your personal road, and stay on it.

Freedom of Choice

You are different from the animal kingdom in that you have true freedom of choice. From a higher awareness, you chose the body you now inhabit along with its characteristics, strengths, and weaknesses. You chose your parents, you chose the time and place that you were born. You chose your basic personality and your basic life path. Whether or not you follow your chosen life path is up to you.

When it comes to following one's chosen life path, from spirit's side we observe a curious phenomenon. Some Participants have chosen an ambitious life path offering a multitude of learning experiences, new philosophies, and considerable soul growth. But what happened? Nothing. Once born into the material body, they forgot their plan, turned off in another direction, or got stuck in a traditional belief system, and then staunchly opposed all efforts to steer them back onto their chosen path.

On the other hand, a Participant may come in with little or no enthusiasm and life plan for spiritual enlightenment, then all of a sudden, they catch fire and achieve substantial soul growth. Life is like being dealt a five-card poker hand. You have the option of discarding and drawing two or three new cards. The strategy you use, though, is up to you. It is your choice as to what you do with it.

In this regard, here is our advice. If a more advantageous opportunity is presented to you than you had originally anticipated, there is nothing stopping you from pursuing it. What others may think concerning your personal decisions is of little importance to you. Ultimately, what is of significance is only what you think of yourself and what you think, feel, and do for others.

One of the biggest challenges in life is figuring out how to do "your thing," and express your freedom of choice without interfering with the individual rights of other Participants. As one practices Limitless Total Love in their interactions with others, this challenge eventually ceases to exist. Remember that "All is One!" You are the other Participant, and the other Participant is you. Whatever energies you extend will return to you. The good you do for others will come back to you. Love always feels wonderful when it returns to you.

The choices you make concerning your life are very important. As a Participant in this Earth Educational Expedition, you have an inner, spiritual mission that extends beyond simply making a living, accumulating money, having children, enjoying outrageous forms of entertainment, and sitting on your sofa watching the latest TV sitcom.

You are not here on Earth as beings disconnected from the rest of creation. You need to recognize that there are vast realms of beings with spiritual consciousnesses available as your support team. It is your choice whether you take advantage of this form of assistance. Search and you will find. If you exercise sufficient determination, you will attract the teaching, the guide, the answers, the ideas, and the concepts that will promote your knowledge, wisdom, and your soul evolution.

- 12 -

GAINING THE MOST FROM YOUR ADVENTURE

Once you begin to practice becoming the actor, the audience, and the director in your life, you realize you have the inherent ability to be in control of your thoughts, words, feelings, and actions. With your acceptance of total responsibility for everything in your life, you can more clearly identify with the source of any and all of your problems. With these realizations comes a *power* over yourself, your surroundings, and the world. You develop the power to achieve your spiritual goals. Following are some ideas and techniques to assist you in working toward and achieving the fourth-dimensional consciousness you seek.

Moving Through Your Lessons More Quickly

It is a Universal principle that each Participant receives the particular lessons that they need, when they need them. As long as you are on Planet Earth, or surfing the galaxy, there will always be another lesson to learn. This schoolhouse's class catalog is truly endless.

A wise course of action is to closely examine each difficulty that you encounter and remember to ask, "Now, why am I confronted with this uncomfortable situation? Why did this happen to me? What am I supposed to be learning from this experience? To solve this problem, what new perspective do I require to modify my past modes of behavior?"

Introspection and analysis of the motives behind your actions will give you a distinct advantage and accelerate your soul evolution to "warp-speed." Rather than dawdling over your lessons by constantly repeating the same errors, you can stop the merry-go-round, get off, and walk the straighter, more direct path of spiritual wisdom. Although you may expect to make missteps as new lessons are presented, you now have new keys to help you complete these lessons in less time, and with honors. With your new perspective, you can accomplish more progress in this lifetime than you had throughout many previous experiences.

Recognizing Your Personal Guidance

Albeit extremely important, this is one of the more difficult tasks for Earth Participants to master. In addition to your soul, your spiritual guides are in constant communication with you. However, are you aware of their promptings?

Each new lifetime, a Participant arrives in a new Earth body accompanied by four innerplane guides. Their job is to protect, guide, and help teach you. They are able to do their jobs most efficiently when you are aware of and ask for their guidance, and then thank them for the assistance they provide.

Spiritual guides communicate with you through your thought processes and your feelings. The main question that arises is, how do you differentiate between your own thoughts and the thought-messages sent by your guides?

If a thought or idea pops into your mind when you were not even thinking about the subject in question, it was a message from your innerplane guides and teachers.

To learn this process takes practice. It is too easy to dismiss the incoming suggestion as coming from your own mind. When you finally catch on to the process, you will most likely feel like "kicking yourself" for all the times you previously received these suggestions and discounted them as a figment of your own mind/imagination, or because of subconscious fear-based blocks.

Most often these messages pertain to suggestions that will enhance your life or the lives of others around you. The messages may consist of thoughts like, "Call on Mr. So-and-So for a business appointment." "Phone your friend, Rita." "Slow down. There is a police radar setup ahead." "That is enough oregano, now add some chile pepper." "It is time for you to meditate today." "Go down to the Mall this afternoon to shop for some shoes." (The reason being we want you to meet someone.) Only if you *ask* will your guides give you the purpose behind their promptings. Even then you may not get an answer. You must discover the reason for yourself. It is more fun for you that way. Plus, it is a lesson in Trust.

You always have the right to question a guide's suggestion. "Thank you. Please show me how I am to fit this into today's schedule." In this case, you may also find it beneficial to reprioritize your schedule. Always feel free to ask your guides for assistance in any harmonious, constructive matter.

This guidance is relatively inexpensive. All that your guides anticipate is a sincere "thank you." The more you become aware of and use these suggestions, the more your life circumstances will be enhanced, and the faster you will progress your soul evolution.

Living in "The Now"

When living on Earth in a material body, how do you determine what you call "time?" Your planet has its own unique built-in clock—its rotation on its axis. You have divided this period of rotation into time cycles. One rotation of the planet itself you refer to as one "day," which is divided into twenty-four hours. A rotation of the planet around the sun is one "year," or 365 days. On Earth, Participants divide the passage of time into three major segments: the past, the present, and the future.

On the higher, spiritual realms of experience—the fourth realm and beyond—darkness does not exist. There is only Light—a blinding, blazing, all-encompassing light by Earth standards. On these realms there is no such thing as "time," as there is no way to calculate it. There exists only "The Now." All time is *Now!*

All thought exists beyond time and space as it travels instantaneously through the Universe. The realm of thought knows only *Now!*

The Now is not the present. **The Now is the past, present, and future combined as One.** Knowledge accumulated from your past experiences becomes the wisdom base for present actions, and present thoughts, words, feelings, and actions determine your future experiences.

When do you design your future? When you get there? Isn't that a little late? Every minute of every day you are choosing your future. This is why it is wise and astute to monitor your self-talk and conversations with others. Otherwise, you may inadvertently create a future that you do not want—for you are continually designing your future in the NOW!

The higher vibrational realms and their associated dimcons are the support basis for everything that exists on the material, first realm of Planet Earth. Each higher dimcon and realm has more inherent power than each lower one. In prayer, this is why you relax and raise your consciousness toward a higher power (more correctly, a conscious higher energy) when you ask for wisdom, healing, companionship, abundance, peace, or the like.

As only "Now" exists in these higher realms, the past, present, and future are not recognized. Therefore, to be most effective when you make decrees or state affirmations, you must word all statements in terms of "Now." Through practice, you will learn to See, Feel, and Know that your requested condition exists *Now!* "I Am *Now* happy and cheerful." "The money for my car payment is *Now* in my possession." "I Am *Now* one with Infinite Abundance!" "I Am *Now* experiencing an intimate relation-ship with a compatible partner." "I *Now* have received an 'A' on my science examination paper."

If you desire a special event or outcome to take place on a future date in time, you still word your decree in the *Now*. "I Am *Now* accepting the managerial position on (future date)." "The rent money is *Now* in my possession before (date due)."

With a fourth-dimensional consciousness you function on Earth in two worlds. Your consciousness is in the heavens, but your feet are on the ground. Increasingly, you will learn new ways in which to handle material earth circumstances from a completely different, spiritual perspective. The more you unify yourself with and become the Twelve Principles of creation, the less you need to labor by the "sweat of your brow." As you evolve through the fourth dimcon, you will learn how to use some powerful tools that are at your disposal. The effectiveness of these tools, however, is much greater when one has achieved a fifth-dimensional consciousness, and progressively increases as you attain higher dimcons. This presents you with a far-reaching plan you may look forward to.

The key to inner peace and harmony is to be in the world but not a part of it; to work as hard as you can to achieve a particular goal, but not be emotionally attached to the fruits of your labors. If you do not accomplish what you have worked for, or received what you have decreed, prayed, or asked for, *so what?* You tried, but what did you learn? Was it within the objectives of your soul blueprint, soul direction, or overall soul evolution to accomplish all your personal desires or receive your personal wants?

The harboring of **emotional expectations,** wherein one's happiness is linked to the outcome of future circumstances and events, is a major source of disillusionment, depression, and despair. Generally, Participants do not realize the degree to which they set themselves up for disaster by creating emotional expectations. How are they created? It is all based upon what you *tell* yourself. You are God, and statements you tell yourself are *true* as far as your soul is concerned.

George is deeply in love with Jane. He says to himself, "I will be happy only if Jane will marry me." Sure enough, Jane runs off and marries Bill. Or John may say, "I will be angry and in a rage if I do not get that promotion." Thomas gets the promotion over John. Tough luck, buddy. Life has just set you up to teach you some lessons.

Everyone has the free will to make their own choices. Life's events and circumstances are usually going to have their own way regardless of the outcome you want. Since when do other Participants and situations need to cater to your whims and wants? You may have your **preferences,** but to base your personal peace and harmony on the outcome of future circumstances and events is to invite disillusion and disharmony into your life.

Ultimately, the question indicating a search for greater wisdom and understanding is, "What is the best course of action for the greater good of all concerned?" With a clearer understanding of the true nature of the Now, it is anticipated that Participants will develop a more Loving and understanding attitude towards one another.

Dissolve in a blaze of golden-white Light thoughts of disharmonious actions and events you are harboring from the *past!* The curtain has closed on them. Retain only what you have learned and gained from your experiences. Be grateful for the growth you have made because of them. The only important moment in your life is *Now,* upon which you are building your future *Nows.*

Here is a point to remember. When you dwell on the past you tend to get caught up in *guilt,* and when you focus on the future you are inclined to attract feelings of *fear*. To maintain a calm, relaxed, and centered demeanor, stay focused on the present tasks at hand, using the wisdom of *The Now!*

Making Correct Decisions

What is a "correct" decision? Depends. Correct in the sense that you proceed into a situation that offers a great degree of harmony, understanding, and freedom from stress, or, correct in the sense that you need to experience a particular circumstance wherein you have lessons to learn and/or have karmic debts to pay?

There is a nearly foolproof technique to assist you to always make correct decisions—from simple, like choosing a restaurant for dinner; to more complicated, like choosing a boy or girl friend, buying a home, or linking up with a business or marriage partner. Once practiced and perfected, you will find this technique an invaluable tool for always making "correct" decisions. Your Higher Self knows what you *need*. Correct decisions may bring you rewards that you have earned. They also may bring you uncomfortable experiences to add to your data bank of knowledge and wisdom, and progress your soul evolution.

This technique involves sequentially directing your attention into your head, heart, and gut, in each place asking the same question and receiving yes, no, or indifferent answers. You then evaluate the results and make a decision.

The first step is to formulate your question. To receive a valid answer, your question must be expressed as concisely and specifically as possible. The key to receiving accurate answers is to first ask the proper question. For instance, "Is this a good day for me to go into town to shop?" "At this time, will entering into a business partnership with Jack be beneficial to me?" When buying or renting a house or apartment, "Will I find peace and comfort in this home?" Or, "Is this the proper place for me to buy/rent?" When contemplating taking a new job, depending upon your priorities, "Will this position bring me the optimum opportunity and advancement I seek?" You get the idea. Work with drafting your own questions.

The second step is to focus your attention in the **center of your head,** your brain-mind. The head processes and analyzes the question through the intellectual mind, and relates the question to the outer, everyday reality. Fear-based responses from the head, however, must be analyzed to determine the source of the fear and then questioned as to whether the concern is warranted or imagined. If imagined, it is most likely coming from inappropriate soul programming, which must first be corrected if you are to receive clear, reliable answers.

Now, ask your question and observe what you *think* about it. Is your conclusion constructive and harmonious to warrant a *yes* answer, neutrally indifferent, or do you foresee major obstacles to pursuing your question?

The third step is to focus your attention in the **area of your heart center.** The heart relates to how you *feel* about the matter in question. Feelings will disclose how the action in question relates to your personal preferences and how it will affect yourself and those intimately connected to you.

Now, ask your question and observe how you *feel* about it. Is your feeling response a comfortable or enthusiastic *yes*, a neutral *so-so*, or a depressing *no?*

The fourth step is to center your attention in **the solar plexus area** in the center of your body. This zone harbors your gut feeling, your intuitive message center wherein you receive answers from your soul and spiritual guides. Your intuition has the potential to provide the most appropriate and enlightened answer to the specific question you are asking.

When you ask your question, what is your *gut level feeling?* Again, is it a comfortable, uplifting *yes,* an indifferent non-response, or a gut-wrenching *no?*

Act upon the basis of your question only if all three answers are "yes." If one or more answer is a "no," either reject the proposal or do not make a decision at this time. You may need to get more information. Unforeseen circumstances may not work to your advantage. **Indifferent answers** leave the decision up to your (the anapersona's) discretion.

Be particularly attentive to your gut level, intuitive feelings.

Take Charge!

If you desire not be governed by changing conditions, you first need to take charge of your life. Rather than waiting for life to happen to you, *you must happen to life!* This principle applies to anything you wish to accomplish, including your spiritual evolution.

Know that *you are not a wimp!* You are The Absolute in disguise!

The Godhead wants the benefit of *your* personal experiences. Not someone else's.

If you are waiting around for God, Jesus, or a Guru to do it all for you, you are basking in the dreamland of nebulous illusions. Great teachers and avatars guide you along the path through their teachings and examples. Every now and then they can even give you a boost up a rung of the ladder, but you must climb another three yourself. *You have to do your part! You have to ask, search, and strive for your own spiritual enlightenment!* Unless you had already achieved enlightenment in a previous lifetime, it is not going to happen by itself.

Remember that this Earth Expedition is a learning experience. If you want to evolve, you need to study, take your lessons seriously, and pass your tests. "Seek and you shall find." You need to walk out on the seashore of higher consciousness and begin to pick up shells, looking for ones you are attracted to, ones that sparkle, have gems embedded in them, and hold these close to your heart.

Rise Above It!

The vast majority of Participants now experiencing Planet Earth have been programmed by society to believe that the normal human condition is to live in fear, chaos, and turmoil. Most of each Participant's disharmonious soul programming was created through fear-based experiences and/or reinforced and perpetuated by the various entertainment, media, governmental, business, educational, and religious institutions. The result has been that most Participants look on the illusions and delusions of the world as the only reality. If one suggests that truth may very well be in the opposite direction, they may be accused of being sacrilegious and in league with the forces of darkness.

Today, if all Participants would choose to live beyond fear and in love, peace, and harmony with one another and their environment, the world would instantly change. The quest for the attainment of "Heaven" would then not be some yearning for a better existence beyond this lifetime, but would *now* be an actual reality *here* on the physical plane.

Each individual Participant forms the basis of the family, the neighborhood, the community, the city, the state, the nation, the world. Each Participant's responsibility is to learn how to function in the highest state of Love of which they are capable. As a spiritual exercise in everyday life, it is each Participant's responsibility to humbly demonstrate the principle of Love through their example.

When a Participant functions through their lower animal nature, they can be easily controlled by self-serving interests. They see life through a dark, smoky glass. Few, if any, of these Participants, even realize they are being controlled. "Know the Truth and the Truth will set you free." One begins to free themselves when they seek to attain a spiritual consciousness, for only then are they able to identify the problem instead of being a part of it. Your personal objective is to transcend duality, and then assist the whole planet to make this same transition.

You can promote unity and oneness by supporting **heart-based** entertainment that inspires Participants to focus on their higher, loving natures. Become aware of the deceptions and frauds perpetrated by society's institutions that are keeping you imprisoned and earth-bound by draining your energy. Search for and pursue your personal freedoms while always respecting other Participants' personal freedoms. Look for opportunities to support thinking and actions that encourage your fellow Participants to achieve higher expressions of Love, Gratitude, Enthusiasm, and Joy in their daily activities.

Humor – Umm, Umm Good!

This life can be fun and exciting if you are determined to make it that way. Whenever appropriate, find humor in and laugh at everything. **Life is to be taken and treated *lightly!*** From a cosmic perspective, nothing on or beyond this Earth is really that serious. When situations get heavy, it is time to say to yourself, and perhaps to everyone concerned, "Okay! It is time to lighten up. Things are getting too dreary around here."

Want to conquer your mood swings? Remind yourself, "I have only one mood, and it is *good!*" With constant vigilance, you can triumph over any disharmonious pattern.

You are The Absolute experiencing this planet! You can do anything you want to do with your life. This can be either a blessing or a curse. However, this is what soul evolution is all about—learning lessons in self-discipline, honesty, responsibility, and harmlessness; respecting others as God; and the big lesson of living in Limitless, Total Love. You can choose between lightness and good humor, or heaviness and despair. Which attitude brings enthusiasm, happiness, and Joy to yourself and others around you? Which do you think reflects the attitude of The Absolute? Love is a joyous, expansive feeling. Why not emulate the highest aspect of your Being?

Communication

Of the multitude of lessons to be learned by Participants on Planet Earth, one of the most important, yet most difficult to learn, is the fine art of communication. In all phases of life, clear, purposeful exchanges of information form the foundation of all harmonious human interactions. At the basis of perfecting this art is thinking about what you are saying, and using words that clearly express what you are thinking.

Calm, constructive communication is the prerequisite to loving, peaceful, and harmonious relationships. However, whenever a stressful situation is encountered within a relationship, then (or in the near future) is the time to discuss, analyze, and resolve the issues. Waiting only prolongs and intensifies your agony or concerns regarding the situation.

Everyone in your life is a mirror of yourself. Hopefully, we are all *loving* mirrors. Are you listening to other's suggestions? Are you eager to transmute your disharmonious patterns of behavior? If so, drop your defenses, relax, keep an open mind and **listen.** This may offer you a great opportunity to transform a disharmonious trait, thereby progressing your soul evolution.

What seems to be most difficult is bringing another's disharmonious words or actions to their attention. It takes the utmost tact, Love and understanding to communicate your personal, hidden thoughts and feelings to others, especially those closest to you. In relationships are you inclined to say nothing regarding issues burning on your mind? Holding back from expressing these thoughts and feelings don't do anyone a favor and may eventually cause you suppressed anxiety, stress, and seething resentment. Thereby, the problem is not transmuted and spiritual progress is thwarted. The most productive approach is to be courageous and say, "There is something that I need to get off my chest and speak with you about. May we discuss it now?" Or, "May I discuss some ideas with you as to how we may improve our relationship?"

The manner in which you present the topic of discussion is very important. The manner in which we use words can result in either harmonious understanding or disharmonious reactions. It is always best to present your inquiry and perspective in the form of *questions*. "Are you aware that every time I either do (this) or say (that), you respond in (this manner)?" You thereby do not directly challenge the other person and put them immediately on the defensive. Asking questions is the key to assisting another to dig within themselves for an awareness of the manner in which they observe, respond to, and feel about their actions.

Is it not true that we all communicate with ourselves more than we communicate with others? A key to your spiritual progress is to carefully monitor your thoughts and self-talk and use your observations to your advantage. What are you thinking? What is behind your thoughts and ideas? Are you using constructive, harmonious, uplifting words. Or, are your thoughts bringing you anxiety or depression?

Considering your higher God nature, are the thoughts and the words you are saying to yourself helping you to solve a present problem, or are they keeping your mind on a merry-go-round? Will your thoughts bring you what you really need in your life? Remember, "You are Gods!" Given enough energy, what you say and tell yourself will eventually manifest—fortunately, unfortunately, or indifferently. The art of constructive communication dictates that you use the utmost awareness and discrimination in your self-talk, as you would in interactions with others.

Honoring Your Body and Your Experiences

On the Astral Plane, many anapersona/souls are patiently waiting for material bodies through which they may progress their evolutionary growth. It is most important for Earth Participants to realize that many souls had desired the very body and the associated lessons you are now experiencing. This particular body you are now using was a gift to you from The Creator.

Remember that you are The Absolute experiencing this first realm of creation on this particular planet, at this particular time. You, therefore, have a responsibility to honor your physical body, care for and maintain it the best you are able, and evolve your soul evolution through the experiences you choose, and with which you are presented.

We on spirit's side observe that, when on the Astral Plane, you asked for, and even begged for this particular Earthly lifetime. However, it is curious that once the anapersona inhabits the physical body and begins to experience its chosen lifetime, it wants to leave! The manner in which a Participant values a bodily lifetime experience may be entirely different from spirit's side than from an Earth perspective.

On spirits' side, the soul views Earth experiences with their corresponding problems and difficulties as valuable learning experiences. Once in a human body, however, the uninformed personality sees these same experiences as conditions to be avoided. The soul-growth gained through these challenging experiences is not readily evident from an Earth perspective. The general acceptance of higher, spiritual truths would significantly reduce the degree of trauma Participants inflict upon themselves, and make their learning processes more fertile and productive.

We desire to impress upon you, as fellow Participants in this marvelous adventure, the importance of respecting and honoring your present bodily experience, regardless of outer appearances. This lifetime is not a "do or die" situation. From where you are now, all that can be asked is that you do your best within the confines of your personal condition, situation, talents, and abilities.

Know that you benefit from any situation or condition with which you are confronted, no matter how uncomfortable or life-threatening it may be. At times, you may feel you are in a maze, having no clue as to why you are there, the solution to the puzzle, or the location of the route to safety. Because of their higher perspective, your spiritual guidance or Divine Spirit will usually provide the answers to your queries. No answer means you are able to solve the problem yourself, or that the quest is a karmic search for knowledge and wisdom.

Everyone, regardless of their state of evolution, has their breaking point. We do not expect you to push yourself to this limit. Given similar situations, some Participants are capable of more development than others. Whatever your lifetime situation, pursue it with grace, dignity, calmness, and Joy! Joy that you feel inwardly and express outwardly! You are thus living this lifetime in the highest consciousness of which you are capable.

On the Road to Limitless Total Love

A major step on the path of spiritual consciousness is learning to express Limitless Total Love in your everyday activities. Limitless Total Love transcends parental love, brotherly love, romantic love, and sensual love because these lesser types of love are, by their very definition, limited to a specific party or action. Limitless Total Love is infinite and transcends the duality of conditional and unconditional love.

Limitless Total Love is a deep feeling of respect, honor, and sincere appreciation that one extends to every person and thing—animate or inanimate—because of the inner realization of its common identity and origin with The Creator.

Learning to express Limitless Total Love takes effort and practice. Try to remember a time when you experienced an exhilarating feeling of love as a spontaneous response to some external stimuli. Now, practice recreating this feeling at will under your conscious direction. The feeling of Limitless Total Love can be consciously developed through the application of willpower, as directed by thought.

To assist you in developing your love/feeling nature, you may find this exercise helpful. Visit a rock shop, arboretum, zoo, aquarium, county fair, or take a walk out into nature. Admire the beauty of the mineral kingdom, the landscape, the hills, the mountains, the rocks, the minerals, the gemstones. Delight in the beauty of the vegetable kingdom, the wide variety of styles and colors of flowers, plants, and trees. Admire the beauty in the animal kingdom, the wild and domesticated animals, pets, birds, fish, and other sea creatures. Appreciate the beauties in the sky, the sun, stars, planets, and Milky Way. Search out the beauties of the human kingdom, how every race, every person has their own individual, unique expression.

Know that everyone is either knowingly or unknowingly reaching for their highest potential. Honor all Life as an extension of The Absolute. Give thanks for the opportunity to experience such a beautiful planet. Feel Love and appreciation for the beauty of all aspects of Life as the artistic expressions of their spiritual creators.

Every living being, whether animate or seemingly inanimate, feels and responds to Love. Limitless Total Love, is the highest vibration a human being can transmit—to themselves, to others, to the environment, to the planet. When you consciously send the rose-pink ray and feeling of Love to anything or anyone, not only do they have the opportunity to respond in the highest manner they know, but whether or not it was accepted, know that the Love you send out will always return to you.

With reference to particular areas of improvement upon which Participants need to concentrate, we suggest that Limitless Total Love is—

- Total Self-discipline to act in a constructive and harmonious manner towards yourself, everyone, and everything.
- Total Honesty and Integrity blended with appropriateness and kindness by living the highest truth that you know.
- Accepting Total Responsibility for all people, events and circumstances you had attracted in your life, without blame or judgment.

- Total Harmlessness by honoring and respecting yourself, others, animals, and all aspects of Mother Nature, because they are all extensions of Infinite Being.

Optimizing Your Experiences

Life is important; yet it is best taken *lightly*. If one looks for it, humor is to be found almost everywhere, in any situation. It is your birthright to live and work surrounded by cheerfulness—allowing time for fun, relaxation, and enjoyment.

It is much more productive to view what might be considered as problems, difficulties, and disasters as simply obstacles to be overcome; roadblocks to be skirted. Even when encountering bodily "death," you now know that the anapersona lives on in a higher realm, continuing its evolution. We all grow as individuals, and as a whole, by recognizing what appears to be unfortunate situations as challenges through which we progress our soul evolution.

A basic experience in every soul's evolution is to follow the crowd. The greater experience, however, is to search for and find your own path, pursue it, grow through the obstacles encountered, and reap the personal satisfaction that comes from achievement. We may learn through other Participants' experiences, but it is up to each of us as individuals to make our own unique mark upon the Universe.

- 13 -

CALL 911! ILLNESS, DISEASE, AND ACCIDENTS

 Within the infinite Universe, everything is connected. All realms are connected. The inner affects the outer, and the outer affects the inner. Since your thoughts, words, feelings, emotions, and actions to some degree affect yourself on all realms, it is important to realize how they have a direct influence upon your material body. Your material body is designed to be ultra-sensitive to your inner mental and psychological states. Your body, therefore, is your greatest teacher.

 The discordant energy created by a Participant's constant disharmonious thought or behavior patterns return to them in the form of a bodily malfunction, injury, accident, disease, or other annoying condition, like premature death. The original source of your disharmony may be either in this lifetime, a previous lifetime or both. Through your discomfort, life is trying to get your attention, and is saying that something you are doing, or have done in the past, is/was out of harmony with the intrinsic nature of *yourself*—God the Absolute.

The Benefits Gained from Illness and Disease

Most Participants view sickness and disease as their adversary, an enemy to be conquered. However, from the perspective of soul evolution, they are your allies.

Over millennia, Participants as a whole have created sickness and disease as the karmic consequences of their disharmonious thoughts, words, feelings, and actions. What most Participants do not realize is that sickness and disease are their greatest teachers, broadcasting the message that humanity is out of harmony with Universal Law. What is out of harmony must be brought back into harmony. As long as the errors remain unchecked, the Laws of Harmony and Karma will bring new diseases to humankind as soon as a cure is found for the old ones. Have you noticed how some of the "old" diseases are now becoming resistant to modern antibiotics?

The source of all imbalances begins with disharmonious thoughts—thoughts out of harmony with your basic God-nature. Persistent disharmonious thoughts create illness in one's emotional body, and if they continue they eventually can cause the death of the physical body. If Participants would choose to learn to live in Limitless Total Love, all illness and disease would disappear from the Earth. Also, Participants' bodily vibrations, as well as the vibrations of the Planet Earth itself, would raise to a point where humankind would function in a higher dimensional physical-etheric experience, and death as it is known today would not exist.

Disharmonious thoughts and emotional reactions inevitably build up toxins in one's material and inner bodies. Sickness and disease are actually cleansers of disharmonious soul programming and the associated toxins accumulated in one's physical, astral/emotional, and mental bodies. The common cold and influenza do a terrific job in this respect. Within reason, the ideal way to handle these "soul cleansers" is to let them run their course without attempting to thwart the process with antihistamines and the like. Otherwise, your case of the cold or flu will have to be done over. The medical profession has recognized the importance of this periodic cleansing process, for without the occasional purging of accumulated toxins, even more serious illnesses may occur.

Illness is a personal teacher for it is usually an indication that an area of one's soul programming requires transmuting. Illness purges the toxins associated with one's disharmonious behavior patterns. In many cases, a Participant may choose to cleanse a serious disharmonious trait carried over from a previous lifetime, in this or a future lifetime. This may be observed in cases where young children have either been born with or contract severe and even life-threatening illnesses or disabilities. Through these physical and emotional ordeals, much is accomplished at the soul level.

When your thoughts, words, feelings, and actions are in total harmony with your true nature as Divine Being, your material body is healthy and functions harmoniously. When ill, you may observe that your body is transmitting messages to you to transmute your concepts and emotions into more constructive forms of expression. Do you attempt to analyze and solve the problem they are urging you to correct?

Illness and disease may occur without a karmic cause—from contact with contagious diseases, or exposure to environmental toxins. The message here is to keep your immune system in good condition, use your awareness to avoid contact with harmful bacteria, viruses, and chemicals, and attempt to avoid being in a contaminated area. It is important for all Participants to respect their planet by not polluting the air, water, and lands upon which they, other life forms, and the planet itself depend for their general well-being and survival. Your planet is the body through which the soul of Mother Earth is experiencing and evolving. It is wise to respect, nourish, and care for the body of Mother Earth as you would your own body. All is one. You are not separate from all of creation. Your responsibilities extend beyond yourself to include the whole planet and ultimately the whole Universe. Yes, what Participants do on their home planet effects the whole Universe!

Modern medical science has found remedies and cures for many serious illnesses that have plagued humanity for millennia. However, curing disease is a double-edged sword. On the one hand, medical cures may keep the human body alive longer to have more experiences. On the other, to cure a disease may prevent a lesson from being learned and the soul from being cleansed of disharmonious aberrations. From the soul's perspective, much disharmonious karma is transmuted through one's pain and suffering.

From a spiritual perspective, each Participant's illness may have a different cause, and thereby require a unique solution. This is the case wherein advances in modern technology have outstripped Participants' ability to use them wisely. Only the awareness and wisdom that comes from a perspective higher than a third-dimensional consciousness can suggest a course of action appropriate to a patient's best soul interest.

For instance, the suicide, assisted suicide, or mercy killing of a Participant with a terminal illness may not be in that anapersona/soul's best interest. In most cases this is not a suitable alternative, for the illness may have to be repeated in a future lifetime. Suicide does not solve a problem—it just postpones its resolution.

From a spiritual perspective, there is no requirement to maintain a Participant on life support systems. As with newborn babies or Participants of any age, if their body cannot survive on its own without minimal basic support, there is no requirement that it be kept alive through extraordinary mechanical means. Many times, as in the case of Participants who are in a comatose condition but on life support systems, the soul is in a state where it is not experiencing a normal life and is learning nothing. Keeping a body in this condition actually restrains the anapersona/soul from incarnating in a new, more useful body and obtaining a fresh start. Conditions like this become lessons for the caregivers rather than for the patient. One's soul consciousness is in charge of their body, and such life and death decisions are best left up to each Participant's Higher Self.

You chose this lifetime and you chose the material body through which you are now experiencing. Your present body carries over unresolved problems from previous lifetimes in its DNA and subconscious programming. These tendencies are reflected in your body's genes and in your psyche. Also, each Participant is responsible for their body's maintenance and well-being. Each Participant, therefore, must accept total responsibility for the state of their physical, mental, and feeling conditions. *Know* that through correct thinking and through claiming your own Power as a "Sun" of God, you have the potential to overcome and transform many, if not most, adverse conditions with which you are confronted.

Cancer

As long as Planet Earth remains a fear-based planet, diseases like cancer actually benefit a Participant's soul evolution. Cancer is an emotional disease originating in one's inner, astral body. This is why it is so difficult for allopathic physicians to cure. When some of the esoteric causes of cancer are examined, you may comprehend why cancer is one of humanity's greatest teachers.

Cancer is a disease which is "eating away inside." One question that might be asked of a cancer patient is, "What thoughts and emotions are 'eating' you?" The breasts and breast areas of both women and men are magnetic/receptive (feminine) in polarity. One root cause of breast cancer is the harboring of anger against women.

Since a woman's breasts represent one's nurturing functions in life, the overnurturing of other Participants to the detriment of one's own physical, feeling, mental, and spiritual requirements, is another common cause of breast cancer. Remember, from a spiritual perspective, your first responsibility is to your own health, well-being, and soul evolution. Your personal requirements must always be held in a balanced perspective while attending to the needs of others. As much as Mother Theresa assisted thousands of others in need, she always took two to four hours of time for personal meditation. Decide what constitutes your primary personal priorities, and resolutely reserve sufficient time for them.

Likewise, the prostate gland in men and the ovaries and uterus in women are dynamic/electric (masculine) in polarity. There are also two primary causes of cancer in these areas. The first is anger against men. Harboring suppressed anger is definitely a detriment to one's health.

The second cause in this regard is thoughts and emotions of rejection by men. If a man or woman harbors self-blame and guilt over the departure, divorce, or abandonment of a man, the resultant trauma may generate prostate, ovarian, or uterine cancer. The lessons here are in self-love, Trust, Knowing that all is well in God's Universe, and detachment—being objective and not taking the situation personally. To release a situation and another person in Limitless Total Love and forgiveness, is the ideal, spiritual attitude that heals all wounds and has no disharmonious repercussions.

Another person does not leave *you,* they choose to leave *themselves* because of their own fears or shortcomings. If they had better coping skills, a more expansive experience base, and/or more appropriate soul programming, the outcome may have been different. Then again, perhaps each person had a different destiny. There are "Y"s in our paths throughout life wherein people need to pursue other directions, other experiences. Other factors are the degree of compatibility between one another, and whether they had common goals to achieve. These are just a few observations on a very complex subject.

Disharmonious thoughts and emotions, as exposed through your emotional reactions, are the root cause of illness and disease. The lessons of Limitless Total Love teach the acceptance of another Participant's right to exercise their free will. It is, therefore, wise to always respect one's right to be "wrong."

Know that at all times, regardless of outer appearances, all is well in your Universe. Work towards being the Master of yourself so as not to manifest disharmonious emotions that may likely manifest as a discomforting illness or disease.

AIDS

For millennia, human sexuality has been out of harmony with Universal Law. (An in-depth discussion of this subject is provided in the section Tapping the Power of Gender). Before and during the last century, there were twenty-nine sexually transmitted diseases (STDs) calling out to get Participants' attention. However, the majority did not hear the message. It was more convenient to blame the disease as the cause of their problems, rather than take responsibility for their lives and acknowledge that their thoughts, words, and actions were at the basis of their discomfort.

Humanity, therefore, called to itself the condition called AIDS (Auto Immune Deficiency Syndrome), a thirtieth, more deadly, more difficult to cure, sexually transmitted disease, that addressed recreational and addictive drug use for good measure. This disease finally brought home the fact to most people that a real problem did indeed exist. In response to the AIDS epidemic, the allopathic medical profession came up with a constructive answer to the puzzle:

The only safe approach to avoid contracting AIDS is to have sexual contact within a sexually exclusive relationship, with a person whom you know has not been exposed to the Human Immunitive Deficiency Virus (HIV).

Now, apply this statement to the lessons behind all sexually transmitted diseases, and you have the basic answer as to under what conditions human sexual contact is in harmony with Universal Law.

Do not think that just because you are on the spiritual path or have acquired a fourth-dimensional consciousness you cannot contract a sexually transmitted disease. These lessons apply to everyone. Wisdom dictates that if you embark upon a new relationship that has sexually intimate potentials, both of you have blood tests to reveal any possible HIV/AIDS or other STD infection.

Accidents: Your Wake-up Call

Accidents, whether vehicular, job, home, sports, or recreation related, can be another form of wake-up call. Accidents by their very nature are sudden and jarring. They jolt you into stopping, thinking about, and hopefully reevaluating your life direction.

You are not living in and experiencing a haphazard Universe. You are connected with everything and everything is connected to you. You are constantly sending out energy vibrations, and the Universe is continually sending you messages and lessons.

Earth is currently a very imperfect, unpredictable planet wherein unexpected events are more the rule than the exception. It may, therefore, be difficult to intellectually determine whether an accident was intended to carry a lesson, or whether it was truly an unplanned event without a specific spiritual purpose. It is wise, though, to attempt to determine whether there was a personal message for you contained in an "accidental" event. Invariably, if you search, you can discover an inner cause behind an accident.

Had an accident? Well, what you may not realize is that your own Higher Self may have purposefully set it up to send you a message or teach you a lesson. Your Higher Self, the consciousness of your soul, has the responsibility for guiding your Earthly sojourns toward your spiritual destiny, your personal *dharma*. Pain, whether mental, emotional, or physical, is one of your best teachers, and your Higher Self is not reluctant to use this mechanism to nudge you onto a higher path.

Automobile accidents are especially significant and may be the easiest to analyze to obtain the message involved. Your automobile represents your direction in life, your life path. The front is your forward direction, the rear of your motor vehicle the past. The left side of your vehicle represents incoming energy and opportunities; the right side is where energies in the form of people, places, or things require releasing or transmuting.

If you have an accident involving the front end of your automobile, question yourself as to whether your present life direction is advantageous to your soul evolution. If the left side is damaged, what incoming information, energies, or opportunities are you ignoring? If hit on the right side, what present condition, habit, pattern, job, or person have you resisted transmuting, or releasing? If the rear of your vehicle is struck, to what past condition or to what old pattern are you still clinging, and need to release?

There are many other messages you can receive through your motorized vehicles. Your tires—are you rolling smoothly down the road of life, or are you causing the adventure to be unnecessarily bumpy? Battery or alternator problems—is someone stealing your energy—perhaps not giving back relative to what you are giving them? The vehicle's frame is bent—perhaps the basic structure of your philosophy needs to be examined. The windshield is shattered—are you harboring illusions that need to be replaced? The list goes on. Put the problem into words that you can apply to your life, and you can open yourself to a valuable source of advice and information.

These same principles can be applied to your material body ailments. There are books available, like *Heal Your Body*, suggesting how to translate the messages your body is sending you by analyzing the particular ailment, or part of the body which is affected. These books examine the problem, the probable cause, and the new thought pattern needed to replace or eliminate the root cause of the problematic programming. Be aware of all the reflections that life is sending you. Thereby, you can greatly progress your personal soul evolution.

- 14 -

ALTERNATIVE ROUTES AROUND THE STORMS, WASHOUTS, AND ROADBLOCKS

There are many obstacles that restrain a Participant's soul progress. These barriers are based upon personality imbalances and disharmonious soul programming, and require transmutation into more harmonious modes of functioning if one is to evolve to a spiritual consciousness. Here are some of the major ones.

Fear: The Barrier to Love

The goal is to be fearless but not foolhardy.

Fear is the greatest barrier to your soul evolution. Fear is the opposite energy to Trust and Limitless Total Love. Fear is the greatest evil, for it is behind humankind's most despicable acts. Your fears block your progress, your path, and your evolution. Fear holds you down and keeps you from transcending the restrictive human condition. It takes consistent, constructive counteraction to replace fear with Trust and Limitless Total Love. Trust is a quality that is developed from within.

You *Trust* the universe and *Know* that no matter what happens through outer circumstances, the *Real You* is always OK; that All is Well in God's Universe, and, therefore, in *yours!* Fear is a paper tiger that will dissolve if you face it down. Know that eventually, Love will dissolve fear.

On Earth, fear is your greatest teacher. Your fears are a self-fulfilling prophesy—a prayer for disaster. What you think about, you get, especially if propelled with enough emotional energy to materialize words or thoughts into physical reality. Again, the energies you send out, return to you. This is why anger begets anger, violence begets violence, fear perpetuates fear, and Love begets Love. One would think that by experiencing the discomfort of the consequences of fear energies returning to them, Participants would eventually seek out the opposite, more comfortable energy, namely Love.

However, it appears that most Participants have been conditioned to thrive on fear and accept it as a way of life. As a result, many Participants have unwittingly become vulnerable to control by unconscious individuals who would manipulate others for their own self-aggrandizement. So you hear a lot of complaining, but the vast majority of Participants feel they are helpless to change the situation. They are caught in a self-created trap.

In the realm of duality, some Participants use fear as a device to control others. Sometimes this is done very subtly, other times very blatantly. Some governments use fear tactics and force to control the populace; some companies use fear messages in their advertisements to encourage you to purchase their products; some special interest groups use fear arguments to pursue their causes; family members use fear threats to control other family members. The list goes on.

Fear tactics may have temporary success, but eventually they create more problems than the perpetrators can solve. One cannot beat the Law of Karma and Reincarnation (see Appendix) into submission. What goes around, comes around. The Law is immutable. You may observe that fear is at the basis of all disharmonious behavior.

Untie Your Knots

Does negativity have you tied up in knots? If you carefully monitor your thoughts, words, and feelings you will soon become aware of the "nots" in your thoughts and speech. "Nots" originate in one's soul programming and produce and maintain fear-based patterns in one's emotional nature and one's actions. The means to eliminate and transform these patterns is to drop the "nots" that are holding you back, restraining your progress.

To untie your knots, first, become the observer of your self-talk and communications with others. Behind all discomfort is some subconscious disharmonious word or thought pattern. Be very cautious in your speech when attempting to use negative words like not, cannot, is not, was not, and the like. You are God, so, whatever you say is true. "I cannot do that!" So, you cannot! "I was not proficient at that task." Since the Universe and your soul knows only Now, it will carry this statement into your future. "She is not a loving person." By making this statement you are actually reinforcing the other's problem and making their efforts to transmute it more difficult.

Carefully reword your statements or questions, if possible, to present the situation from a constructive perspective. "I can do anything I have the desire to accomplish." "What training do I need to achieve that objective or goal?" "What suggestions do you have that would help me perform that task more efficiently?" Or, "With a different approach, I may be more proficient at that task." "She feels unloved. Let us send her Love and show her more empathy and consideration."

Beware of "knotty" questions like, "Don't you want to go to the mall with me?" Perhaps you may replace this with, "Would you like to go to the mall with me?" Negative questions are difficult to respond to.

You will discover that if you transmute your self-talk and use positive, constructive, dynamic words in your thoughts, affirmations, meditations, and communications with others, you will quickly transform your life and advance your personal soul evolution.

Judgment

If you want to be judged, go ahead—judge others!

Judgment is a feature of the third dimcon because it is based upon duality—the concepts of good and bad, right and wrong, better and worse. Since Limitless Total Love and unity of understanding and purpose prevail in the fourth and higher dimcons, judgment does not exist. Observations, yes. Judgments, no.

Judgment is a barrier to one's spiritual progress. *Awareness* is not to be confused with judgment. When Participants judge another's actions, or a situation in general, they do so from a very limited perspective. It is simply not possible for an Earth Expedition Participant to be fully aware of another's soul programming, their motives, lessons, limitations, and all the karmic implications behind a given situation.

One makes a judgment when they assert and attach a definite conclusion to a situation as a condition of fact. The problem lies in the word "fact." A situation that appears to be a fact is only a relative reality. Like truth, fact and reality are relative to each individual Participant's perceptions. To state a condition or situation as a "fact" is a judgment. So many diverse factors form the basis of any given situation or condition that it is virtually impossible for anyone to be totally cognizant of all sides of the matter.

Being aware is different. Awareness says, "From my limited perspective, this appears to be the situation. However, I do not know the whole story." If you go further into judgment, know that The Law of Cause and Effect is always in force. Whatever energies you extend, will return to you.

Have you ever been stopped by a police officer for a traffic violation where you were required to appear before a local magistrate? If ever you are, ask yourself, "Now, what was that all about?" Within a few days you will get your answer. Had you had been judging someone else's actions? The lesson—be aware and observant, but do not judge others.

Here is an observation regarding the relationship of "time" and judgment. It appears that most Participants are overly obsessed with the past, especially as concerns others. They firmly believe that actions a person had performed in the past are a positive indication of what that person is today, and that person must be severely reprimanded and punished by the media and Earth tribunals for their past transgressions. This reflects a judgmental attitude which can produce severe karmic implications and lessons in compassion, understanding, and forgiveness.

First, this perspective reflects a lack of Trust that there is perfect justice in the world, and it exhibits a lack of understanding that, from a spiritual perspective, no Participant secretly gets away with anything. Besides being an extension of God the Absolute, one cannot hide from their own soul and the karma it has recorded.

Secondly, this demonstrates a lack of comprehension of the continual process of transformation—that no one is the same today as they were yesterday. The question that must be asked is, "Has this Participant learned from their past mistakes and thereby evolved to a higher level of consciousness? Or are they presently repeating the same disharmonious behavior patterns?"

As an individualized expression of The Absolute, each Participant in the whole Universe is equal. In infinity, there can be no more God or no less God anywhere. However, no two Participants are identical at the personality or soul levels. The beauty inherent in the creation of individualized beings is that each soul has its own unique programming, knowledge, and wisdom. Each material body has its own unique height, weight, skin color, facial, and bodily appearance, mental capacity, personality traits—and experiences.

Beings with a spiritual consciousness use awareness and discernment to perceive another's personality and soul traits. Since there is no judgment, there is no discrimination. There is a difference between discernment and discrimination. One is based upon awareness, the other on judgment.

The Astral Plane – A Barrier to Progress

The ethers of the Astral Plane house the long, complicated history of the descent of spiritual beings into astral, physical-etheric, and material forms. Beginning millions of years ago, this realm has been infused with all the error events that caused beings with a spiritual consciousness to descend into the restrictive confines of material bodies.[12]

This is why the Astral Plane is referred to as the realm of emotion and sensory gratification, for these were at the basis of this devolution and descent into matter. Since your astral body corresponds to the vibrational frequency of the Astral realm, it is also referred to as your emotional body. As a Participant evolves to a fourth-dimensional consciousness, their astral body is sublimated in importance to their spiritual Body of Light. This transition requires that a Participant cleanses their astral body of sensory cravings and addictions. Mental and emotional illusions must also be transmuted, as these aberrations result in delusions—not a spiritual attribute.

Do you enjoy the high you get from emotional exhilaration and the low you achieve from depression? The Hermetic Principle of Rhythm states: "The measure of the swing to the right is the measure of the swing to the left." As you refine your fourth-dimensional perspectives, you will realize the wisdom of keeping the swings of your moods and feeling nature within a more steady, narrow range. The more you live in Limitless Total Love, the more your perspective of the world changes—you feel and demonstrate more inner exhilaration and peace of mind, body, and soul in your life. What more do you really need?

Examine your life and search for ways you cave in to the whims of your astral-emotional nature. Make note of these, and during your meditations decree, see, feel, and know that these sensory cravings are *now* dissolved from your soul data bank. Incorporating Patience, Persistence, and Perseverance in this process will facilitate the manifestation of this goal.

---

12. For detailed information, read *The Evolution of Man,* published by Mark Age.

Remember, **what is astral is not spiritual.** It is very easy to be confused by the two. Astral *psychic* phenomena are different than spiritual *mystical* occurrences. It is wise to exercise awareness and discern one from the other, as they originate from vastly different sources. The Astral Plane houses a very broad range of consciousness. On the lower astral levels reside demonic entities and Participants with the lowest consciousness who are usually up to mischief. Those yearning for a higher, spiritual awareness may be sincere about helping you, however they are limited by their third-dimensional consciousnesses.

It takes experience and discernment for you to distinguish the difference. Use awareness and listen to your Heart and your intuition. They will tell you whether an innerplane experience you encounter is appropriate for you.

You may think of the third dimcon, and the Astral Plane to which it is related, as a huge block of Swiss Cheese. The Swiss Cheese represents the denseness of matter. When engrossed in the third dimcon, it is very easy to become lost in the maze of holes, and very difficult to find your way out. As you venture out through a hole, and you encounter fear, guilt, and anger, the Swiss Cheese heats up and melts. Again you find yourself stuck in the gooey mess.

As you are sincerely trying to make constructive progress in your life towards a spiritual consciousness, when you have blocks that still require transmutation, you only heat up the Swiss Cheese and find your headway thwarted. You need to constantly remind yourself to *stay calm and relaxed when in the midst of chaos.* The true seeker will be aware and take advantage of the opportunities with which they are presented to break through the blocks in the Swiss Cheese. Currently, the holes are getting larger, so you may more easily find the escape route.

This is why daily meditation is so important. Meditation is the only mechanism that will get you out of the denseness of matter, the sticky block of Swiss Cheese. If you desire to achieve a spiritual consciousness, *stay out of the Astral Plane.* One goes out into the Astral Plane through their solar plexus. In meditation, we suggest you go *through* the Astral Plane *into the spiritual realms.*

To reach the spiritual realms, raise your consciousness up through the top of your head, into your Higher Self, the spiritual consciousness of your soul. Once in the point of your Higher Self, you are beyond time and space. You can then place your attention in the infinite point in the center of your head, to be in union with your Divine Spirit. From there, you can travel anywhere in the spiritual realms, and beyond—up through the Godhead to the Source of everything, God The Absolute.

Controlling Others

Any form of exercising control over others is an illusion. Although all Participants are playing out their chosen roles as strong/weak, rich/poor, healthy/sickly, the ruler/the subject, all are intrinsically equal —equally God, for everyone is an extension of The Absolute. Everyone in any social position deserves to be treated with the respect due them as a Participant in this grand adventure. Rank and status are illusions— simply characteristics of a role through which one plays out their karma and learns their lessons through their interaction with others.

Intimate relationships are a great training ground for the practice of detachment and the respecting of another's freedom of choice. When control or domination issues arise behind disputes and conflicts, you immediately know you are looking a learning opportunity right in the face. It is best you stop right there and examine your motives. If appropriate, ask the other person about their motives. In what area is transmutation required?

It is unwise to judge another Participant's "rank" by their outer appearances, for they may be in a position to present you with some very important lessons. There are times when an anapersona with a highly evolved soul will choose a lifetime as a very simple, humble, uncomplicated man or woman, eking out a living by offering some menial service to others. Perhaps lessons in humility and frugality were required for them to attain a higher degree of consciousness.

You are the God of your life. You have the ability to develop absolute power and control over yourself. However, it is not permissible for you to exercise undue influence, power, and control over others. When you exert control over others, you are restraining their soul evolution and are interfering with their individual freedom of expression—their free will.

Would *you* like to be in their position? Would you like to have your free will restrained? Always be mindful of The Law of Karma and Reincarnation. "Treat others as you would like to be treated." The energies you extend to others *will* return to you. Conversely, the degree and quality of respect you demonstrate toward others will eventually be showered upon yourself.

Excessive Ego

Ego is the sense of self as an individualized being. Ego is *great* when it nurtures self-esteem and self-worth, but it can be taken too far when it manifests as an exaggerated sense of self-importance. As a result, a Participant's outlook may be overly concerned with their own personal status, activities, or needs. Ego needs to be put into a proper, broader perspective. You were created as an individualized aspect of The Absolute to have individual experiences. Your individuality is both a reality and an illusion, for simultaneously, each individual Participant *is* The Whole, The All.

We attract many lessons brought on by the sense of self. Ego is one of the trickiest and most subtle aspects of self with which we are confronted. Ego works in some very devious ways to get your attention. Arrogance is an example of an error which enters the personality through one's thoughts, then is exhibited through one's words and actions.

Cousins of arrogance are willfulness and spiritual pride, which originate in the ego and then lurk in the personality. Whenever you realize you are not acting in a loving, non-judgmental manner, you need to be aware and astute enough to bring yourself back into balance.

It is unwise to place too much value on your individual self-importance. No matter what a person's social rank in human terms, we are all servants of one another, and all share the responsibility for the evolution of the whole of humankind.

No one is isolated from anything or anyone else. Whatever you do for yourself as an individual, you do for your family, your friends, your community, your nation, your planet, your galaxy, your Universe. If you desire to progress your soul evolution in an efficient and effective manner, it is well to keep this point at the forefront of your awareness.

Every person *is* yourself. You are the animals. You are the environment. You are the Earth. You are everyone and everything. Your responsibility is not only to yourself, but to the whole. Continually ask yourself, "How will my proposed action contribute to my own soul evolution as well as the overall evolution of Planet Earth, and the All?"

To attain a fourth-dimensional consciousness, it is wise to be humble, and constantly honor and show respect for the first, second, and third dimcons, as they have taught you countless lessons. The lessons from the first dimcon are taught through forest fires, floods, hurricanes, tornados, and other disasters; the lessons in Love and beauty are taught by the insects and animals of the second dimcon; and millions of lessons are taught throughout one's progression in the third dimcon.

Rather than criticize and condemn the path you have traveled, thank and bless it for the strength and wisdom you have gained through its experiences.

Willfulness

From a spiritual perspective, willfulness is exercising your gift of free will in a manner in opposition to the will of your God-self. An act of willfulness produces disharmony or destructiveness to yourself, others, animals, or the environment. To what extent is your willfulness interfering with your soul evolution? Despite promptings, suggestions, or experience to the contrary, have there been times when you obstinately said, "I want to do *(this!)*," knowing that in some manner your actions may have discomforting or disharmonious repercussions? It takes a certain amount of humility to lay aside your ego and wilfulness, to realize that everyone is but a part of the whole, and that the whole does not revolve around one Participant's egocentric personality.

The harmonious management and direction of one's willpower is a major challenge throughout the total progress of one's soul evolution. The lessons of the third dimcon do require that one exercises their willpower outwardly in the material world to achieve material results. It is only through a multitude of experiences, resulting in knowledge and wisdom, that one learns what actions are harmonious and which are disharmonious. The Law of Karma assists Participants in learning the difference.

In the fourth dimcon, wherein one's *inner* reality takes on more importance, the exercising of one's will suggests a different approach. An important lesson one learns is to release all addictions to material attachments and circumstances. This is accomplished by the Participant coming into harmony with the higher direction of their soul and spirit by saying, "Not *my* will, but *yours* be done, in and through me." As the occasion arises, it follows that you ask, "What is *your* will in my life?" —and then be aware of any answer you receive. The answer may come from a variety of sources—it may instantly pop into your mind, it may be triggered by a magazine article, a film, radio or television story, or even through someone's comments.

There is no guarantee that you will immediately receive an answer. Some things you have to figure out for yourself to benefit your evolution. If you do not know the ideal course of action, the choices you make will provide you with the answer. Experience is always the best, albeit harshest, teacher.

Energy Blocks

The disharmonious statements and scripts a Participant accumulates in their soul programming in reaction to the strains of Earth living, become energy blocks in one's physical, emotional, and/or mental bodies. These energy blocks greatly affect one's physical, feeling, and mental health and well-being. These blocks exist until the Participant dissolves them.

The best technique for dissolving energy blocks is performed during your daily meditations, and consists of four steps.

1. Raise your consciousness to the level of your Divine Spirit.
2. From the neutral point in the center of your head, visualize yourself in the center of your body and in the center of your soul.
3. Visualize a blazing golden-white Light, and feel Love radiating from this point throughout your material body and your soul.
4. Finally, decree the following statements with *feeling,* knowing that the condition is transformed:

"All mental disharmonious statements and energy blocks, be dissolved!

All emotional disharmonious statements and energy blocks, be dissolved!

All physical disharmonious statements and energy blocks, be dissolved!"

The dissolution of the energy blocks may then occur instantly, or may require repeated use of the decrees. It is a good idea to integrate this technique in your daily meditations, as energy blocks can creep into your psyche without your awareness. These healing decrees are included in both the Progressive and the Advanced Consciousness Raising Meditations. Order information is available at the end of this field guide.

The Power of Thought-forms

Thought, word, action! Thoughts are *things* that have the potential to produce actions. Every minute, through their thoughts, words, and actions, each Participant, either consciously or unconsciously, is affecting their personal life's destiny, as well as that of the whole planet.

When a thought is given enough energy, it materializes on the astral realm as a literal "thought-form." As viewed from the spiritual realms, a dense, black astral cloud is seen enshrouding Planet Earth. Over thousands of years, this dark astral layer has accumulated from Participant's disharmonious thoughts, words, and actions of anger, violence, hostility, greed, and lust. It is worse and more irritating than smog. However, if you have been brought up in smog and that is all you know, clear, fresh air is a foreign concept!

Look around you and observe the increasing crime, violence, greed and corruption, sexual aberration, and the corresponding incidence of disease! What Participants are not recognizing is how they are unconsciously reinforcing and perpetuating this disharmony. This dense residue of disharmonious thoughts, words, emotions, and deeds perpetuates error and fear among the populace, making it more difficult for Participants to live in harmony and Limitless Total Love.

These disharmonious thought-forms unconsciously influence and impede all Participants, particularly immature and morally weak souls. The mass obsession with crime, violence, war, murder, and lust, as reflected and reinforced in all forms of mass media, is having disastrous effects. When filtered through and imbedded in the minds and souls of millions of people, these impressions are being lodged in the astral realm as thought-forms. What you put out returns to you. These thought-forms eventually take on physical manifestation to become a reality in the environment, thereby compounding what problems already exist.

The continual bombardment of disharmonious thoughts and ideas through the verbal, visual, and emotional imagery projected upon the general public by spiritually unconscious Participants in the news and "entertainment" industries, perpetuates and increases the problems. The more spiritually evolved Participants on Planet Earth have been demanding change for a long time, however their voices have been drowned out by forces seeking only financial gain and world control. Where chaos exists, the masses can be more easily dominated. This results in the loss of personal freedoms and basic human rights.

Each individual Participant has a responsibility for the whole. If there is an error, an imbalance somewhere in society, then it is the responsibility of *each individual* in that society to help correct the disharmonious situation. These disharmonious thought-forms around Planet Earth need to be dissolved if Earth is to become a Love-based planet.

How can you assist the planet to rise above the extremes of duality? Each individual Participant has the responsibility to avoid contributing to the disharmony that presently permeates the ethers around Planet Earth. On the inner, this is accomplished by searching out and transmuting all fear-based programming in your psyche, and by sending prayer-decrees of Love, peace, and harmony to the planet. On the outer, it is accomplished by not participating by thought, word, or action in fear, greed, and lust-based activities, such as violent and overtly sensual "entertainment" productions, whether printed, auditory, and/or visual. These productions reinforce conflict and duality by appealing to humanity's lower animal nature. Are you supporting these productions by participating in them?

Collectively, you are the Gods of Planet Earth. What you hear and watch—you *think* about. What you think about—you *create*. You are *NOW* creating your present and future reality. Do you choose to live on a Love-based planet, or a fear-based planet? Each moment you are deciding. What is *your* decision?

Inertia

Do you feel too comfortable in your present life situation to exert sufficient effort to progress your soul evolution? Are you content with your status quo even though you have the potential to expand into higher realms of consciousness in this lifetime?

Are you adhering to a fear or judgment-based religion which you feel is no longer serving a progressive purpose in your life? Are you fearful of leaving the security it has provided you in the past? Do you feel apprehension at the thought of venturing out to explore new avenues in search of higher truths?

Are you in a family, friendship, or personal relationship situation wherein you perceive that the person(s) around you are not supportive of your breaking loose from traditional ways of relating to the world? Do you fear their lack of approval over what you sincerely believe you need to do with your life? Do you feel uneasy at the thought of leaving a restrictive or abusive relationship because of the material comfort and financial security it offers you?

What you do in these situations is really up to you to decide. You may be in a vacation lifetime wherein you simply planned to enjoy a comfortable lifetime that presented few challenges. But if you really think and feel that with just a little more effort you could make great strides in your inner development, it may be to your advantage to confront them, overcome the obstacles, and jump into the river of spiritual progress. It only matters what you think—not what others think—for others may be attempting to control you to justify their own beliefs and pursue their own agendas.

If you have the ability, desire, and determination to make substantial progress in your soul evolution this lifetime, you will be eternally grateful for doing it now, rather than waiting for some subsequent bodily experience. Once you embark upon the spiritual path, you will be rewarded with the support you need. You must *Trust and Know* that your real needs are always supplied, especially when you decide that your primary need is to progress your soul evolution. Inner strength is developed and accumulated through conquering obstacles and adversities as they are presented. Soul progress is the only item of value you can take with you when the time comes to leave the material vehicle behind.

– 15 –

TAPPING THE POWER OF GENDER

A husband is united with his wife and they become one.

The Principle of Gender – Gender is in everything. Everything has both its Masculine and Feminine Principles. Gender manifests on all realms.

The whole universe reflects perfect balance. Everything is balanced through polarity and gender. There is power in balance. In balance, there is harmony. The Principle of Gender is one of the basic Laws upon which the Universe was founded. There is power in the polarity of gender. A flashlight or automobile battery has two poles: positive and negative. A light bulb connected to just one grounded (negative) pole will light only when an energized (positive) wire is connected to the other pole. The circuit is thereby completed. Gender functions in a similar manner.

Gender is a specific form of polarity. The soul of each Participant is androgynous or neutral in polarity, being neither electric nor magnetic. However, when Participants with a third or fourth-dimensional consciousness take on a human body, polarity shifts take place between the body and the soul.

Ideally, the bodily energies of adult men are outwardly electric/dynamic in polarity and those of adult women are outwardly magnetic/receptive in polarity. Thereby, the two genders are polar opposites. Some characteristics associated with the electric/dynamic energies are outgoing, bold, adventurous, rational, serious, self-assertive, goal-oriented, self-determined, opportunistic, and, in the extreme, aggressive. Keywords associated with magnetic/receptive characteristics are warm, loving, compassionate, nurturing, supportive, sharing, sensitive, intuitive, light-hearted, and joyful.

During a human incarnation, in order to maintain a neutral polaric balance between body and soul, the soul of an adult man becomes magnetic/receptive (the anapersona being electric/dynamic), and the soul of an adult woman is electric/dynamic (the anapersona being magnetic/receptive). Children, whether male or female, are neutral in polarity until they reach a point of maturity whereupon they may realize and express either their electric-male or magnetic-female natures. Some male and female Participants, though, remain neutral in polarity throughout their entire lifetimes, never realizing or expressing either an electric or magnetic nature. In the expression of some personalities, the polarity is even reversed, the male being magnetic/receptive and the female exhibiting an electric/dynamic nature—a submissive, dominated man or an aggressive family matriarch, for instance.

As a Participant achieves a fifth-dimensional consciousness, both their physical body and soul become androgynous, being dynamically and magnetically balanced, inwardly and outwardly. These Participants no longer required a partner of the opposite sex for the completion of a spiritual power structure. Although men are still outwardly men and women are outwardly women, a polaric balance exists between their outer gender and their reserve storehouse of inner qualities.

There are many esoteric subtleties regarding heterosexual relationships that are not widely recognized, such as the relationship between gender and the development of spiritual power. As expressed by Participants with either a third or fourth-dimensional consciousness:

1. An individual Participant has a certain amount of power in his or her own right.
2. The power potential of two people of the same sex is just that, the power of two.
3. For two Participants of the opposite sex, the power potential is *four times or more* that of a single individual, depending upon how effectively it is generated. Within meditation and prayer groups composed of equal numbers of male and female Participants, the power factor is likewise *squared*.

The ideal purpose behind the union of male and female genders is to complement one another, and together create a synergy that potentially may produce more strength and power than either could possibly generate individually. The ideal situation occurs when the two partners are generally compatible, with a harmonious balance in their polarities. Thereby, when purposefully directing their unified energies, the couple may effectively achieve their individual and common goals.

Sexual intercourse is performed in harmony with Universal Law in a dedicated, committed, heterosexual, sexually exclusive union. The two Participants are *dedicated* to assist one another in their soul evolution, in an intimate relationship *sexually exclusive* of other partners. They are *committed* to supporting each other's individual goals, and the attainment of their mutually agreed upon goals. They expect their union to be of a long-term duration. Under these conditions, their sexual activity is a sacred act, full of beauty and grace—a spiritual union.

Spiritual beings on the higher realms then work with the two partners to harmonize their polaric energies into one strong, unified power source. The creative electric/dynamic and magnetic/receptive powers of the universe are thereby joined and balanced between the two, as *one*.

Whenever this unified pair is focused and works together in harmony to achieve a worthy, common goal, it has the ability to consciously generate four or more times the innerplane power than a single person with a third or fourth-dimensional consciousness.

Within all male/female relationships, particularly dedicated, spiritual unions, there is a definite purpose behind the interactions between the genders. The intention is the spiritual expectation that each partner assists the other to progress their soul evolution. Part of this process entails assisting one another to work out their individual karmas.

In an intimate spiritual relationship, the two partners are powerful mirrors to one another. Either consciously or unconsciously, Participants tend to pick partners who are strong in the areas where they are weak. Participants experience great difficulty seeing their inner selves and the ramifications of their outer actions clearly. Great progress is made in close, intimate relationships wherein one's disharmonious work areas become glaringly evident to the other partner. The spiritual objective is to assist in strengthening and transforming each other's weaknesses, thereby progressing the soul evolution of both partners.

Progress and transformation are most comfortably and best achieved when these observations are communicated in a constructive, kind, questioning, and loving manner. Condemnation and destructive criticism are demeaning and judgmental, and disclose a lack of respect for the other person, as well as a lack of self-love. You must first forgive yourselves for *your* transgressions, and then treat others with kindness and understanding. There would be considerably more harmony in intimate relationships if both parties clearly understood the spiritual goals of partnerships before beginning their intimate alliance.

All Participants need to recognize they are learning many important attributes from their gender opposites, thereby achieving a balanced polarity within themselves. There is a crossover effect where each individual may grow more through the experience with their polar opposite than they could through their own individual experience or with a member of their same gender. Women are striving to balance their outer magnetic/receptive natures by becoming more electric/dynamic inwardly, and men are attempting to balance their outwardly electric/dynamic natures by becoming more inwardly magnetic/receptive. One must eventually achieve this polaric balance to attain a fifth-dimensional consciousness. Balance is the key word here.

Women assist men to be in touch with, recognize, and identify their feelings, and to be sensitive to the feelings of others. Men, thereby, learn through experience to express and communicate their personal feelings. Women also demonstrate and share what intuition is all about, and how to recognize and trust it. A man's task is to get in touch with his Heart and listen to what it is saying to him; to learn to be more compassionate, understanding, and loving; to learn the limits of the intellectual mind and the unlimited potentials of the intuitive mind. Generally, men's task is to balance their heads and their Hearts.

Women predominately think through their feelings and emotions. Through the example and loving encouragement of men, women strengthen their intellect to better confront and solve everyday Earth problems in a more rational, organized, and practical manner. Men's task is to encourage women to express their feelings clearly and logically so as to be understood by others (men in particular), and to distinguish disharmonious emotions from harmonious feelings. Women also ascertain from men how to direct their willpower in a manner whereby they may achieve their own personal dreams and goals.

Both genders are learning lessons in responsibility, honesty and integrity, self-discipline, harmlessness, and clear, loving, open communication, to name a few. Between two partners dedicated to the progression of their mutual soul evolution, there are no obstacles that cannot be over-come, and no limit to their spiritual achievements. The goal toward which all Participants are working is to express Limitless Total Love in and through every thought, word, and action.

At the close of the twentieth century, the majority of women strove to do their part in balancing their outer magnetic/receptive nature by becoming more electric/dynamic inwardly. Some women even went beyond that elusive balance point and became too outwardly dynamic.

The majority of men, however, were clueless as to what was expected of them—that they also needed to transform *their* temperaments. What women did intuitively, most men have not grasped. Men need to accept that women are *their* teachers in learning what feelings and intuition are all about, to be sensitive to the feelings of others, how to be aware of and in touch with their own feelings, and how to communicate them. How many men talk about their *feelings?* A major task for everyone is to learn to lead with their spiritual Hearts.

The objective of intimate relationships is that both sexes assist and encourage one another to evolve spiritually. As we enter the new millennium, it is now men's opportunity and responsibility, individually and as a group, to progress their soul evolution by paying more attention to what women are saying to them and what the Universe is encouraging them to accomplish—to balance their outward dynamic natures by becoming more inwardly magnetic.

Hopefully the day will arrive when the ideal goal regarding human sexuality is achieved—when men are men, and women are women—each balanced in their outer and inner, dynamic and magnetic natures.

The Lessons of Romantic Love

Romantic Love is the opposite of Limitless Total Love.

One must first experience romantic love in order to understand Limitless Total Love. Romantic love is initially and primarily based on superficial physical and psychological factors which, when viewed from a spiritual perspective, are illusions. It is being caught up in the moment with unrealistic expectations and ideals, instinctual and emotional factors, and, primarily, subconscious programming. It is the pursuit and quest for physical and emotional sensual gratification based on the excitement and adventure of newness, variety, and infatuation.

One learns about romantic love in their teens and twenties. This is when one learns what love is not. As a romantic love relationship progresses, the couple is confronted with the practical aspects of everyday life. Romantic love tangles one's emotions. When conflicts arise, the manner in which they are resolved determines the nature of the lessons both parties are learning. Where there is conflict, both Participants have something to learn.

The greatest trap in romantic love is *judgment*. Judgment pulls one out of Total Love, and throws them back into a third dimensional mode of functioning. Romantic love is an external love, based upon outer concerns, whereas Total Love is an internal Love, that comes from deep within the Heart. An intimate relationship based solely on romantic love will most likely burn out and end in disappointment and disillusion. The ideal union fulfills each partners' needs through an objective outlook, and is dedicated to the achievement of common goals.

What does romantic love teach Participants? It teaches that a true, harmonious relationship between a man and a woman entails awareness, commitment, loyalty, acceptance, open communication, tolerance, kindness, respect, responsibility, and honesty. Think about these qualities and their implications. Contemplate how you may apply these qualities to all your relationships—intimate, family, friendship, business, or otherwise.

The Role of Sex in the Human Drama

Sex is a powerful, sacred gift bestowed upon humankind. As with the granting of any gift, the recipient is also given the responsibility of using it wisely. It is each Participant's task to learn and demonstrate this, by determining the optimum utilization of their personal sexual energies.

The lessons involved in learning the appropriate use of sex are guided by the precepts of the Law of Harmony and the Law of Karma and Reincarnation. When one incurs karma through the misuse of sex, they are encouraged to learn the proper use of their sexual nature. When sex is dis-graced through its disharmonious use, Participants attract to themselves illusion, delusion, sickness, and death—mentally, emotionally, and physically.

Sexual expression is an energy that is particularly actuated by Participants in the third dimcon. They place great importance upon their sexuality, and sex in general. To Participants with a fourth-dimensional consciousness, sex is of little importance for, having mastered their physical energies, they have become less desirous and needy in that area. In the fourth dimcon sexuality is acknowledged, enjoyed, and appreciated, but it is not an energy that prevails. There are other significant compatibility considerations that come before sex. Sexuality is primarily a third-dimensional energy.

All realms, as well as your outer and inner bodies, are interconnected. When two heterosexual people first engage in sexual intercourse, they become attached at their solar plexus areas by bright red astral cords. This is an innerplane, astral connection undetectable to most humans' sight. A few talented Participants with astral vision can observe these cords. Can you imagine how some sexually promiscuous Participants must look from the inner planes? Like a heaping serving of tangled spaghetti!

Human beings are not rabbits, acting solely through instinct, although many humans have been performing as such. Out of ignorance, sex has been treated too lightly and frivolously—as a toy. The result has been the degradation and desecration of a sacred gift. Human sexuality was designed to be awarded due respect, for it has an inherent power that is rarely recognized.

The contemporary practice of engaging in casual sex, or two people having sexual intercourse within their first few meetings, is not in harmony with spiritual principles. This type of behavior is not only a misuse of sex, but it clouds one's perspective in evaluating the purpose and objectives of the relationship. It takes many encounters, under a variety of circumstances, to clearly observe and appraise all facets of another Participant's personality and potentials. Compatibility issues on the domestic, physical, feeling, mental, and spiritual levels also need be examined. Regarding intimate relationships, when subjectivity (one's illusionary emotional desires and expectations) rules over objectivity (clear thinking and freedom from personal desires, prejudices, and interpretations), the outcome usually has uncomfortable repercussions.

Wisdom shared from a spiritual perspective suggests that a couple date in a platonic manner for at least ten months before engaging in sexual relations. Although one never knows everything about another, this exploratory period enables the couple to perceive one another in an atmosphere where objectivity may prevail. The potential compatibility, practicality, and longevity of their relationship may then be more adequately evaluated as well as the prospective partner's admirable qualities, quirks, and shortcomings. When appropriate, these factors need to be discussed openly and appraised. It is rare that the potential for an objective commitment between two people can be evaluated and entered into in less than ten months time. Even then, only in years hence are certain traits exposed or come into play.

To achieve higher expressions of relating to your sexuality, we suggest you work to evolve above and beyond the influences and persuasions of your hormones. True, this requires that you exercise self-discipline, awareness, objectivity, and restraint, but this is what self-mastery and spiritual soul evolution are all about.

The misuse of sexual energy has pulled Participants off the track, gotten them confused, and has caused the greatest problems. When you have these energies in balance and use them properly, everything in your life works smoothly and wonderfully. However, unless you are centered and grounded, it is easy for the sexual energies to pull you emotionally off balance. By placing inordinate importance upon, or becoming addicted to sex, Participants have become trapped in their sensual-emotional natures, and have found it very difficult to escape and evolve to the higher, spiritual dimcons.

When two Participants come together in body, mind, and spirit, they indeed have made a contract with spirit. They may not realize it in their mind or other natures, but they have made an agreement. If they choose to break their agreement, they should make it a clean break, separate, and go their individual ways. Each may then attract another polarized mate that can aid in the balance of body, mind, and spirit.

Generally, if one of the parties to this sacred union has a sexual affair with a third party, the power bond between the two original mates is shattered, and the power link between them is greatly diminished.

There can be exceptions in this circumstance. One occurs when a karmic encounter is required to bring loving closure to an intimate past-life relationship—even in the middle of a Participant's current primary relationship. A story that illustrates this situation is presented in the book by author Robert James Waller, *The Bridges of Madison County,* and the subsequent motion picture of the same title. This type of encounter, the totality of which covers a period of only three or four days, is guided by spirit and brings loving closure to a past-life intimate relationship that had previously ended on a discordant note. The intense feelings of Love that emanate from such an encounter remain with the Participants throughout their current lifetimes and beyond.

Another exception occurs when a third party engages in a love affair with one of the partners in a dedicated relationship to present them with a karmic lesson. This type of situation is usually the result of a past-life love affair situation involving one or more of the Participants that did not end in Love and forgiveness by the other partner. The Participants preplan these karmic situations before they incarnate in their present human bodies.

As one might observe, there are many factors going on behind the scenes of the human drama that are undetectable and unexplainable through the five physical human senses. By applying spiritual insights and principles, these situations can be dealt with in a calm, comfortable, harmonious manner, thereby bringing closure to a karmic situation and lesson.

Indeed, these situations provide an endless supply of challenging learning experiences. How does one tell the difference between a secret affair and a spiritually guided karmic encounter? The aware approach is to first ask your spiritual guidance or Divine Spirit why you, or your mate, met this person, what was the past-life connection, and what is the proper approach to handle this particular situation. You may receive an answer in words or as an image. Also, always stop, check your head-intellect, heart-feelings, and gut-intuition before blundering into a potentially disharmonious situation. As you become more spiritually aware, you can develop your ability to receive immediate answers from your guides or Divine Spirit.

The Phenomena of Energy Exchange

Another topic relating to one's everyday living, and sexuality in particular, is that of *energy exchange*. Every Participant is energy in motion. Any and every action generates energy. Consider two people passing each other on the street. One asks the other for the time of day. The other relays the information. This encounter generates an energy exchange between the two individuals.

A Participant has a long conversation with a friend or relative. There is a stronger energy exchange between the two individuals than in the previous example. When two people engage in sexual intercourse, there is a *very* strong energy exchange between the two. When used consciously and with a focused intention, this energy may be directed to fulfill a need, accomplish a goal, or help another Participant, for example.

Of course this raises a pertinent question, particularly regarding casual sex. What types of energies are being exchanged between you and the other person? What energies are you absorbing? Do you know that these energies or traits may stay with you for a period of time? The technique of aura cleansing, performed by a specialized practitioner, may be useful to transmute either your or another's disharmonious vibrations and energy patterns. You may also use technique #7 described on page 170, adapting it to this situation.

Honoring Your Chosen Sexuality

Before a Participant took possession of their present physical body, they planned this lifetime and chose their sex—male or female. (For karmic reasons, there may occur a physical or psychological combination of the two, as in a hermaphrodite or a person born with a bi-sexual orientation). Before inhabiting their new body, Participants make an agreement with the Board of Karma that they will accept and work with their chosen sexuality, and not resist or disclaim it. Some Participants, however, upon incarnating in the material body, forget their agreement and endeavor to modify or reverse their chosen sexuality.

From a spiritual perspective, homosexual or bisexual relationships do not generate spiritual power. Perceptions to the contrary are illusions. Participants with a homosexual or bisexual orientation are functioning in the third dimcon, continuing to work on their Search for Self. Participants may graduate into the fourth dimcon only when at least 90% of all issues concerning their Search for Self have been resolved.

As with heterosexual promiscuity obsessions, homosexual or bisexual inclinations or preferences are usually carried over from previous lifetimes and are, thereby, ingrained in the Participant's mindset, DNA, and soul programming. As with any other habit or addiction, a great expense of effort and constant vigilance are required to transmute this programming. Each subsequent lifetime then becomes an opportunity for a Participant to transmute these dispositions into a purely monogamous, heterosexual orientation. The primary thrust of a single Earth lifetime may be devoted to transcending this and other blocks to one's spiritual soul evolution.

Expressing Your Sexuality Responsibly

The original intent was that sexuality be used wisely and responsibly. If you are not in a position, or do not desire to be a father or mother to a child, question the wisdom of engaging in sexual intercourse. Exercising abstinence is likely indicated, especially for adolescent youths. Clear thinking, the exercising of one's willpower, and the mastery of one's emotions are always precursors to correct action.

Using birth control methods to prevent conception is assuming responsibility for your sexuality. If there is a soul waiting or destined to be born to a particular female, usually by prior agreement, either the mother-to-be will know this intuitively and refrain from using birth control procedures, or the new soul will circumvent the birth control measures and be conceived in spite of them.

When Participants choose to engage in sexual activity, they must assume the responsibilities associated with their actions. Also, even when birth control methods are used, the chance always exists that conception will still take place. In the case of conception due to rape or incest, the wise question to be asked of your or another's Higher Self or Divine Spirit is, "What is my or the other Participant's, karma from a previous lifetime that attracted this experience?"

Also, Participants change sexes between their various incarnations—from male to female and female to male—to learn certain lessons and play out their karma. There are no accidents in this regard.

For instance, the man who engages in the sexual assault of a woman, will, in a future life, reincarnate as a woman, to thereby experience the implications of his previous actions. Remember that karma is life, and life is karma. This does not mean that all rapes are karmic, for perhaps the woman did not take proper precautions or ask for spiritual guidance and protection. Also, a woman may sometimes sacrifice her life to benefit humanity, and progress her own soul evolution. In such cases, however, she may still have the trauma of the experience to release in a future lifetime.

From a spiritual perspective, abortion is not an acceptable method of birth control. The general karmic rule is that if a woman has an abortion, she will either be sterile the rest of this lifetime, or in her next lifetime. Perhaps by prior mutual agreement (for karmic or other reasons), there was a soul desiring this particular woman to be its mother. If a woman is considering having an abortion, it is preferable she ask her Higher Self and Divine Spirit if under the circumstances, this is a karma-free, acceptable course of action for her to take.

Perhaps you can see the folly in the actions of a woman who is unable to conceive a child, or a couple wherein the man is sterile, attempting to circumvent their karma by using artificial or surrogate means to have a child. Some scientific procedures to induce conception have produced an instant karmic response by giving the woman more than she asked for—quintuples or sextuplets. Circumvent karma in this lifetime, and you only postpone it to be repeated in a future incarnation.

– 16 –

YOUR RELATIONSHIP TO THE OTHER KINGDOMS ON PLANET EARTH

Until he extends the circle of his compassion to all living things, man himself will not find peace. Albert Schweitzer

On Planet Earth, there are four basic kingdoms which function through their respective levels of consciousness:
1. The Mineral Kingdom, which has a first-dimensional consciousness
2. The Vegetable Kingdom, which also has a first-dimensional consciousness
3. The Animal Kingdom, functioning through the second dimcon
4. The Human Kingdom, the majority of which has a third-dimensional consciousness, with several thousand people functioning through a fourth-dimensional or higher, spiritual consciousness

Each of these kingdoms relates to Earth's environment through their own mind category, soul programming, and level of understanding. Each kingdom has its own evolutionary path toward which they are striving to attain the next, higher dimcon.

The Mineral Kingdom of Mother Earth

Participants functioning through the third-dimensional intellectual mind have difficulty relating to the idea that the Mineral Kingdom, which appears inanimate to the five physical senses, is indeed alive, is conscious, has intelligence, and possesses its own unique type of soul. Actually, this kingdom is supported by a myriad of nature spirits, devas, and angels. From the magnificent vistas of rock formations to the beauties of natural stones, geodes, and gemstones, the Mineral Kingdom provides humanity with much beauty and enjoyment.

This whole planet, Mother Earth, is an intelligent organism, and has an evolving soul with its own evolutionary pattern. Participants have caused themselves many problems because they have not respected and acted responsibly towards Mother Earth and the various kingdoms she supports.

A Universal Principle states, "If you take something from any kingdom, you must give something back in return." When being given something or taking something from a kingdom, the very least that is expected is a simple "thank you," delivered with feelings of love and appreciation. An example of this is saying "grace" at mealtime, thanking the beings that produced the food for their efforts. Where individuals or business enterprises harvest the fruits of a kingdom for personal use or monetary gain, wisdom dictates they return a portion of their benefits to the various kingdoms functioning on the Earth.

For inner peace and harmony, Mother Nature requires that portions of her natural wild aspects—beautiful plains, forests, mountains, canyons, and deserts—be set aside for her peace and solitude. These primeval areas are best isolated from the intrusions of humanity and industrial operations. National and State Parks and Forests, so chosen for their natural beauty, old growth woodlands, and other sensitive features, are intended to serve this purpose.

When the inherent unity of humanity with the kingdoms of Mother Earth is not appreciated and respected, the forces of nature revolt by causing earthquakes, hurricanes, tornados, and even oil spills from tankers. When human beings learn to live in harmony with themselves and with nature, these disruptive conditions will not happen.

Whenever there is a conflict between groups of people, whether it be wars, or even the polarization of spectators at an athletic event bent on having their favored team win, strains and stresses are placed upon the Planet. Thoughts are things that have far-reaching effects. More harmony will prevail on Planet Earth when disputes were settled peacefully, and when sports fans say, "May today's best team be the winner!"

The Vegetable Kingdom

Nothing will benefit human health and increase chances for survival of life on Earth as much as the evolution to a vegetarian diet. Albert Einstein

The nature spirits, devas, and angels of the Vegetable Kingdom extend their love to humanity by supplying it with a wide variety of resources and pleasures. Its plants supply food products for animals and humans, its trees provide timber, and the variety and colorful beauty of its plants and flowers provide Participants with much enjoyment. The Vegetable Kingdom also supplies the Animal and Human Kingdoms with a continual fresh supply of oxygen, a necessary element for their bodily existence.

The forests and grasslands have endured the most abuse by humanity. Trees are a replenishable resource when properly managed. The practice of clear-cutting a forest (cutting down all of the trees in a large area or mountainside leaving only stumps and bare ground) has been especially devastating to the Vegetable kingdom. It is one thing to spot cut mature trees in a forest for their log and lumber uses, thereby leaving a large percentage of the trees still standing. It is something else entirely to clear-cut and destroy a whole forest.

The clear-cutting of forests may be financially and economically effective, however, this practice utterly destroys a forest, and eliminates the nature spirits and devas that produced the timber to begin with.

Where the replanting of trees is required, it is preferable to do so with the same variety as those harvested, thereby restoring the forest's original natural beauty.

As the human race seeks to evolve to higher modes of expression, the adaptation of its appetites and bodily nutritional requirements to a vegetarian, vegan, or raw foods diet would facilitate its spiritual advancement. Fruits, nuts, and vegetables contain a full range of vitamins, minerals, and enzymes. Digestive and systemic enzymes are vital to the youth, vitality, energy, healing, and maintenance of every human body organ and function. However, cooking temperatures over 112° F. destroy enzyme activity. If in harmony with your nutritional requirements, a raw foods diet can be especially beneficial for the rejuvenation and longevity of your material body. Many recipe books are available on the subjects of vegetarian, vegan, and raw foods cuisine, to assist you in making healthy, tasty, palatable dishes.

The Animal Kingdom

As long as men massacre animals, they will kill each other. Indeed, he who sows the seeds of murder and pain cannot reap the joy of Love.
Pythagoras

Animals dominated Planet Earth long before *Homo Sapiens* arrived on the scene. The animals were created to reflect the beauty of the Absolute through their unique life expressions. As humanity evolved, it was given stewardship over the animals with the responsibility of being their protectors and guardians. It was intended that the Animal Kingdom progress its soul evolution by emulating the love and guidance bestowed on them by their human counterparts. As has been necessary, they have been a source of tools, clothing, and food. Some species have been companions for humanity.

The animal kingdom was put on Earth for the same reason the human kingdom exists on this planet—to evolve through learning the lessons of love. Observe the higher range of the animal kingdom, the loving, domesticated cats and dogs. On the other end of the spectrum, observe the savage prey animals. Note that under conditions of duality, humans have a similar range of consciousness—wild, angry, and violent in the lower forms and loving, peace-seeking, and harmless in the more evolved Participants.

The indigenous Native Americans reverently honored and prayed to the animal soul before going on a hunt. They thanked the Animal Kingdom and asked its permission and forgiveness for sacrificing some of their fold to supply food, clothing, and tools to their more intelligent human guardians. These original Americans honored, loved, and respected the Animal Kingdom on which they depended for their survival.

It is an acceptable action for Participants to hunt down and kill wild animals as a food source out of the necessity for survival. However, to kill animals for fun, adventure, sport, recreation, and trophies especially, is out of harmony with the Laws of the Universe. Alternatively, photographing various aspects of the Animal Kingdom on film with still, motion, and video cameras is fun and adventurous recreation that is in harmony with natural Law.

All Participants need to work together to bring themselves into harmony with the Laws of Nature. Humanity has induced fear in animals by terrorizing and killing them. As it encompasses evolving souls, the Animal Kingdom must be awarded the Love and respect it deserves. Humanity's goal is to acquire a reverence for life—to become harmless. To achieve this, it is desirable that all humans assist each other to be more Loving and live in peace and harmony—together, and with *all* of Nature.

The souls of four-legged, warm-blooded animals function at the higher levels of the second dimension of consciousness, very close to the Human Kingdom. Loving, domesticated pets are at the highest level. Human beings occupy sophisticated animal bodies, there being only a relatively small difference in genes between them. The upper part of the Animal Kingdom and the Human Kingdom itself, are very close in their soul vibrations.

The souls of all life forms on Planet Earth, and throughout the Universe, are continually climbing the evolutionary ladder leading to higher levels of awareness, understanding, and expression. The animal souls have their own evolutionary purpose and destiny and were created to evolve into the Human Kingdom. The higher, more evolved essences of animal group souls eventually become new, individualized human souls.

For this reason, it is preferable that human Participants eat a vegetarian diet, including little or no meat of the four-legged, warm-blooded animals. At times, some human bodies require two to four ounces of animal meat at a meal to balance their thyroid energies or fulfill other bodily requirements. The meat of fish and poultry may still be considered part of a vegetarian (albeit not vegan) diet, as these animals' soul vibrations are more distanced from the Human Kingdom.

Your Responsibility to Planet Earth

Planet Earth has supported a multitude of life forms for billions of years. If it is going to continue to provide these experiences, it is desirable that Participants develop a long-term outlook towards maintaining Earth's beautiful and productive environmental resources.

It is the responsibility of the Participants functioning on each dimcon to assist progressing the soul evolution of the life forms on dimcons of lower vibration. The evolution of the Earth soul is dependent upon the evolution of the human Participants. Earth cannot evolve to a higher dimcon unless a majority of the human race itself evolves.

The disharmony inherent in duality greatly disturbs Mother Earth and her soul, as exhibited by the number of fires, earthquakes, volcanic eruptions, hurricanes, and floods that are being experienced on her surface. Even oil spills and other ecological disasters have been a manner in which Mother Earth attempts to admonish Participants to give something back for what they have taken, and to stop robbing the planet of all its natural beauty and resources.

We remind you that the Law of Harmony and the Law of Karma and Reincarnation are always in effect and operative throughout every life experience. There are severe karmic penalties for Participants who misuse and abuse the Mineral, Vegetable, and Animal Kingdoms. Limitless Total Love means honoring and respecting all forms of life, for all life is God.

Participants are learning to use common sense when interrelating with the cycles of Mother Nature. As with everything else in the universe, Nature has its own cycles. There are cycles of hot and cold, wet and dry, windy and calm, expansion and contraction. To farm on the rich soil of a flood plane is ideal, but to also live there invites disaster.

All Participants have the duty and responsibility to be more sensitive to the true range and measure of *their real* needs and the needs of the planet they inhabit. Participants must take into account the future needs of their descendants by limiting their present consumption and by replacing outmoded, resource-wasting technology with more advanced conservation techniques. Remember, you are your own ancestors and most people will be your own descendants. Under what conditions would you desire to live in the future?

- 17 -

ADDING THE MISSING INGREDIENT

Two thousand years ago, a Word was disclosed as the secret of transforming yourself and the world to a higher, spiritual level of consciousness. What was that word? **Love!**

The admonitions were:

Love God with all your heart, with all your soul, with all your mind, and with all your strength.

Love one another. Love your neighbor as you love yourself.

[These statements imply that you first develop and deepen Loving yourself, for you are the highest aspect of Self, The Absolute.]

Love your enemies [who in reality are your brothers and sisters, and yourself].

Generally, Participants in this Planet Earth Educational Expedition have been quite successful in developing their intellectual minds and exercising their willpower. What Participants have been challenged to achieve, though, is the acquisition and expression of true Limitless Total Love. To be a well-rounded Participant, however, requires that you work toward bringing your Mind, Will, and Feeling natures into an equal, harmonious balance.

It appears that most Participants on Planet Earth lack awareness of what the word "Love" really means, and how to relate to it. To the intellectual mind, the above directives regarding Love do not make sense when an apparently hostile situation is staring you in the face. Why? Because Love is not an intellectual concept. Love is a *feeling* that comes from one's spiritual Heart. Not only is Love a feeling, Love is a *Power*—a power so paramount, that it produced the Universe, and everything and everyone in it. Through meditation and the use of constructive affirmations such as "I am Love," the expression of Limitless Total Love that you radiate in your life will vastly increase.

What does the statement "Love one another" mean? This is a very broad subject that can encompass a whole volume in itself. We offer a few basic ideas you can practice in your daily life:

1. Exhibit respect for all Participants and everything created.
2. Provide appropriate assistance to others, within your ability to respond to a given situation.
3. Through your example, and by offering suggestions, assist others to diminish their fears, raise their consciousness, and act in the highest manner that they know. Thereby, everyone's soul evolution progresses.

Limitless Total Love is a spiritual quality, a Quality of The Absolute. The Universe, with its twelve realms and thirteen dimcons, was created through the principles of Life, Light, and Love. Love is a transformational power. Love has the power to produce anything—a substance, an object, or effect—where nothing existed before. Love can transform fear into Trust. Love is the greatest comforter.

When thoughts, words, and actions are encompassed in Love, there is harmony. Actions that lack the quality of Love invariably result in disharmony. Love can transmute disharmony into harmony. Love has the ability to disarm evil. Love can tame the Beast—within others, and within yourself. There are no limits to the transformational power of Love.

Although we were all created out of Love, how to Love, how to consciously produce the *feeling* of Love at will, is the major learning task of each Participant throughout their Planet Earth sojourns. With continual practice, the expression and transmission of Love eventually becomes an automatic response to any and all situations. Your goal is for Limitless Total Love to become an integral component of all your thoughts, words, and actions.

The Role of Love in Your Soul Evolution

Soul evolution is a rung-by-rung process up the long, high-reaching ladder of spiritual progress. Soul evolution involves realizing a more accurate truth today than you knew yesterday, and then applying this higher truth in your life. Trekking along the spiritual path, your first steps involve the learning and understanding of various spiritual principles and truths. Your next steps comprise implementing these truths and principles in your outer world of tangible reality.

As you toil farther along the path, you learn that spiritual truths and principles, like thoughts, are *things*. Since nothing can exist outside of infinity—The All—these truths and principles are *alive* and have an infinite life and existence of their own. The most effective way of implementing these spiritual Principles in your daily life is, through meditation, *to become these Principles.* In particular we are referring to the Primary Principles of Life, Light, and Love, and the Personal Principles of Trust, Confidence, Knowing, Courage, and Fortitude.

This being a new, unique approach to perceiving the inner realities of life on this planet, your intuition may tell you one thing, and your intellectual mind may attempt to negate your progress by telling you that you are crazy. This is because your intellectual mind cannot easily relate to abstract, intangible concepts.

Since your intuitive mind knows better, it is up to you to direct your *willpower* toward transcending the theatrical façade of material reality by focusing your attention on new, higher, transcendental realizations. It is all a matter of perception. What made sense to you yesterday, no longer makes sense to you today. What was previously a reality, no longer has quite the same glitter and shine. Old concepts begin to tarnish in the light of new, higher perspectives.

Eventually, you will no longer look outside yourself for the Higher Source of who you are. You then realize that *you are that Higher Source.* You simply need to reprogram your brain-mind and psyche to come into alignment with your new, developing self-image.

During your daily meditation time, you can very effectively facilitate this reprogramming by—

1. raising your consciousness to a higher vibrational frequency—to your Higher Self, the consciousness of your soul, or better yet, your Divine Spirit.
2. stating, with *feeling,* constructive statements to implant and reinforce your new paradigm like, "I Am That I Am!" "I Am the infinite, creative, primordial Light of God The Absolute." "I Am all Life. ... I Am all Light. ... I Am all Love. ..."
3. concluding your meditation by sitting in silence for twenty minutes or more, whereupon your spiritual guides may assist you in your transformation.

Repeat this process daily over an extended period, ideally, the rest of your bodily lifetime on this planet. *The Basic Consciousness Raising Meditation* on the compact disc included with this field guide is specifically designed to assist you in this regard.

The next step is for you to apply these new philosophical concepts, particularly Limitless Total Love, to the practical realities of your daily life. To implement this, ask yourself appropriate questions, like, "On a Love-based planet how would I handle this unexpected condition with which I am now confronted?" "How can I transform this difficult situation so that it is resolved in Love for the greater good and evolution of everyone concerned?" Simply put, "How can I resolve this situation in Limitless Total Love?"

Everyone, particularly those attempting to restrain your spiritual progress, may not be entirely comfortable with your decision to progress your soul evolution. However, Total Love does not require you to please another Participant at your own expense. You are free to choose your own life path.

Your giving something to another Participant is a choice. However, for one's own soul evolution, everyone needs to help themselves to the best of their abilities. It is admirable to help another when they are down and need a lift; but if by assisting another to the point whereby they do not attempt to help themselves, you can end up taking on the other person's karma.

One perception of Total Love is: Giving another not what *they* think they need, and not what *you* think they need, but what they *really* need. This may take some reflection on your part. However, your intuition and gut-level feelings will invariably give you an answer. There are times when a Participant needs to learn through experiencing a hard lesson. Examples are prison sentences for criminal offenses; dissolving an abusive partnership; the refusal of further financial support for individuals who have the ability—but are reluctant—to sustain themselves.

The more consciously you attempt to focus on expressing Limitless Total Love in all aspects of your life, the more quickly you will evolve to higher dimcons of experience.

- 18 -

TRANSFORMATION

Now is the time for many to step off the merry-go-round and free themselves from reincarnating on Planet Earth.

With the Aquarian Age bringing in increasingly higher transformative energies, a tremendous opportunity now exists for a great many Participants in this Planet Earth Educational Adventure to realize their true natures, spiritual potentials, and cosmic destinies. Through the marvels of modern-day communications, new and more accurate perceptions of reality can travel around the planet at lightning speed. However, simply acquiring information and knowledge is not enough. Spiritual progress and soul evolution do not take place unconsciously. Since you are the actor on the stage of your life, you will attain your spiritual goals only if you apply the utmost thought, willpower and feeling towards your transformation.

This lifetime is your opportunity to transform whatever disharmonious traits you acquired in the past, and apply more accurate concepts and spiritual techniques in your life. You can thereby substantially progress your soul evolution.

As everyone is unique, no two souls are ever exactly at the same place in their evolution. It is not realistic to expect that all Participants on Planet Earth can achieve a fourth-dimensional consciousness within this lifetime. New experiences, the development of the intuitive mind and the learning of various third-dimensional lessons all take time, perhaps requiring many future lifetimes. What matters is that every person strives to perform in the highest manner of which they are capable, whatever their present level of consciousness.

As with the achievement of any goal, advancement along the spiritual path requires dedication, study, and practice. A major step forward is the completion of 90% of your Search for Self. The Search for Self begins to accelerate when one comes to the realization that, as an individual, they are something far greater than the short-lived material awareness of their brain-mind consciousness.

When one can view themselves as a vast energy field that encompasses and interpenetrates everything in the Universe, they have achieved a self-image that is more in harmony with their true divine nature. The conclusive step is to identify yourself as One with The Absolute, the Source from which everything is but a vibratory extension. You thereby Know that you are One with not only The Absolute, but with all of creation.

One technique to facilitate the resolution of your Search for Self is to repeat with *feeling,* affirmations such as, "I Am That I Am. I Am the Absolute experiencing Planet Earth as (your name). I Am The All." To achieve any goal, such as acquiring a fourth-dimensional consciousness, one must constantly think, envision, feel, and know that they are *already there*—in the *Now*.

When this first Search is sufficiently completed, the next quest is your Search for Truth. Your personal truths are what you tell yourself they are. Spiritual advancement simply involves seeking a clearer understanding, aligning yourself with higher spiritual realities, and then practicing and living your new truths daily.

Although clear analytical thinking is advantageous, spiritual understanding is not solely an intellectual process. The intellect serves a particular purpose in assisting Participants to sort through the myriad of seemingly conflicting philosophical ideas and concepts. However, the intellect alone cannot bring you to the inner realization of higher, more accurate truths. It is only through your intuition and the Knowing of your spiritual Heart that a spiritual truth may be identified, confirmed, and then realized.

The intention is that you evolve beyond the dense atmosphere of Planet Earth. This planet was never intended to be your final destination. There are more beautiful and expansive environments ahead on higher vibrations of expression. Since your material, etheric, and astral bodies are physical, the true divinity of your being is more fully reflected and expressed when functioning through a spiritual body. This is what Participants of this Planet Earth Educational Expedition are working toward—functioning through their Body of Light.

Along the path of soul evolution, each Participant takes one step at a time, for one cannot jump levels or dimcons without first experiencing them. It is required that you work through your lessons and pass the tests that each level offers. The more you take steps to expand your spiritual awareness in this lifetime, the more wisely you will be able to plan your next incarnation.

There is a vast expansion in a beings' spiritual awareness between the third and the fourth dimcons. Through their more developed intuitive minds, Participants with fourth-dimensional consciousnesses are able to accurately comprehend the abstract nature of their existence. Also, these Participants can more readily communicate with spiritual beings beyond the confines of the tangible Earth environment. Many other spiritual talents are developed and expressed in the fourth dimcon.

To achieve a fourth-dimensional consciousness, it is not sufficient to simply lead a "good life" and do all the "right" things. Awareness, discernment, and a minimal amount of wisdom are necessary requirements for Participants desiring to graduate to the fourth dimcon.

A major step toward acquiring a spiritual consciousness is to identify with your **Higher Self** soul consciousness This is accomplished through meditation. It is very important to consciously connect with this higher aspect of your individualized nature.

Your **Divine Spirit** is the highest aspect of your individualized being. It is your personal genie that is able to provide your needs, heal your physical body, and dissolve impurities, blocks, and imbalances. As a Participant in this Cosmic plan, your ultimate destiny relates to the evolution of *consciousness,* the objective being total union with your Divine Spirit, and then the Unity Point at the level of the thirteenth dimcon.

In the fourth dimcon, one is just getting their feet wet regarding the practical use of spiritual principles. When you attempt to manifest your needs and desires from this level of consciousness on Earth, much Patience, Persistence, and Perseverance is required.

You will get the most out of this lifetime only if you attack it aggressively. Awaken the Sleeping Giant within you. Here are some suggestions and techniques to assist you in working toward the achievement of a fourth-dimensional consciousness:

1. Meditate daily for twenty minutes or more. Devote at least five minutes in praying for the transformation of Planet Earth to a Love-based planet.
2. Be aware of your flaws and work areas. Direct your willpower and feelings toward turning your weaknesses into strengths.
3. Understand the nature and function of your soul and become aware of areas that require reprogramming and blocks that need dissolving.
4. Be conscious of all emotional reactions within yourself and act to transform their cause. Become the actor on the stage of life, not the re-actor.
5. Act only in harmony with yourself and with others in ways that will progress your soul evolution.
6. Consciously develop your intuitive mind.
7. Observe your dreams and record them in a journal.
8. See and feel yourself as a spiritual being, directly connected from your human mind/lower self, to your soul's Higher Self, your spirit Highest Self, the Manifest, The Creator, and The Absolute.
9. Practice living in Limitless Total Love. Learn to *feel* Limitless Total Love at will and consciously project it towards all life, seen and unseen.

10. Assume total responsibility for your life, including everything that you do or that happens to you. Look for the inner cause of adversity, even though the outer cause may not appear to be your conscious creation.
11. Become harmless, respecting all life for its own unique place in the process of soul evolution. Treat nature and all animals in a respectful, loving, humane manner.
12. See and feel yourself in the unity and oneness of all of life and all that exists.
13. Be happy and cheerful, excited and enthusiastic about Life. Do not permit yourself to feel unhappy or depressed.
14. Develop a sense of Power that arises when you are in harmony with the highest spiritual truths.
15. Always live in and demonstrate the highest standards that you know.
16. Reach for your highest potentials.

The basic reason you were created as an individualized aspect of The Absolute is to contribute to the wisdom of the whole—The All. The greatest role you can perform in a lifetime is to be of service to others. You accomplish this by being compassionate towards everyone, by sending Love to others and to the Earth, and by assisting others to progress their soul evolution, either through your example, or through your welcomed suggestions.

Be particularly aware of influences or situations that either raise your vibrations or lower them. Remember that everything vibrates—thoughts, feelings, colors, sounds, rhythms, atoms. Things that may raise your vibrations are calming—mellow new age or classical music; spending time in the trees, meadows, lakes, streams, and seashores of nature; quiet, peaceful buildings; the companionship of compatible friends. Situations that tend to lower your vibrations are those in which you feel your inner nature being crushed by disharmony—situations that appeal to the gratification one's lower, sensual nature, whether it be through sight, sounds, emotions, or actions.

Endeavor to express the will of your higher God-self through your thoughts, words, and actions. Maximize your potential by putting theory and knowledge into practice. Sit down at the control module of your life and *take charge!*

Become multisensory by working to integrate and balance your left and right brain functions—your intellect and your intuition. You thereby go beyond your five physical senses to receive the answers to your questions, and to relate to the world, and the Universe in general.

Continually ask yourself, "Are my thoughts, words, and actions creating harmony or disharmony?" "What will be the karmic consequences if I pursue this particular course of action?" "Is this situation going to serve my best interests?" "How will this person fit into my life at this time?" Listen to your intuition and your gut feeling for the answers.

This is an individual trip. Nobody is going to raise your consciousness except YOU. Yet, at the same time, this is a group effort. When you feel blocked, ask for assistance. All Participants need to assist one another when appropriate. Seek out good friends to get constructive feedback regarding your experiences, and discuss how to put spiritual theories to practical use.

Life is an interesting paradox. Within the infinite spectrum of consciousness, you are "i," the personality, and "I," the Godhead. You are not just a *part* of this spectrum, you are the whole spectrum, all of the "time." This is what is meant when we say, "Besides simply having a material experience, you are an infinite being having an infinite experience. You are The All." To reinforce this concept in your mind and your being, state to yourself, "I Am infinite! I Am The All!" When you make this statement you are affirming a higher, spiritual truth.

No one in the whole Universe is greater than you. Likewise, no one is lesser than you. No one is greater or lesser than anyone else. Status is an illusion. With focus, study, dedication, and practice, you can achieve anything you desire, including the advancement of your soul evolution. To realize this, and then think, feel, and act in harmony with your Self—the highest Principles of The Absolute—is what soul evolution is all about.

Your Relationship to Government

You are a sovereign being, not because the Constitution or some law says so, but because that is your intrinsic nature as God The Absolute. The founders of America, now a union of 50 sovereign states, affirmed this principle in the Declaration of Independence of 1776 which stated:

> "We hold these truths to be self-evident, that all men are created equal, that they are endowed by their Creator with certain unlienable [sic] [incapable of being surrendered or transferred] Rights, that among these are Life, Liberty, and the pursuit of Happiness. That to secure these rights, Governments are instituted among Men, deriving their just powers from the consent of the governed."

Ever since this Declaration and the Constitution of the united States of America were ratified, there has been a concerted effort to subvert them—by non-spiritual individuals seeking power and control of the people. Thomas Jefferson had warned against this possibility. America originated as a **republic,** wherein the people are sovereign over the government. Since then, through legal and legislative manipulations, America is now a **democracy,** wherein the people are *citizens*—subjects of the government. The simple truth is that you are still a sovereign, but you need to reclaim and reestablish your *legal* sovereignty.

On Love-based planets, people in government have but one objective—to assist all life forms in the progression of their soul evolution. There are no professional politicians, as everyone volunteers for various roles and shares in the tasks. Man-made rules and court systems do not exist, for everyone lives in Limitless Total Love, respecting each other's free will, their person, and property. Peace and harmony prevail.

The Magical Qualities of Total Love

If you believe what I tell you,
you can do works greater than I have done.

Do you desire to create a harmonious, Loving, compassionate atmosphere in your personal universe? Would you like to rise above the commonly accepted human condition and live a truly gratifying, magical life, filled with wonderment and contentment?

How is this possible? By identifying with your true, Highest nature, and then implementing these Principles in your life. Earlier in this book we listed the Three Primary Principles of God The Absolute, who is *you*. Are you applying these Principles in your life? Have you become these Principles? *Are* you these Principles—*Now?*

Are you *thinking* only thoughts and using words that will bring you what you want—thoughts and words that are constructive, harmonious, and in line with your real needs and desires?

Are you using your *willpower* to direct your thoughts in a manner that will bring peace and harmony not only to your personal world, but to the lives of others?

To manifest the outcomes you desire, are you combining the *feeling* of Limitless Total Love with your thoughts and willpower?

Yes, that missing ingredient in the magical soup is Limitless Total Love. Total Love is so powerful that even expressing it alone, without a directed thought, can produce miracles. This has been demonstrated many times through documented experiments in which Participants sent Love to individuals in need of healing, either to enhance conventional medical techniques, or to be used in place of them. In some studies, it was found that the most effective technique was to be non-specific as to the outcome—a person received healing by simply receiving non-directional thoughts and feelings of Limitless Love. Thereby, the healing powers throughout the Universe did their job by bringing the person back into wholeness.

Basically, there are five principles behind the working of any "miracles"—instant healing, instant manifestation, levitation, invisibility, teletransportation, etc. These Principles are—

Oneness – Seeing, Feeling, and Knowing that you are The All.
You are The Absolute, The Creator, The Manifest.
You are One with all **Life** in the Universe.

Focused thought (Mind) – Being able to concentrate your attention on one specific idea for five minutes or more without allowing distractions.

Willpower – Visualizing your dynamic energy radiating throughout the Universe.

Limitless Total Love – You *are* LTL. You radiate LTL to the whole Universe.

Knowing – You have mastered Trust, Confidence, Knowing, Courage, and Fortitude. You Know that you Know, thereby transcending doubt and fear.

The mastery of these, and other Principles take dedication and perseverance to accomplish. Just Know that anyone and everyone can achieve this mastery over the material plane either in this lifetime, or in a future lifetime. Nothing is impossible when you identify with your True Self. "I Am The All! I Am All that exists!"

Establishing the Golden Age Upon the Earth

Within the infinite Universe, all time is measured in what those on Earth best relate to as "cycles." There are the cycles of expansion and the cycles of contraction; cycles of devolution and of evolution; cycles of separation from the will of The Creator, and of again returning to the harmony of the will of our own God-Self.

The time has now arrived for Planet Earth to return to the oneness of the Whole. Many universal and galactic cycles have simultaneously culminated to effect this change. In accordance with the Procession of the Equinoxes, Planet Earth is now entering the Aquarian Age, a vibration which represents the freedom and independence of the individual, and fellowship and harmony among humanity. These powerful influences are intended to assist all beings on all realms to evolve to higher modes of expression on their paths to eventually be totally unified with their Divine Spirits.

The prospect for a Golden Age on Planet Earth is likely, but is going to manifest only if Earth becomes a Love-based, spiritual planet. The two prerequisites to facilitate this are: 1) that a majority of humanity decrees and prays for the transformation of the Earth to that of a Love-based planet, and 2) that a sufficient number of Participants achieve a fourth-dimensional consciousness.

Any form of prayer for the transformation of Earth is acceptable. However, **fewer words produce greater focus, and when combined with the visualization of golden-white Light and the *feeling* of Limitless Total Love, together they produce tremendous power.**

Therefore, we offer the following technique as a suggestion:

1. Raise your consciousness to your Divine Spirit, or higher.
2. Visualize your representation of Planet Earth either through your third eye, or the planet as centered in the radiant, infinite point in the middle of your head.
3. Next, visualize and *feel* the Earth enveloped in a blazing sun of golden-white Light and Love. Say, **"To all Life on Planet Earth, I radiate Light, Love, Peace, and Harmony."**
4. Then, for a suggested period of five minutes, continue the visualization of Earth dissolved in a blaze of golden-white Light, and repeat with *feeling* every 30 seconds or so, **"Only Limitless Total Love, *now* exists on Planet Earth."**

Collectively, you are the Gods of Planet Earth. If Planet Earth is to become a Love-based planet, only you can make it happen. Respecting your free will, beings with higher consciousnesses outside of this planet will assist you only if their help is requested.

All progress in life comes down to the individual. Everyone contributes their own talents, knowledge, and wisdom. The whole is made up of individuals. The more people pulling in the same direction towards Love, Unity, and Oneness, the sooner the Golden Age will manifest.

The basic principle for changing the future is to effect change in the present, for everything is *Now*. If people desire the planet to be a harmonious, constructive place in which to live, everyone needs to present or be presented with images that reflect that reality *Now*.

If you wish the world to be a happier, more secure, and peaceful place to live, then contribute your harmonious energies to effect this goal within yourself as well as the whole world. On a broader scale, it is required that all fear-based organizations and institutions be transformed so as to become Love-based. This will be accomplished as people connected with governments, religions, news and entertainment programming, education, business and industry choose to raise their consciousnesses and act in harmony with the higher, intrinsic nature of their Being.

The way you may contribute to the manifestation of these transformations is to continually ask yourself, "If I am now living in Limitless Total Love, and this is now a Love-based planet, in what manner do I best express myself in the world?" If you desire to change your reality, it is required that you transform the manner in which you relate to your Self, and, thereby, the people and the environment around you.

Once you feel you are achieving more harmony within yourself, and are beginning to express this new Loving paradigm in your daily life, encourage others to do likewise. You then become a beacon of Light and Love shining out to humankind. As the Master Jesus asserted,

"I Am the Light of the World. Follow my example."

Appendix

THE LAWS OF SPIRITUAL ENLIGHTENMENT AND SOUL EVOLUTION

There are twenty-two Laws that govern the spiritual development and progress of Expedition Participants at all phases of soul evolution. And yes, they even apply to the Participants on Planet Earth! These Laws are in constant operation and function to guide and direct your spiritual progress. If you can keep these Laws at the forefront of your awareness, you can precisely chart a course that truly supports the advancement of *your* soul evolution.

In the third dimcon, numerous man-made laws were devised and implemented to help humankind get along with one another. As Participants enter the fourth dimcon, they honor and respect man's applicable rules, but they live totally under God's spiritual Laws.

"There is no justice in this world," is the phrase we often hear from various Expedition Participants. But, once the functions of these Laws are clearly understood, you will see that *perfect justice* permeates the universe. All lessons are learned. All debts paid. All souls eventually evolve.

Following is a brief explanation of eight of these 22 Laws including some of their applications. The basis of this short presentation was a series of monthly lessons over a period of two years channeled by St. Germain, as transmitted through Judith Ann Gordon. The entirety of the explanation of the 22 Laws by St. Germain will be published in a separate book devoted solely to this purpose.

The Law of Total Love

This is the fundamental Law at the basis of the other Laws. Total Love comes from your Higher Self and deep within your heart. It is total, unequivocal acceptance of yourself and of another human being, in a state of total peace and serenity. Total Love is non-judgmental.

You work on Total Love your entire lifetime, for its achievement is the ultimate goal in your soul's evolution. There are times in your life when you think you are living in Total Love, however, your everyday world continually tends to pull you in and out of it, back and forth, like a yo-yo. Ninety-nine percent of the population of this planet are learning, each minute of each day, about Total Love.

It is through the exercise and projection of Total Love that you evolve and become enlightened. Total Love is being filled with happiness and joy in the presence of another with no strings attached, giving those who exhibit disharmonious behavior the benefit of the doubt. Total Love is just being you, blissfully and joyfully; happy with you, happy with the world and happy with those around you, no matter what they do. As this Law has extensive implications, it has been elaborated upon throughout this field guide.

The Law of Karma (Cause and Effect) and Reincarnation

Karma is a Sanskrit word meaning "action," the action of cause and effect. Dharma is your unique soul's path as guided by your Divine Spirit and represents your individual truth. Dharma is your spiritual blueprint for pursuing your soul's destiny.

Karma is the energy of cause and effect you generate as you move along the path prescribed by your dharma. Karma relates to your responses to the situations you encounter as you travel along your path.

Whenever you deviate from your path, you create uncomfortable karma that pushes you back on. When you are following your path, your good karma rewards you and propels you forward.

Karma means that each thought, word, and action you activate in your life eventually returns to you—harmonious or disharmonious, comfortable or stressful. Your karma may not return in exactly the same manner as it went out, but it returns in a manner that emphasizes either your harmonious actions, or an error, in which case it teaches the applicable lesson. For example, reacting to a situation in anger may later result in a tire coming loose from your motor vehicle.

The Law of Karma is related to the Law of Harmony. When a person's actions are disharmonious, the Law of Karma functions to correct the error through an appropriate lesson. Thereby, the situation and the person's psyche is brought back into harmony. Through the Law of Reincarnation one says, "Let's do that last lifetime's lesson over until we get a passing grade!" "Good, we perfected that lifetime's lessons! Next trip to Planet Earth, let us enroll in another subject."

Karma is life, and life is karma. Karma brings you rewards as well as a long list of lessons. You keep learning and repeating your lessons over many lifetimes to bring yourself more into harmony and spiritual excellence. Each time you have reincarnated you have been presented with both old and new lessons to learn. Those lessons you had not mastered in past incarnations receive particular emphasis.

The major lesson The Law of Karma and Reincarnation teaches is that if you act in Total Love, the rewards of Love will return to you.

The Law of Harmony

"What is out of harmony will be brought back into harmony." Harmony is the state of peace, balance, unity, and oneness. It is being in conformity and alignment with the intrinsic qualities of God The Absolute. Balance is staying steady and stabilized on the tightrope representing higher, spiritual ideals, without falling off into the pit of disharmony.

The distinction between harmony and disharmony is based upon the attributes and qualities of God The Absolute, for these are fundamental to our individualized natures. When your thoughts, words, and actions emulate the Qualities of God The Absolute, you are in harmony with yourself and with your spiritual nature.

The populace on Planet Earth must come into harmony before they can move forward into overall, sustained enlightenment. The major areas where humankind's disharmonies exist are through the misuses of money, power, sex, and drugs.

Discernment, self-discipline and Love form the basis of harmony in your life. Discernment is a personal issue. Discernment is viewing yourself in your own reality and learning to know your truth—what is right for you and what is not. Your truth may not be someone else's truth. It is acceptable to redefine your truth when a more comfortable, more accurate truth is presented to you. You will recognize these higher truths as they tend to bring more harmony to situations. Ask yourself, "Is my current truth bringing harmony to this situation, or do I need to find a more constructive approach to achieve this goal?"

The Law of Harmony will always prevail. When you act in disharmony, you will create an appropriate lesson to restore harmony. When you live in harmony, the Law will support you. The purpose of your life is to learn, through your daily experiences, to think, speak, and act in harmony with, and thereby exemplify, the Constant Qualities of Life, Light, and Love. You then not only advance your personal soul evolution, but both directly and indirectly assist others to follow your example.

The Law of Wisdom

Wisdom is that inner Knowing as to what is correct understanding and action. Wisdom transcends karma. It rises up and above any karma, whether from the distant past or the immediate now. In the third dimcon, you may have asked a question and received the answer from spirit in bits and pieces during the course of many hours of meditation. It may have been many months before you had a perspective and a concept of what spirit was trying to tell you.

Wisdom is more plentiful and more readily available once you progress into a fourth-dimensional consciousness. In the fourth dimcon, the reception of Wisdom changes, for it comes to you in bigger pieces along with greater understanding.

In our daily lives, we are all working towards achieving more Wisdom. Besides originating from deep within yourself, you may acquire Wisdom in many ways. It may reach you through someone who shares your spiritual interests, a book you are reading, a motion picture you are watching, or a magazine article you may turn to; anything that might trigger a Knowing in the deeper part of your being. Wisdom makes your lessons much easier to work through.

Any Wisdom that you acquire, in this and previous lifetimes, always remains with you in the depths of your Heart. Each time you move through a difficult lesson, in addition to knowledge, you gain Wisdom. Wisdom is the greatest gift spirit can give you. As you grow and become more aware, the Wisdom you acquire begets more Wisdom.

The Law of Soul Evolution

When expressing through a bodily vehicle, all life forms have some form of cognizant and memory mechanisms through which they think, reason, evaluate present experiences, and recall past events and learning situations. On Earth, animals and human beings have physical brains and thinking minds which serve these purposes.

A soul is both a record keeping and a guidance mechanism. A soul is supplied with a customized basic operating system appropriate to a specific species, which records all the thoughts, feelings, actions, and occurrences experienced by that particular life form.

There are three layers of soul relevant to Planet Earth. The first layer is the soul of Planet Earth itself, from which emanates all spiritual evolution. Very closely bound to the soul of Planet Earth is the soul of the Mineral and the Vegetable Kingdoms. The second layer is the soul of the Animal Kingdom. The third layer is the human soul which has been given intellect, free will, and free choice. Soul also extends to many dimcons beyond this level of physical experience.

On Earth today, human souls have experienced the third dimcon from one to over two hundred lifetimes on this planet. Visualize the range of these souls represented as a bell-shaped curve. (see Diagram J) At one end of that bell curve are the younger souls that have been on Earth approximately one to thirty lifetimes. At the other side of the curve are the older souls that have been here one hundred, two hundred or more lifetimes. It is taking Participants more lifetimes than is necessary to attain a spiritual consciousness.

Diagram J: Current Population Distribution Relative to Number of Lifetimes on Planet Earth

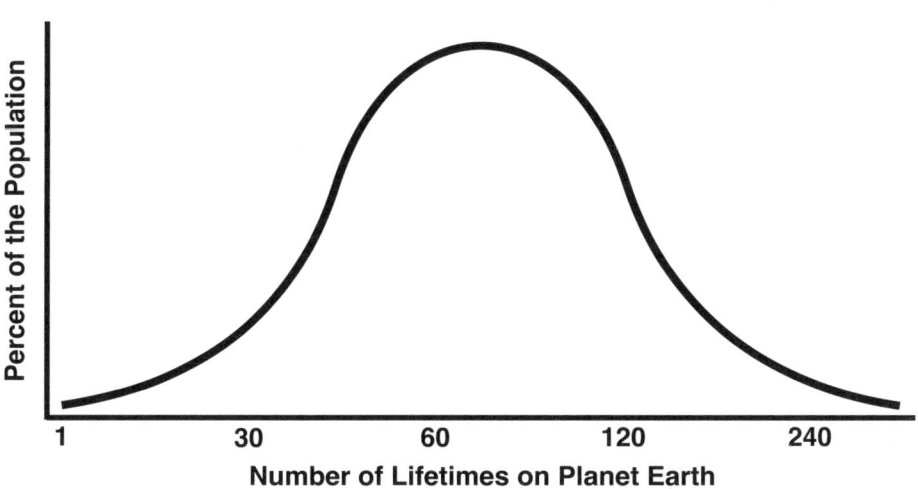

Your Higher Self and Divine Spirit are constantly pushing you to accomplish your maximum potential. If you resist this forward progress, you will experience disharmony in the form of illness, accidents, and robberies. These uncomfortable occurrences are your soul's attempts to get your attention. Realize the importance of following your soul's direction.

It is not enough to live a "goody-two-shoes" lifetime to achieve a spiritual consciousness. You will find it vital to take necessary risks and seek experiences that will allow you to grow and evolve. Your soul knows your divine path. It is so important to meditate, get quiet, centered, and balanced, as this is when your soul can come in and direct you. Upon graduation from Planet Earth, you then experience and evolve up through the spiritual realms and dimcons.

The Law of Free Will

Free will means one's freedom to choose. The Law of Free Will is one with which Participants struggle the most. Do you really have free will? Well, yes and no.

When one is functioning through the third dimcon, situations wherein free will is an issue cause the greatest turmoil and, therefore, receive the greatest consideration. Early in one's life, issues concerning free will are very important. As you move on in life, the Law of Free Will takes on an entirely new perspective, wherein you begin to evaluate the relationship between your will and God's will. You ask, "Am I going to follow God's plan for my life or am I going to go with my plan and my will?"

Through experience you learn that when you are willful about a course of action, things have not gone smoothly and worked out in the best interests of yourself and others. As you evolve, you realize the wisdom in doing the will of your God-self, because it has the insights necessary to constructively direct your life.

As one develops Trust and Love within themselves, their personal will harmonizes and merges with God's will. They become one—fused together. Then, when you are well grounded and very clear, you know what you must do in any facet of your life. When you are one with God and in alignment with your soul and your Higher Self, your choices will always be appropriate to the circumstances.

Each Participant has the God-given right to choose their own future and their own destiny. The greatest evil is for a person to interfere with or obstruct the harmonious exercising of another's free will. In world governments there presently remains a small minority who wishes to control the thoughts and actions of the people. These greedy individuals seek power and control through selfishness, fraud, and violence. This situation will not be allowed to continue. The Law of Free Will always prevails.

The Law of One

This Law is the most vast of the metaphysical Laws for it takes us to the single point of energy in the Universe that is God and All That Is—to the Oneness. What we need to grasp is that we are all part of this Oneness; not separate from it.

Each time you learn a lesson and you take a spiritual step forward on your soul's path to enlightenment, the whole of that Oneness is also elevated to a higher level. Likewise, when you get stuck, fall asleep, or take a step backwards, the greater part, the Oneness, is also pulled down.

This is why your thoughts, words, and actions are so important—for they either elevate The One, or they pull it down. Our greater spiritual responsibility is not only to the self, but to The One, the whole, that greater part.

It is wise to monitor yourself and ask, "Are my thoughts, words, and actions conducive to expanding and uplifting the whole, or will they degrade it and drag it down?" The key is to not participate in negative, detrimental situations, and say, "I choose to not partake in this activity. I choose to stay in peace and go a different way."

The Oneness of which you are a part includes all the solar systems, all galaxies, the entire Universe. Life exists everywhere in the Universe, and the entire Universe is your schoolroom. You need to recognize that the other person is you and you are they. Everyone needs to exercise more caring, Love, and gentleness for all life on Planet Earth.

The Law of Patience, Persistence, and Perseverance

You work with this important Law in your everyday life. The first component of this Law, Patience, has two cousins—Persistence and Perseverance. Patience is that quiet waiting—being calm and peaceful with simply waiting. When you fall into its opposite mode, being impatient, restless, nervous, tense, overbearing, and even obnoxious, you short-circuit whatever you have been asking for or working toward.

The Law of Patience, Persistence, and Perseverance can be continually applied in many areas of your life—personal, family, and business. It is particularly emphasized at times when you or loved ones are very ill, when there is sadness and sorrow in your life, and when certain stressful processes and developments occur that take time to resolve.

The more you attain that state of being the calm observer of life's experiences, the more you come into harmony with the Love, peace, and power of your Divine Spirit.

DEFINITIONS

The All – The whole of everything that exists. The consciousness and energies of God The Absolute which extend throughout all creation.

anapersona – The part of a triune being that has a continuous consciousness that directly experiences an environment in some bodily form. It chooses and exhibits a unique personality with particular talents and abilities. It consciously and unconsciously programs its soul through its experiences.

astral body – A physical, inner-plane body vibrationally situated between your physical-etheric body and your spiritual bodies. It is composed of refined light particles like photons. The astral body is the seat of one's emotions, and its higher aspects may be referred to as the mental body.

Astral Plane – The Astral Plane is a physical, non-spiritual, temporary learning environment that straddles the second and third dimcons. It lies within the earth's energy/gravitational field. It is primarily a way-station for animal and human consciousnesses evolving up through the second and third dimcons, awaiting return to another earthly material body for continuation of their soul evolution.

The Astral Plane consists of seven major levels of experience. The lower levels are relatively dense and house beings still caught in their lower animal natures. The upper astral levels accommodate souls yearning to move into a higher, spiritual expression.

Astral beings are to be distinguished from spiritual beings. Any human astral being functions only within the third dimension of consciousness.

consciousness – The quality or state of being aware and cognizant of one's external environment and of one's internal thought, volition, and feeling processes. It is the inherent characteristic of awareness that gives life forms the intrinsic capacity to think, learn, grow, and expand in instinct, intelligence, knowledge, intuition, and wisdom.

dimension – The degree or measurable range over which something extends. A realm of existence or level of consciousness.

dimensions of consciousness (dimcons) – Dimcons are analogous to different levels or degrees of awareness, learning experience, understanding, and wisdom, similar to graded school systems. There are thirteen dimcons in this Universe system. Each higher dimcon allows its inhabitants a broader perspective and comprehension of Love, Truth, and Wisdom. Dimcons are not related to dimensions of place, time, and space. Each dimcon is divided into seven major levels or progressive steps.

duality – 1. The extreme aspect of polarity that exists on fear-based planets wherein Participants experience both harmony and disharmony relative to Natural Law. Duality is experienced as the opposing forces of good and evil; Trust and fear; Love and fear; Love and hate.

2. The condition in one's consciousness of separation, division, and isolation from their Divine Source, their intrinsic spiritual nature and everything that exists.

emotions – Feelings that have been distorted by the illusions presented to one's consciousness through the disharmonious programming inherent in duality. This condition is prevalent on fear-based planets.

etheric, ethereal – Of or relating to the spiritual realms. Lacking material substance. Non-atomic matter. Not to be confused with the physical-etheric realm.

evil – 1. Power used as force directed toward interfering with another person's freedom of choice (free will).

2. Intentionally harming another person's body or possessions.

3. The use of undue negative influence on a person through the indoctrination of false truths (brainwashing).

4. The negative energy resulting from erroneous soul programming whereby a person has denied their inherent goodness (Godness).

5. The use of mental, emotional, or physical fear tactics to direct a person's focus toward disharmony and doubt, whereby they can be controlled

evolution – The process of continuous change, development, or growth from a lower, simpler condition to a higher, more complex condition or state of existence.

fear – An error condition in a person's consciousness based upon a lack of Trust, manifesting as a disharmonious, self-defeating emotional reaction to a situation wherein one anticipates great physical, emotional, or mental harm to themselves or to others.

fear-based planet – A planet in any solar system where the vibrational frequencies have degraded to the point wherein its third dimcon inhabitants experience aspects of fear.

feelings – harmonious psychological sensations of Love, Compassion, Enthusiasm, and Joy experienced as a constant state or mode of being.

fraud – An intentional perversion or concealment of truth to induce another to part with a valuable possession or to surrender a legal right. A false representation or concealment of a fact which should have been disclosed, with the intention to deceive another so that he shall act upon it to his legal, financial, or bodily injury. Deceit or trickery used to gain an unfair advantage over another.

God The Absolute – The highest aspect of The All which is the Limitless Prime Source and Master Mind behind all creation. Infinite, unmanifested potential. Primordial consciousness, will, feeling, energy, and creative power.

God The Creator – The infinite point constituting the Twelve Basic Principles, or Energies, inherent in the creation, formation, and structure of everything in our Universe system.

God The Manifest – The point of consciousness in which the Twelve Basic Energies of God The Creator are combined and blended, then radiate out to create, maintain, and transform all the realms and dimcons of our Universe system.

This **Unity Point** of manifestation may be thought of as **the thirteenth dimcon,** as all individualized life and all forms of environmental substance have their origin, are unified in, and radiate throughout the Universe from this infinite creative point.

Heart – Refers to the spiritual center located in your heart chakra. It connects your feeling nature with the expression of universal Love. The heart chakra serves as a bridge between energies of the human, lower self, and the Higher Self of the soul.

Hermetics – The study of spiritual science and technology. Hermetic Principles explain the basic conditions, structures, and premises behind the creation and continuing existence of our Universe and everything in it.

Higher Self – The master intelligence of the soul. The Higher Self resides one dimension of consciousness higher than the lower self, which houses our present human consciousness. The Higher Self offers accumulated wisdom, truth, and guidance from the soul's data bank to the lower self via the intuitive mind.

infinite – Being limitless and without boundaries. Endless and inexhaustible with no beginning or end. All encompassing beyond measure or comprehension.

infinity – Limitless space, distance, time, quantity, or number.

Joy – The highest feeling of delight or bliss which transcends the duality of happiness and sadness. The ecstatic feeling that comes through Knowing you are unified with all Life—The All.

karma – The action of cause and effect. The universal law whereby the thoughts, words, and actions a person thinks, expresses, or does eventually returns to them, so they may either learn through evaluating the consequences of their actions, or enjoy the rewards.

Knowing – Intuitive knowledge that transcends doubt. Knowing comes from ones own inherent Wisdom and the vast universal reservoir of Knowledge and Wisdom. Spiritual Knowing is free from doubt and confusion as to a spiritual principle or a proper course of action. Since Knowing is not an intellectual process, it cannot be explained intellectually.

Life – The Primary polar neutral principle of Mind, which sources all consciousness and intelligence.

Light – 1. The Primary polar dynamic principle of Will, which sources all electric power and authority. 2. The effulgent, golden-white Light that emanates from the combined balance of all twelve Principles of Creation, and radiates at various frequencies throughout the spiritual and higher realms.

Love – The polar magnetic principle of Feeling, which sources all magnetic power and psychological sensation.

Love-based planet – The planet in any solar system whose inhabitants choose to live in and express only Limitless Total Love.

oneness – The state of consciousness whereby a being realizes only good (God) and their unity with The All—everyone and everything in the universe. This state exists and is experienced in the spiritual and higher dimcons.

The Pleiades – A star cluster containing hundreds of visible and etheric stars providing an educational environment for spiritual beings functioning between the fourth and the ninth dimensions of consciousness.

polarity – The condition whereby two principles complement or are diametrically opposed to each other. Qualities or conditions having contrasting properties or opposite extremes. Regarding electricity, the relative condition of opposite charges having two poles, referred to as positive and negative.

reaction – 1. The disharmonious emotional response generated by an erroneous, fear-based, or otherwise limiting idea or statement recorded in a Participant's subconscious soul programming.

2. An emotional signal from a Participant's Higher Self indicating that he or she is being confronted with a work area of unfinished business.

realm – A dimension of place or existence within a universe system, occupying a specific, distinct range of vibrational frequencies. There are numerous octaves of energy frequencies within a realm. (For instance, human beings' hearing is within a range of vibrational octaves; their vision is within a higher vibrational octave.) A realm offers a place of existence for the experiences of beings functioning through various dimcons.

soul – The master data recorder of an individual's entire past and present life experiences. The Higher Self is the intelligence of the soul that feeds information and guidance to one's consciousness through the intuitive mind. Beings (creatures) in the first and second dimcons are grouped into collective souls. Humans and etheric beings with a third or higher dimcon have individualized souls.

soul evolution – The process wherein all collective and individualized life progresses successively higher through each dimcon by acquiring knowledge and wisdom through countless personal experiences.

spirit – 1. The intrinsic essence of all consciousnesses. 2. A general term applied individually and collectively to all beings having etheric form and functioning through the fourth to the twelfth dimensions of consciousness.

spiritual – That which relates to the fourth or higher dimensions of consciousness, or to the fourth and higher realms.

trauma – A fear-based brain-memory or soul program created by a Participant's reaction to a stressful, shocking, or violent experience that resulted in mental, emotional, or physical harm, or death.

Trust – The understanding that spirit will supply all of one's real needs, and those requests which are in harmony with one's karma, lessons, and destiny.

Truth – The only absolute Truth is God The Absolute, the highest consciousness within the infinite spectrum of awareness. Each individualized being has their personal truths that form the basis of their unique perception of reality. These relative truths are altered and transformed as one evolves.

universe system – An organized network of many realms. All realms are connected sequentially. The vibrational range of each realm is separated from the next by "transformers" of both power and vibrational frequency. Each realm has its own unique energy spectrum, and each realm is connected to and based upon another, like the links of a chain.

vibrational spectrum – A progressive scale of measure of infinite range that depicts the specific or average rate of rhythm, vibration, or cycle pertaining to anything in the Universe.

Wisdom – Spiritual truth as confirmed through experience, and applied to a course of thinking, speaking, and acting that is in harmony with the nature of The Absolute.

RECOMMENDED READING

Seat of the Soul, by Gary Zukav

The Illustrated Brief History of Time; The Universe in a Nutshell, by Stephen Hawking

God and the Astronomers, by Robert Jastrow, Warner Books, Inc.

How to Know God; The Seven Spiritual Laws of Success, and many other books, by Deepak Chopra

The Kybalion – Hermetic Philosophy, Yoga Publication Society
(an excellent reference book, although at one point, the authors appear to be confused regarding the relationship between the intrinsic natures of human beings and God.)

The Tao of Physics, by Fritjof Capra.

Journey to the Fourth Dimension, by St. Germain as transmitted through Judith Ann Gordon.
Available through Pleiadian Connection – see page 291.

Evolution of Man, Mark Age, PO Box 10, Pioneer, TN 37847, USA; http://www.islandnet.com/~arton/markage.html; telephone: 423: 784-3269

Developing Intuition, by Shakti Gawain

Soul Retrieval, by Sandra Ingerman

Chakras, by Patricia Mercier

Heal Your Body, Heal Your Life, by Louise Hay.

Meditation, An Eight-Point Program, by Eknath Easwaran

Everyday Grace – Having Hope, Finding Forgiveness, and Making Miracles, by Marianne Williamson

A Guide to Rational Living, by Albert Ellis

Don't Sweat the Small Stuff – and its all small stuff, by Richard Carlson

Stop the Anger Now, Ronald T. Potter-Efron, M.S.W., Ph.D.

Astrology for the Light Side of the Brain, by Kim Rogers-Gallagher

Bringers of the Dawn, by Barbara Marciniak.

New Teachings for an Awakening Humanity, Spiritual Education Endeavors Publishing Company

Absolutely Effortless Prosperity, by Bijan

The Four Agreements, by Don Miguel Ruiz

Ponder on This. A compilation from the writings of Alice A. Bailey and The Tibetan Master, Djwhal Khul

The Rainbow Book, The Fine Arts Museums of San Francisco.

The Twelfth Planet (and other books in the series), by Zecharia Sitchin

The Biggest Secret; Children of the Matrix, by David Icke

Inspirational Reading:

Autobiography of a Yogi, by Paramahansa Yogananda

Life and Teaching of the Masters of the Far East, by Baird T. Spalding

NOTES ON THE CONSCIOUSNESS RAISING MEDITATIONS

A series of three *Consciousness-Raising Meditations* are available on audio Compact Discs— *Basic, Progressive* and *Advanced*. A *Basic Mediation* CD is included with this book. These meditations are primarily designed as a successive program to assist you in connecting your consciousness with the major aspects of your individualized being, and with your highest nature, The Godhead.

You may use the *Basic Meditation* for as long as you desire. However, we suggest that you practice the *Basic Meditation* daily for at least 30 days to acquaint yourself with the terms and techniques before moving on to the *Progressive Meditation*. Your Divine Spirit will advise you when you are ready to practice the *Advanced Meditation*.

Following is a brief description of each meditation's program:

The Basic Consciousness-Raising Meditation:
- begins with a 20 minute guided meditation with verbal visualization-feeling notes.
- assists you to ground and protect yourself, clear your physical bodies, align all of your inner bodies, and clear and activate your seven major chakras.

- guides you in raising your consciousness to your Higher Self, the consciousness of your soul—and to your Divine Spirit, in union with all life in this Universe.
- assists you to unify with the Three Primary Principles of Life, Light, and Love and the Five Personal Principles of Trust, Confidence, Knowing, Courage, and Fortitude.
- concludes with a five minute meditation for the transformation of Planet Earth to that of a Love-based planet, and 15 minutes of silent meditation.

The Progressive Consciousness-Raising Meditation:
- begins with the same program as the Basic Meditation but without the verbal guidance notes.
- guides you in further raising your consciousness to God the Manifest, God The Creator, and God The Absolute.
- includes a guided meditation that introduces you to techniques for the dissolving of mental, emotional, and physical energy blocks, for the dissolving of various impurities in your body, and assists you in strengthening, balancing, and stabilizing various aspects of your bodies.
- contains a feeling-visualization for the development of your Body of Light.
- concludes with a five minute meditation for the transformation of Planet Earth and 20 minutes of silent meditation.

The Advanced Consciousness-Raising Meditation:
- includes the same program as the *Progressive Meditation* minus the clearing and activating of the seven major chakras.
- additionally assists you to unify with the Four Elemental Principles of Air, Fire, Water, and Earth, and includes Five Sutras with their associated colors: Companionship, Bodily Well-being, Infinite Abundance, Infinite Wisdom, and Creative Mastery.
- concludes with a five minute meditation for the transformation of Planet Earth, and 20 minutes of silent meditation.

BOOK AND MEDITATION CD ORDERING INFORMATION

Additional books and meditation Compact Discs are available through your local bookstores, or through the Pleiadian Connection website:

http://www.pleiadianconnection.org

BOOKS:

Accelerating Soul Evolution – Personal and Planetary,
by Ralph Genter

Journey to the Fourth Dimension,
by St. Germain as transmitted through Judith Ann Gordon. 8.5" x 11" spiral bound, $28.00 including shipping and handling. Available through Pleiadian Connection, P.O. Box 51808, Albuquerque, New Mexico, 87181-1808, USA

AUDIO COMPACT DISCS and TAPES:

1. Basic Consciousness Raising Meditation
2. Progressive Consciousness Raising Meditation
3. Advanced Consciousness Raising Meditation

Comments regarding the Basic Consciousness Raising Meditation CD enclosed with this book

An outline of this meditation's program is on page 288.

With persistent daily use, this series of meditations will assist you in clearing all disharmony from your seven major astral energy centers, and in raising your consciousness through the Astral Plane, into the spiritual dimensions of consciousness.

If we were to put the highest principle into words, it would be, **"I am!"** Because we are gods, any word we add after the statement **"I am"** is true. Be conscious of this when performing this meditation.

If you choose to meditate longer than the programmed 15 or 20 minutes and not be interrupted by the closing statement, please turn off your CD player before beginning your silent meditation.

When you feel you have mastered this Basic Meditation, you may move on to use the Progressive Consciousness Raising Meditation.

See the previous page for information regarding obtaining additional books and meditation CDs.

Since these meditations put you in an altered state of consciousness, never listen to them while driving or engaging in an activity requiring your full conscious attention.

The format and text of these meditations are subject to future refinements and upgrades. The purpose of the meditation on this CD is to reinforce a positive and constructive attitude towards healing and body-mind-psyche wellness. It is not intended to replace competent professional medical advice, care, and treatment.